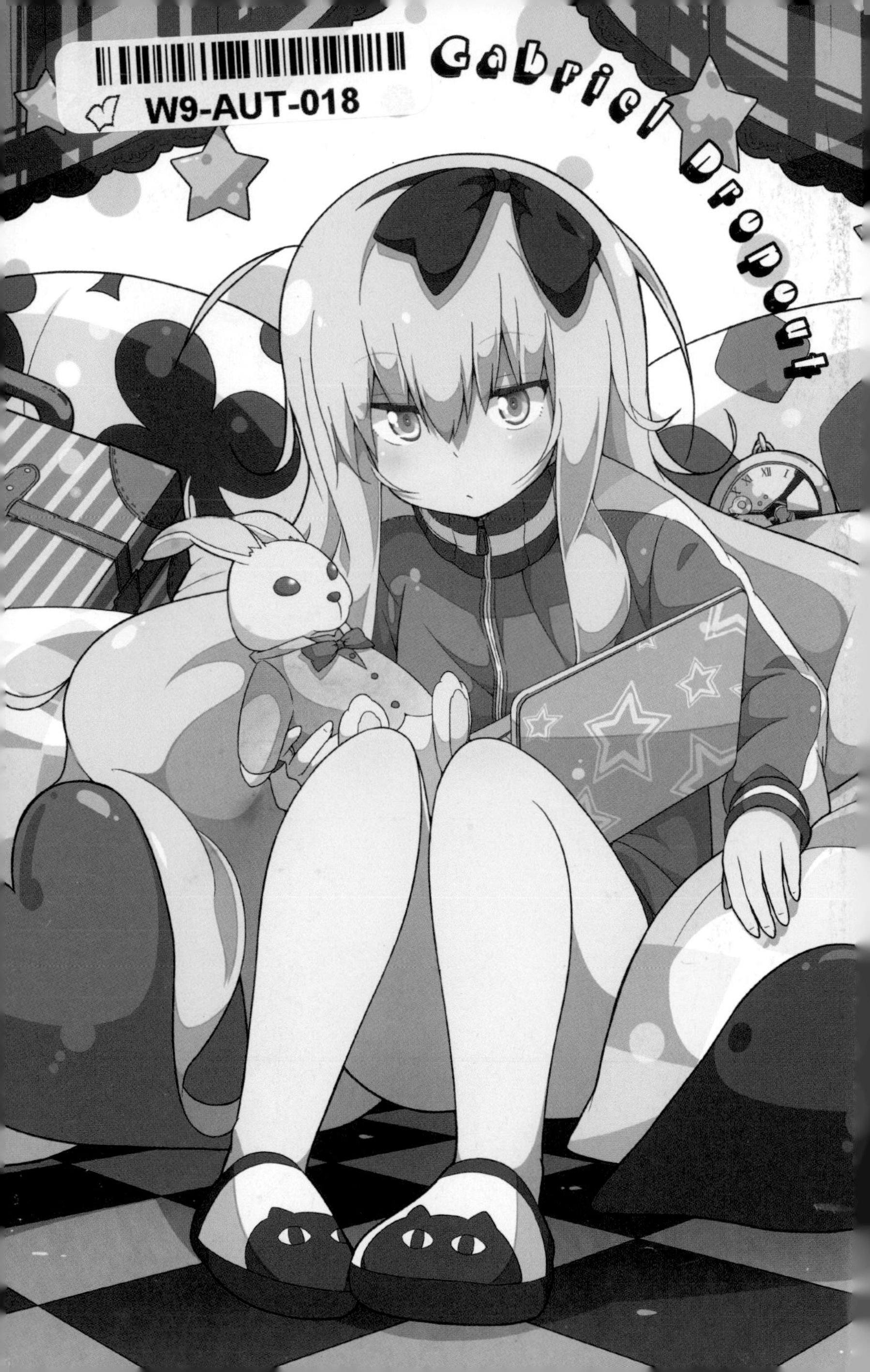
Gabriel Dropout

Contents

Gabriel
DropOut

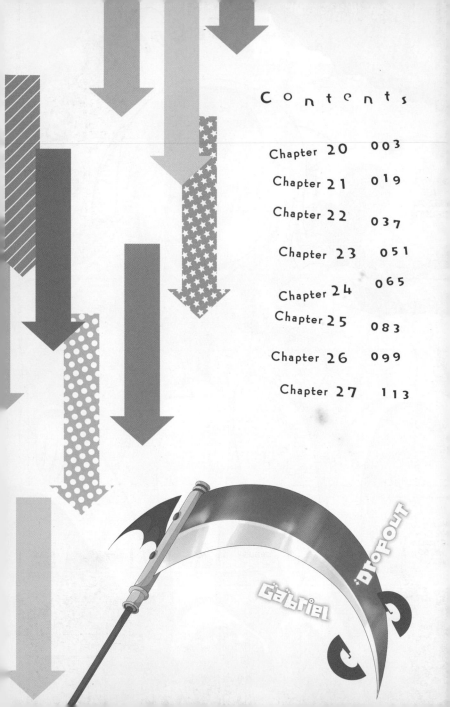

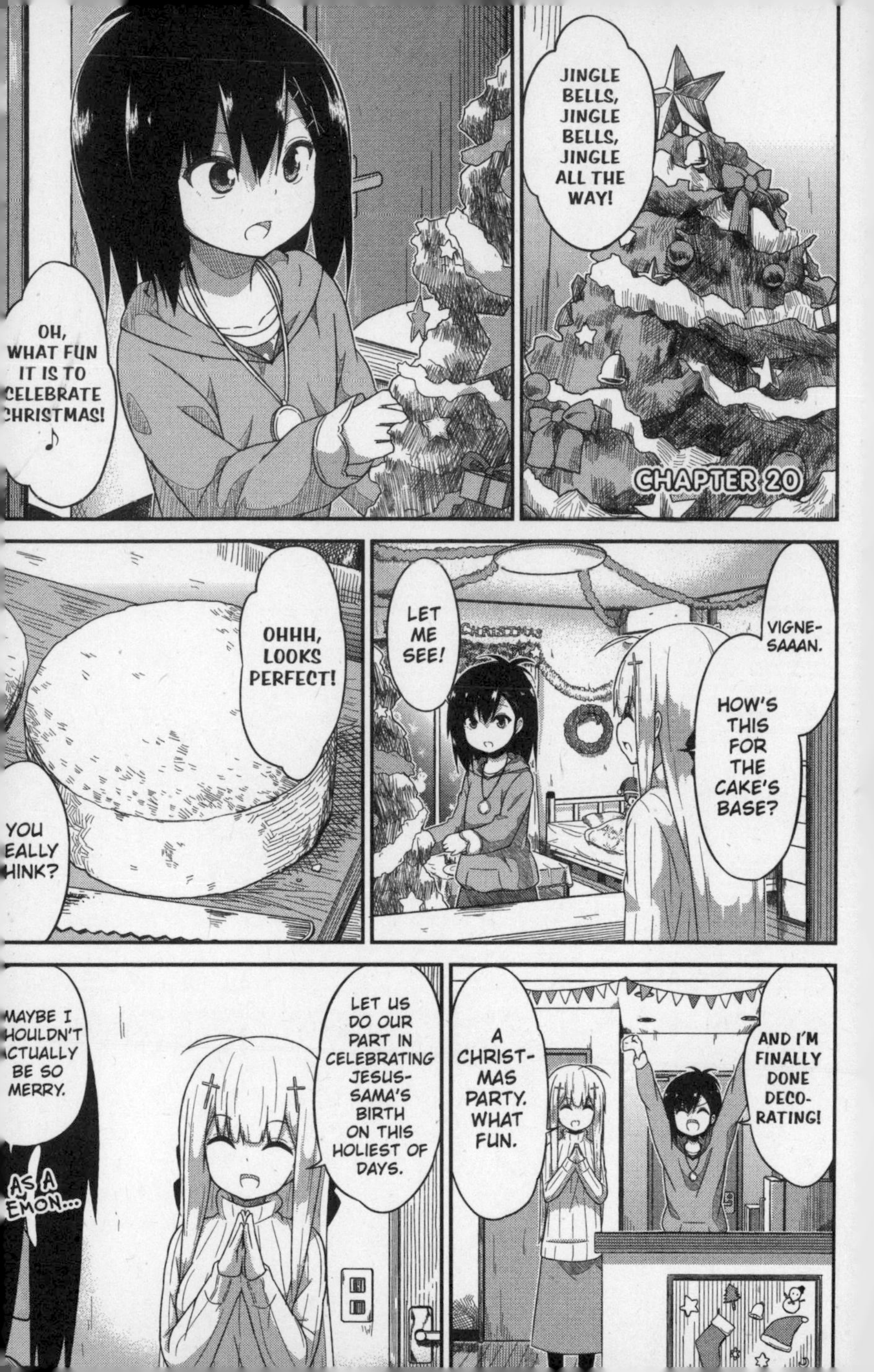
JINGLE BELLS, JINGLE BELLS, JINGLE ALL THE WAY!
CHAPTER 20
OH, WHAT FUN IT IS TO CELEBRATE CHRISTMAS! ♪
VIGNE-SAAAN.
HOW'S THIS FOR THE CAKE'S BASE?
CHRISTMAS
LET ME SEE!
OHHH, LOOKS PERFECT!
YOU EALLY HINK?
AND I'M FINALLY DONE DECO-RATING!
A CHRIST-MAS PARTY. WHAT FUN.
LET US DO OUR PART IN CELEBRATING JESUS-SAMA'S BIRTH ON THIS HOLIEST OF DAYS.
MAYBE I HOULDN'T CTUALLY BE SO MERRY.
AS A EMON...

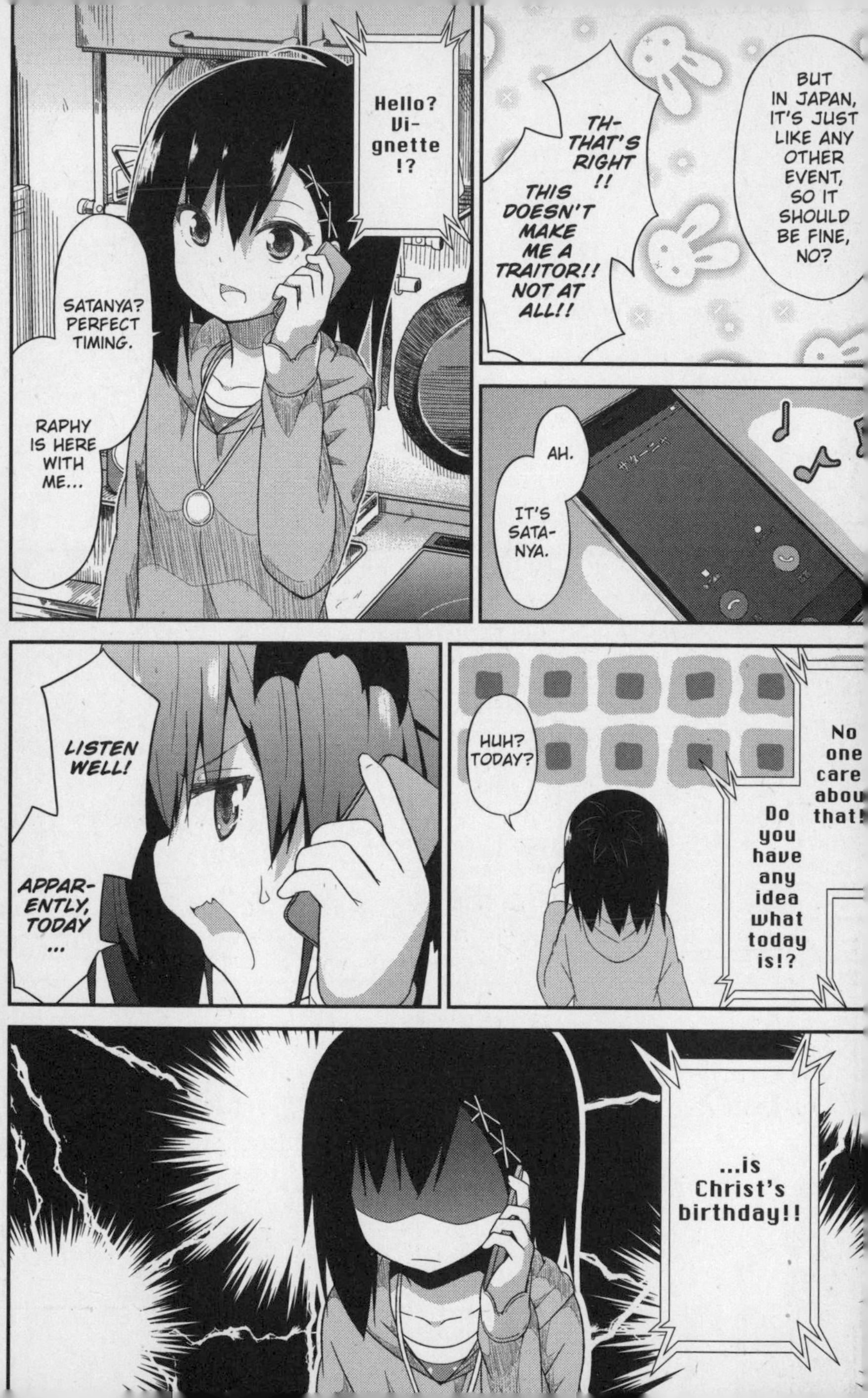
BUT IN JAPAN, IT'S JUST LIKE ANY OTHER EVENT, SO IT SHOULD BE FINE, NO?
TH-THAT'S RIGHT!!
THIS DOESN'T MAKE ME A TRAITOR!! NOT AT ALL!!
AH.
IT'S SATA-NYA.
Hello? Vi-gnette!?
SATANYA? PERFECT TIMING.
RAPHY IS HERE WITH ME...
No one care abou that!
Do you have any idea what today is!?
HUH? TODAY?
LISTEN WELL!
APPAR-ENTLY, TODAY ...
...is Christ's birthday!!

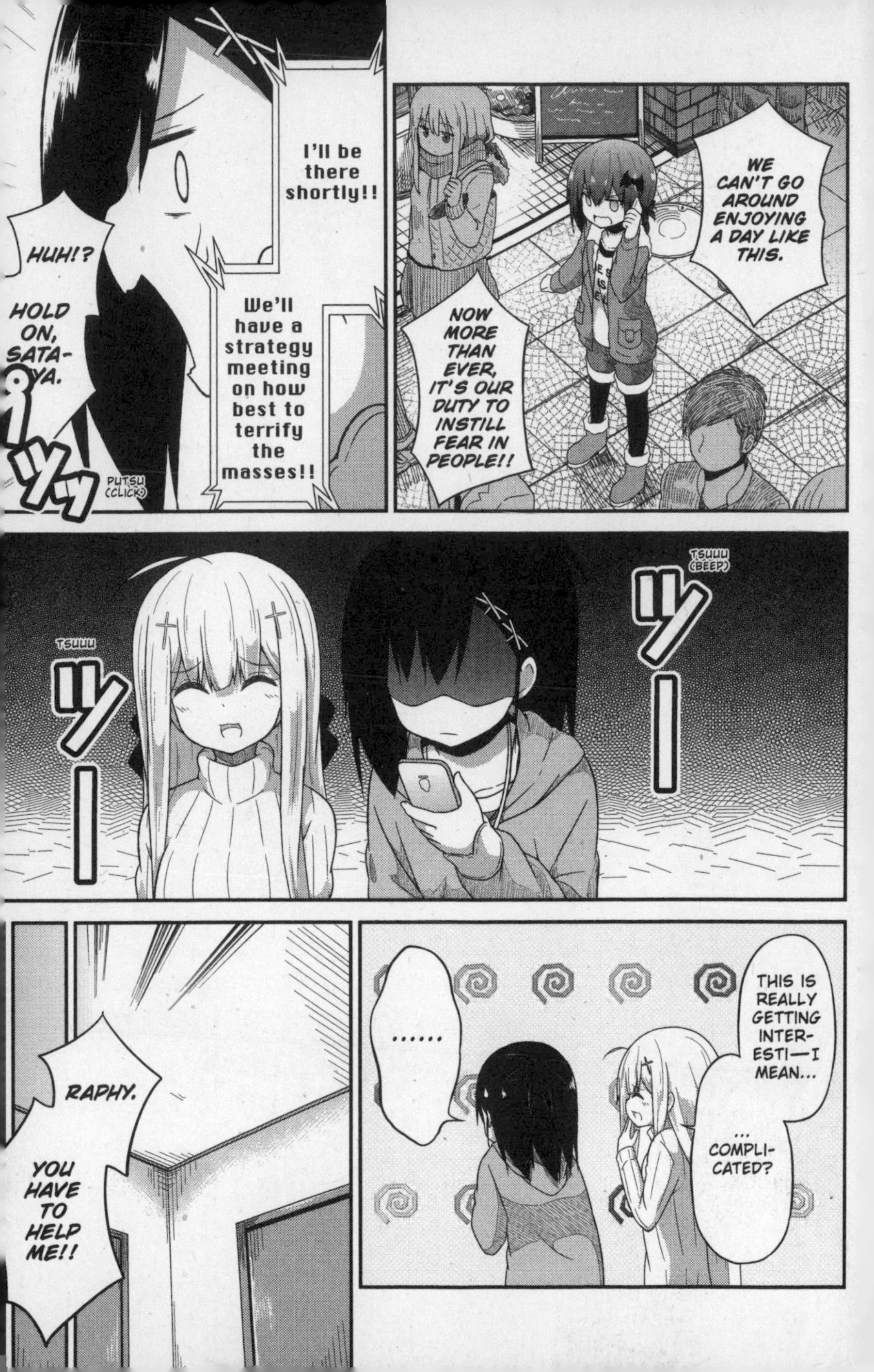
WE CAN'T GO AROUND ENJOYING A DAY LIKE THIS.
NOW MORE THAN EVER, IT'S OUR DUTY TO INSTILL FEAR IN PEOPLE!!
I'll be there shortly!!
We'll have a strategy meeting on how best to terrify the masses!!
HUH!?
HOLD ON, SATA-NYA.
PUTSU (CLICK)
TSUUU (BEEP)
TSUUU
THIS IS REALLY GETTING INTERESTI—I MEAN...
... COMPLICATED?
......
RAPHY.
YOU HAVE TO HELP ME!!

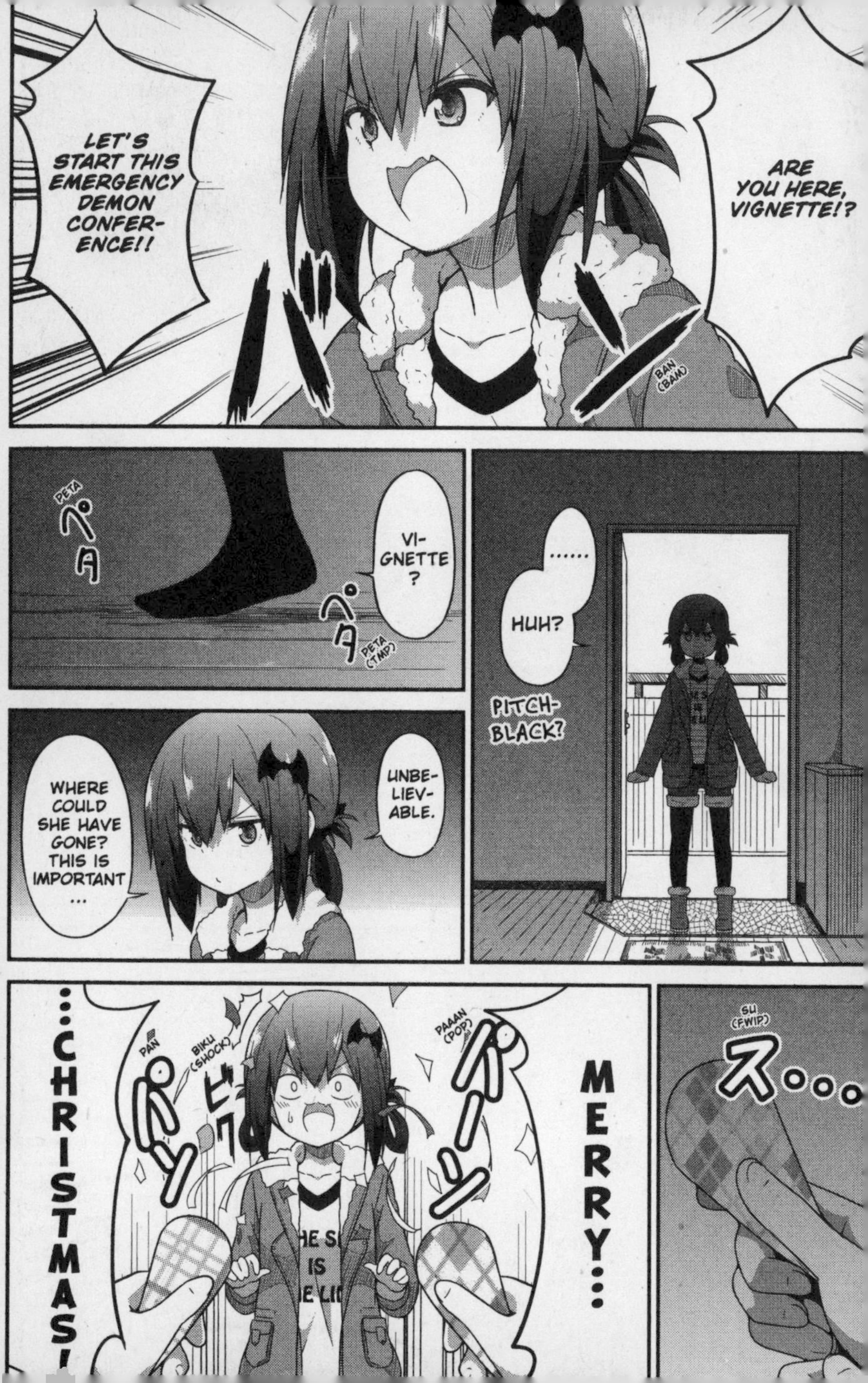
ARE YOU HERE, VIGNETTE!?
LET'S START THIS EMERGENCY DEMON CONFER-ENCE!!
BAN (BAM)
......
HUH?
PITCH-BLACK?
PETA
ペタ
VI-GNETTE?
ペタ
PETA (TMP)
UNBE-LIEV-ABLE.
WHERE COULD SHE HAVE GONE? THIS IS IMPORTANT...
SU (FWIP)
ス…
MERRY...
PAAAN (POP)
パーン
BIKU (SHOCK)
PAN
パン
...CHRISTMAS!

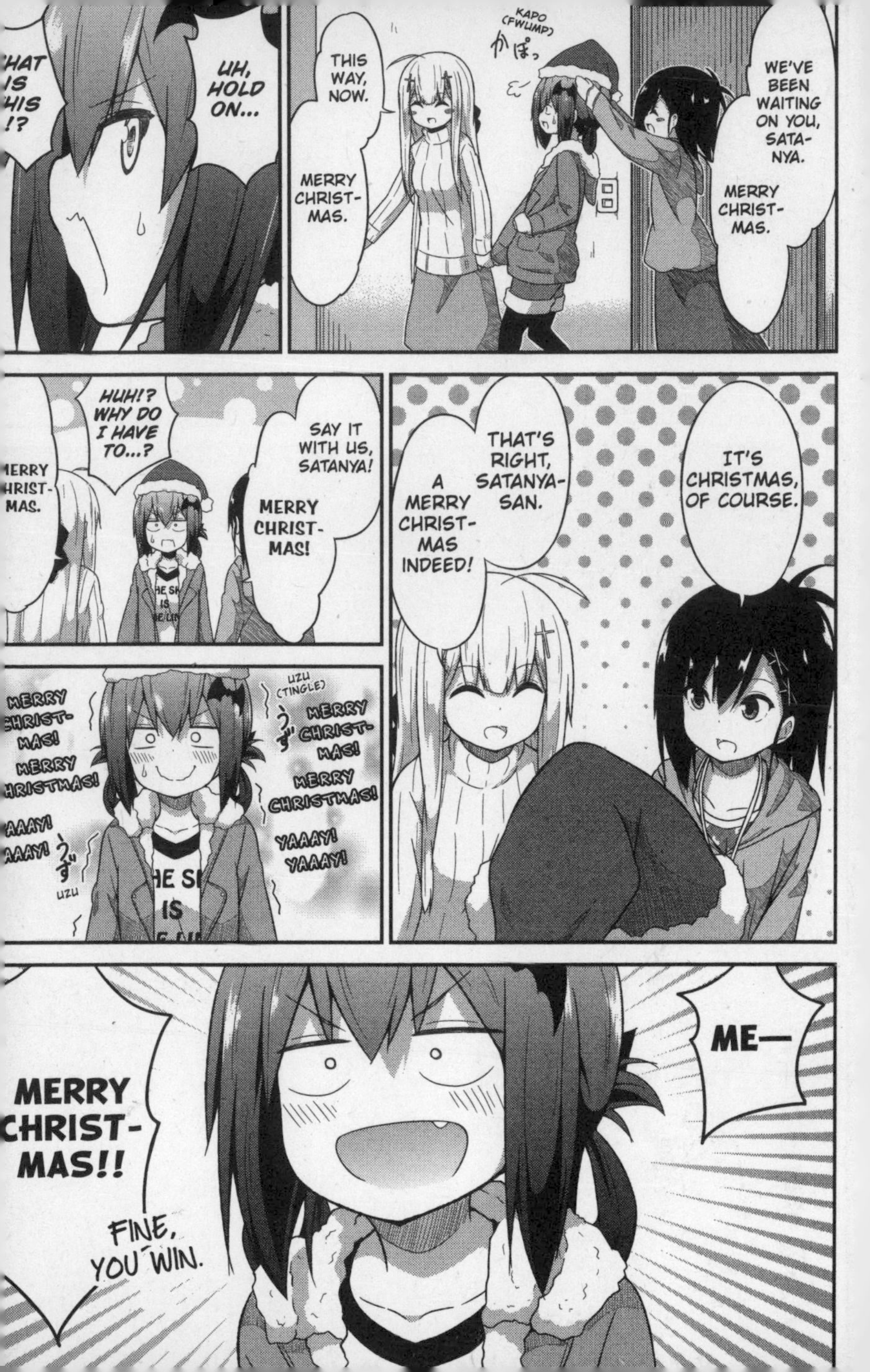

KAPO (FWUMP)
かぽっ
WE'VE BEEN WAITING ON YOU, SATANYA.
MERRY CHRISTMAS.
THIS WAY, NOW.
MERRY CHRISTMAS.
UH, HOLD ON...
HAT IS HIS !?
IT'S CHRISTMAS, OF COURSE.
THAT'S RIGHT, SATANYA-SAN.
A MERRY CHRISTMAS INDEED!
SAY IT WITH US, SATANYA!
MERRY CHRISTMAS!
HUH!? WHY DO I HAVE TO...?
ERRY CHRISTMAS.
UZU (TINGLE)
うず
MERRY CHRISTMAS!
MERRY CHRISTMAS!
YAAAY! YAAAY!
ERRY CHRISTMAS!
MERRY CHRISTMAS!
AAAY! AAAY!
うず
UZU
ME—
MERRY CHRISTMAS!!
FINE, YOU WIN.

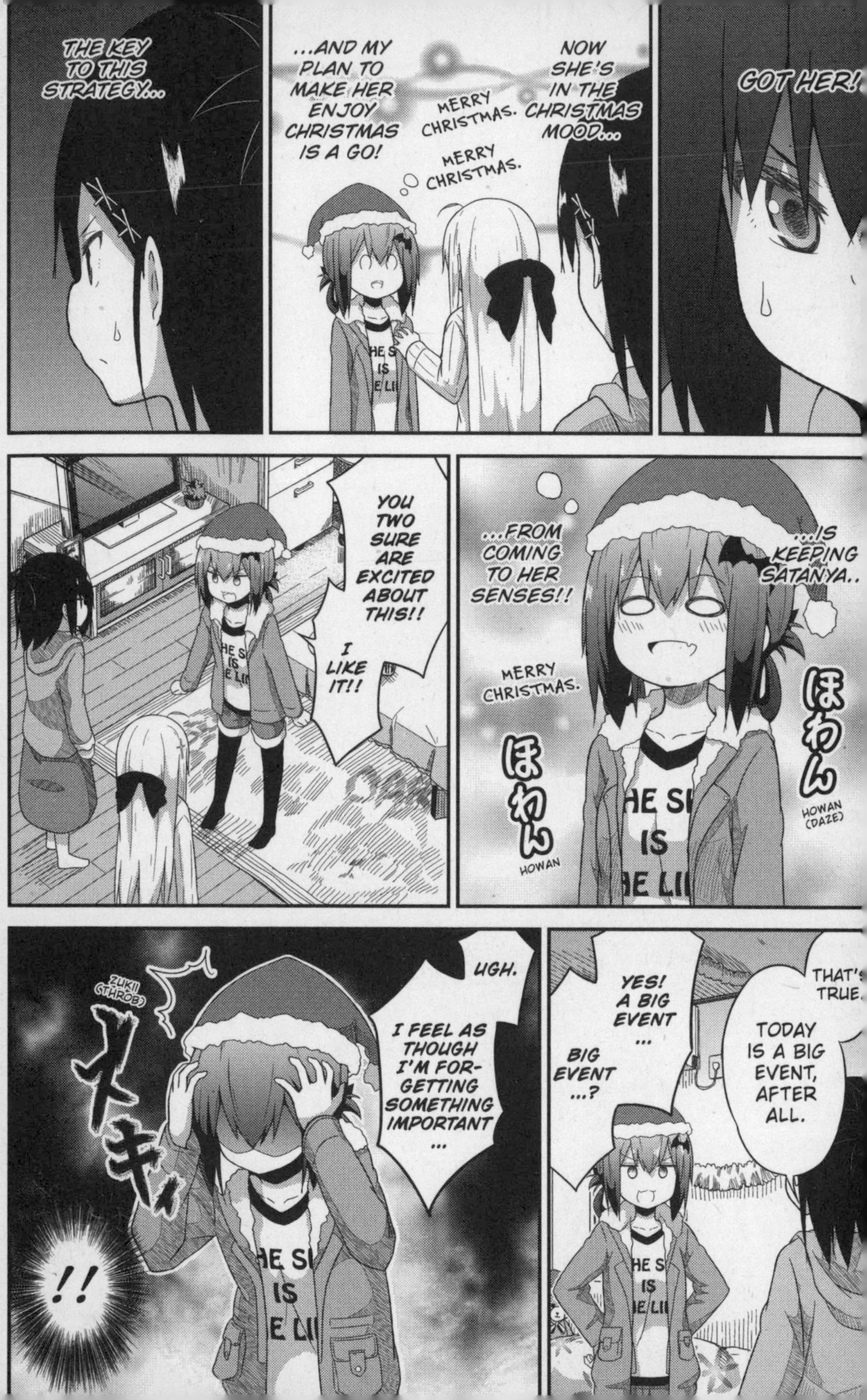
GOT HER!
NOW SHE'S IN THE CHRISTMAS MOOD...
MERRY CHRISTMAS.
MERRY CHRISTMAS.
...AND MY PLAN TO MAKE HER ENJOY CHRISTMAS IS A GO!
THE KEY TO THIS STRATEGY...
...IS KEEPING SATANYA...
...FROM COMING TO HER SENSES!!
MERRY CHRISTMAS.
ほわん
HOWAN (DAZE)
ほわん
HOWAN
YOU TWO SURE ARE EXCITED ABOUT THIS!!
I LIKE IT!!
THAT'S TRUE.
TODAY IS A BIG EVENT, AFTER ALL.
YES! A BIG EVENT...
BIG EVENT...?
UGH.
I FEEL AS THOUGH I'M FOR-GETTING SOMETHING IMPORTANT...
ZUKI! (THROB)
ズキ
!!

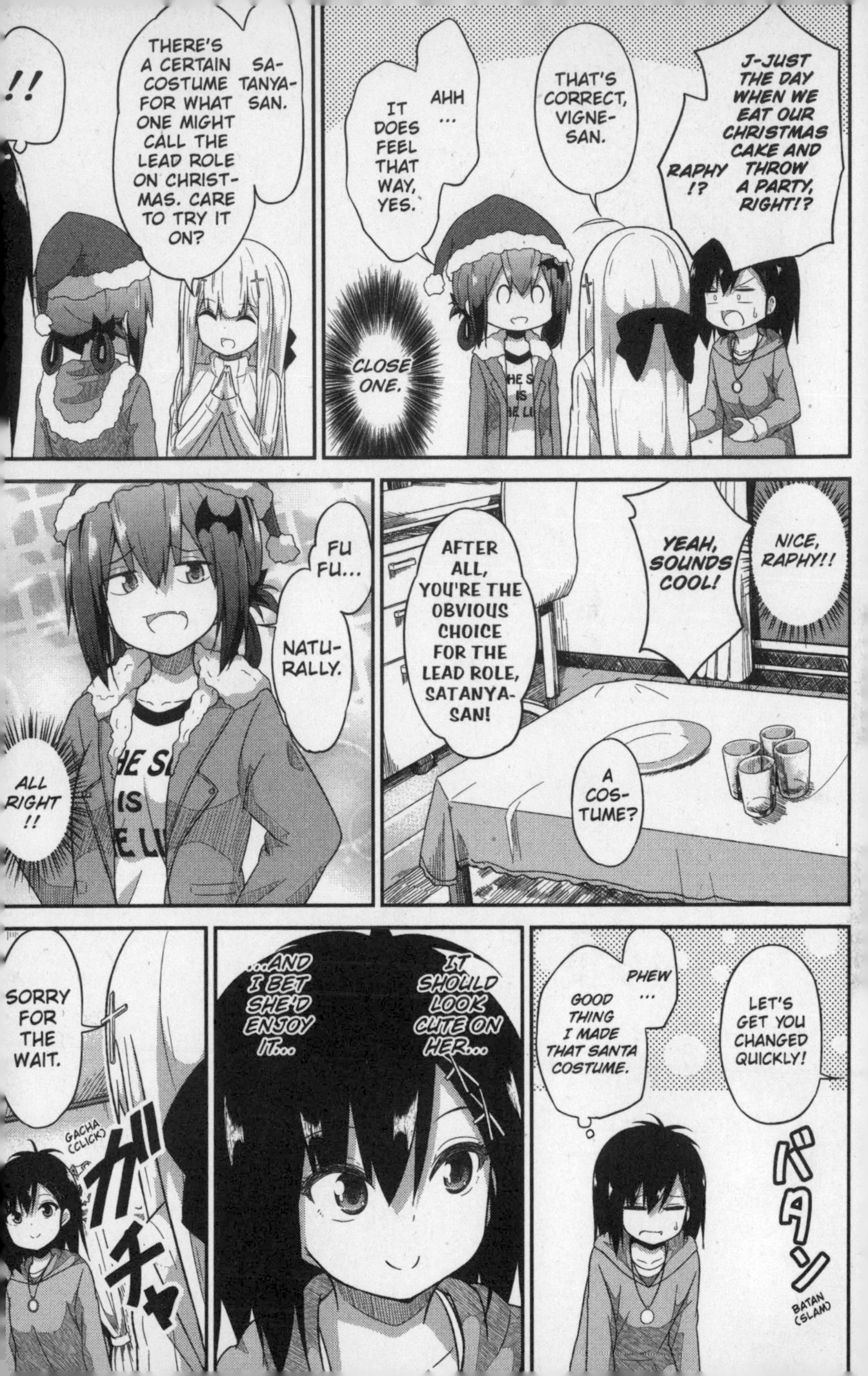
J-JUST THE DAY WHEN WE EAT OUR CHRISTMAS CAKE AND THROW A PARTY, RIGHT!?
RAPHY !?
THAT'S CORRECT, VIGNE-SAN.
AHH ...
IT DOES FEEL THAT WAY, YES.
CLOSE ONE.
SA-TANYA-SAN.
THERE'S A CERTAIN COSTUME FOR WHAT ONE MIGHT CALL THE LEAD ROLE ON CHRISTMAS. CARE TO TRY IT ON?
!!
NICE, RAPHY!!
YEAH, SOUNDS COOL!
AFTER ALL, YOU'RE THE OBVIOUS CHOICE FOR THE LEAD ROLE, SATANYA-SAN!
A COSTUME?
FU FU...
NATU-RALLY.
ALL RIGHT !!
LET'S GET YOU CHANGED QUICKLY!
PHEW ...
GOOD THING I MADE THAT SANTA COSTUME.
バタン
BATAN (SLAM)
IT SHOULD LOOK CUTE ON HER...
...AND I BET SHE'D ENJOY IT...
SORRY FOR THE WAIT.
ガチャ
GACHA (CLICK)

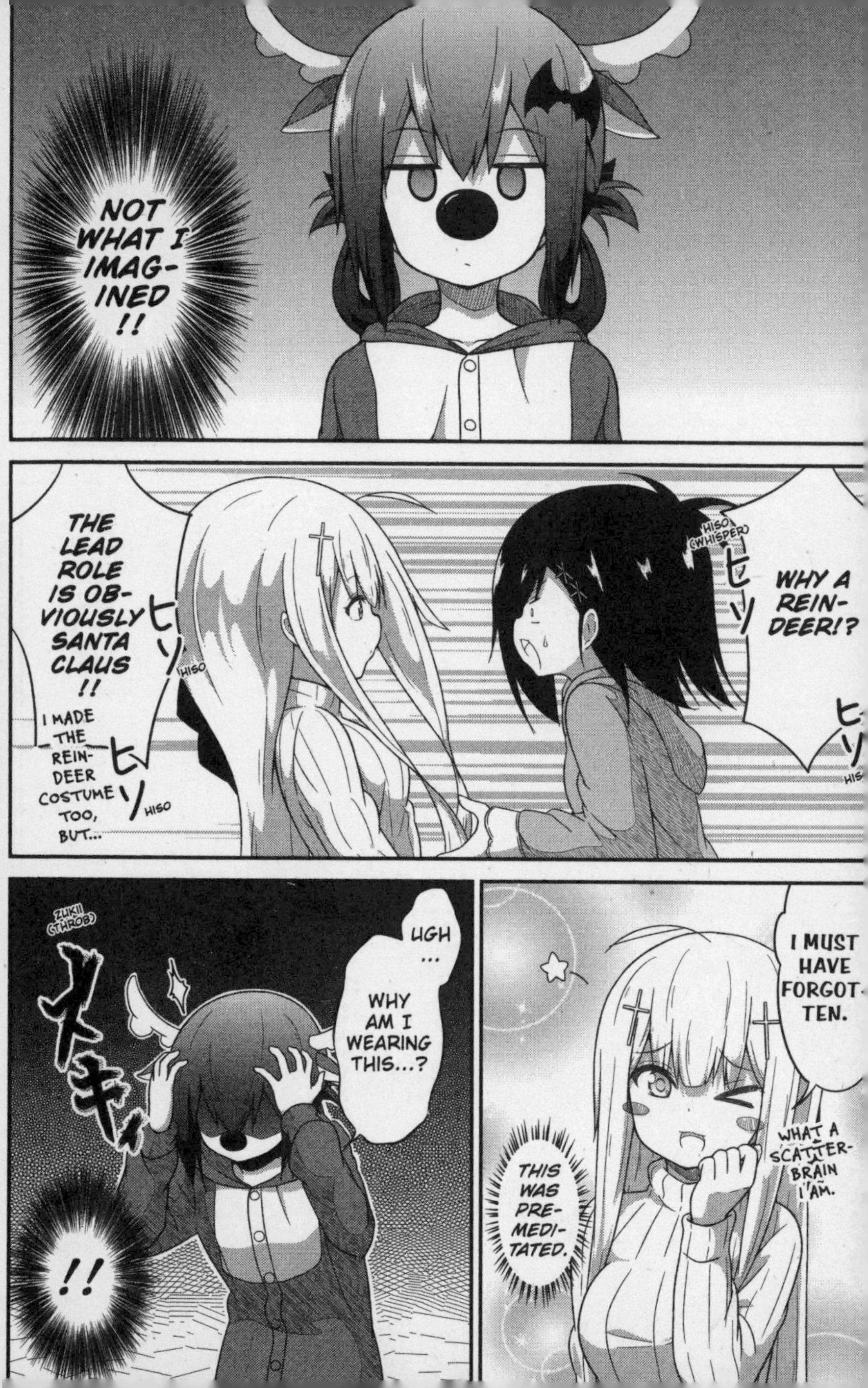
NOT WHAT I IMAGINED!!
HISO (WHISPER)
ヒソ
WHY A REINDEER!?
ヒソ
HISO
THE LEAD ROLE IS OBVIOUSLY SANTA CLAUS!!
ヒソ
HISO
I MADE THE REINDEER COSTUME TOO, BUT...
ヒソ
HISO
I MUST HAVE FORGOTTEN.
WHAT A SCATTERBRAIN I AM.
THIS WAS PREMEDITATED.
ZUKII (THROB)
UGH...
WHY AM I WEARING THIS...?
!!

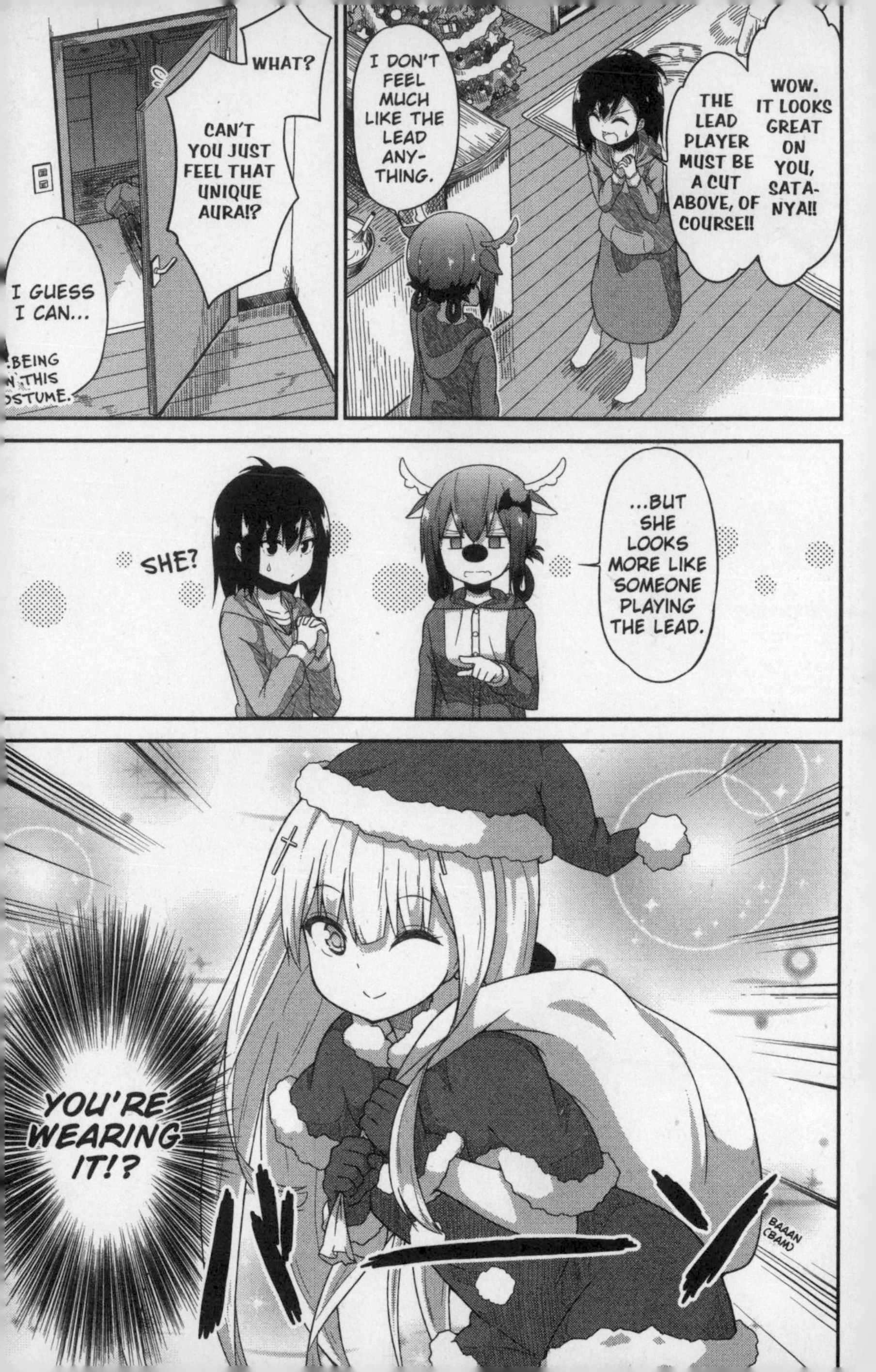
WOW. IT LOOKS GREAT ON YOU, SATA-NYA!!
THE LEAD PLAYER MUST BE A CUT ABOVE, OF COURSE!!
I DON'T FEEL MUCH LIKE THE LEAD ANYTHING.
WHAT?
CAN'T YOU JUST FEEL THAT UNIQUE AURA!?
I GUESS I CAN...
.BEING N THIS OSTUME.
...BUT SHE LOOKS MORE LIKE SOMEONE PLAYING THE LEAD.
SHE?
BAAAN (BAM)
YOU'RE WEARING IT!?

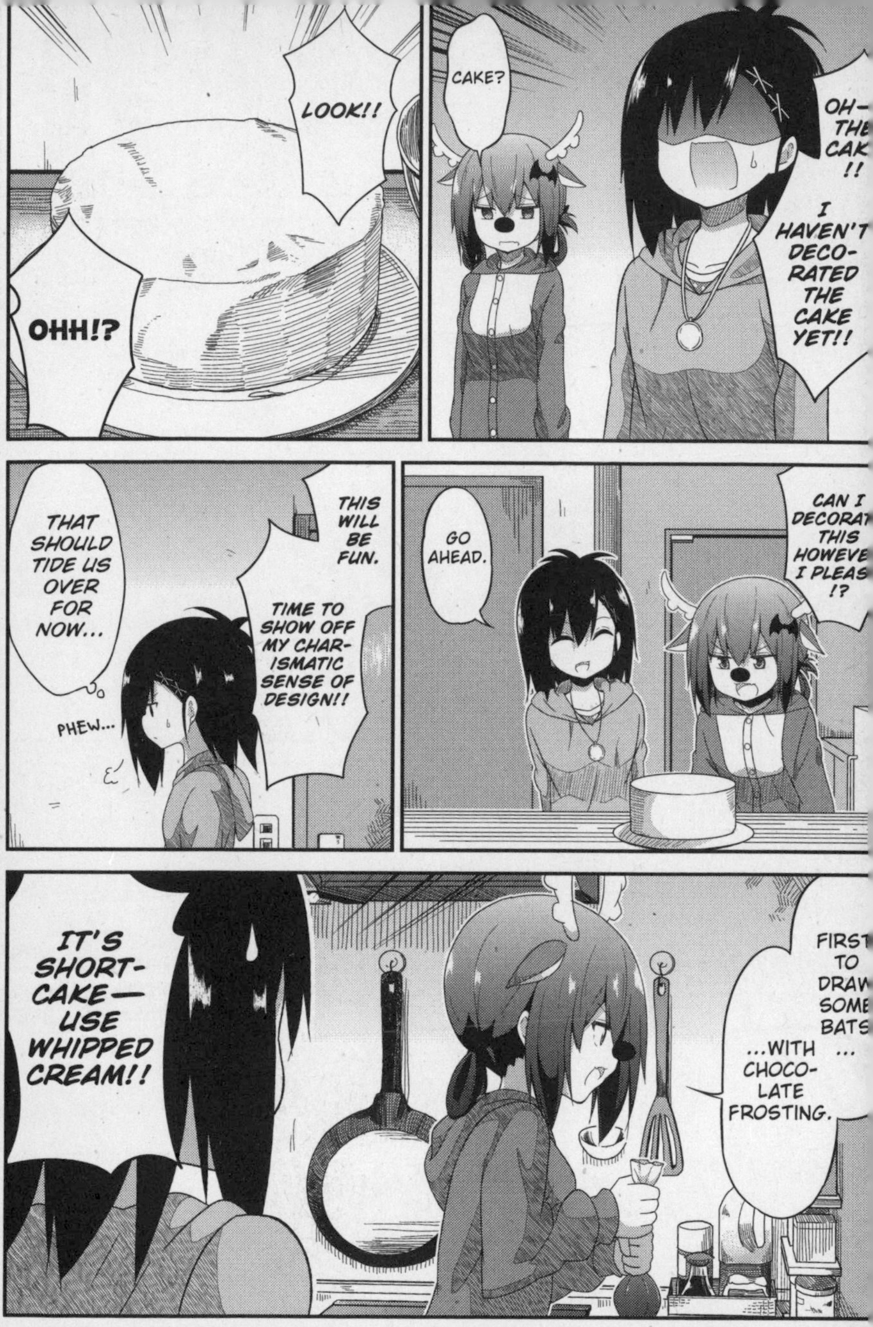
OH— THE CAK !!
I HAVEN'T DECORATED THE CAKE YET!!
CAKE?
LOOK!!
OHH!?
CAN I DECORAT THIS HOWEVE I PLEAS !?
GO AHEAD.
THIS WILL BE FUN.
TIME TO SHOW OFF MY CHARISMATIC SENSE OF DESIGN!!
THAT SHOULD TIDE US OVER FOR NOW...
PHEW...
FIRST TO DRAW SOME BATS ...
...WITH CHOCOLATE FROSTING.
IT'S SHORTCAKE— USE WHIPPED CREAM!!

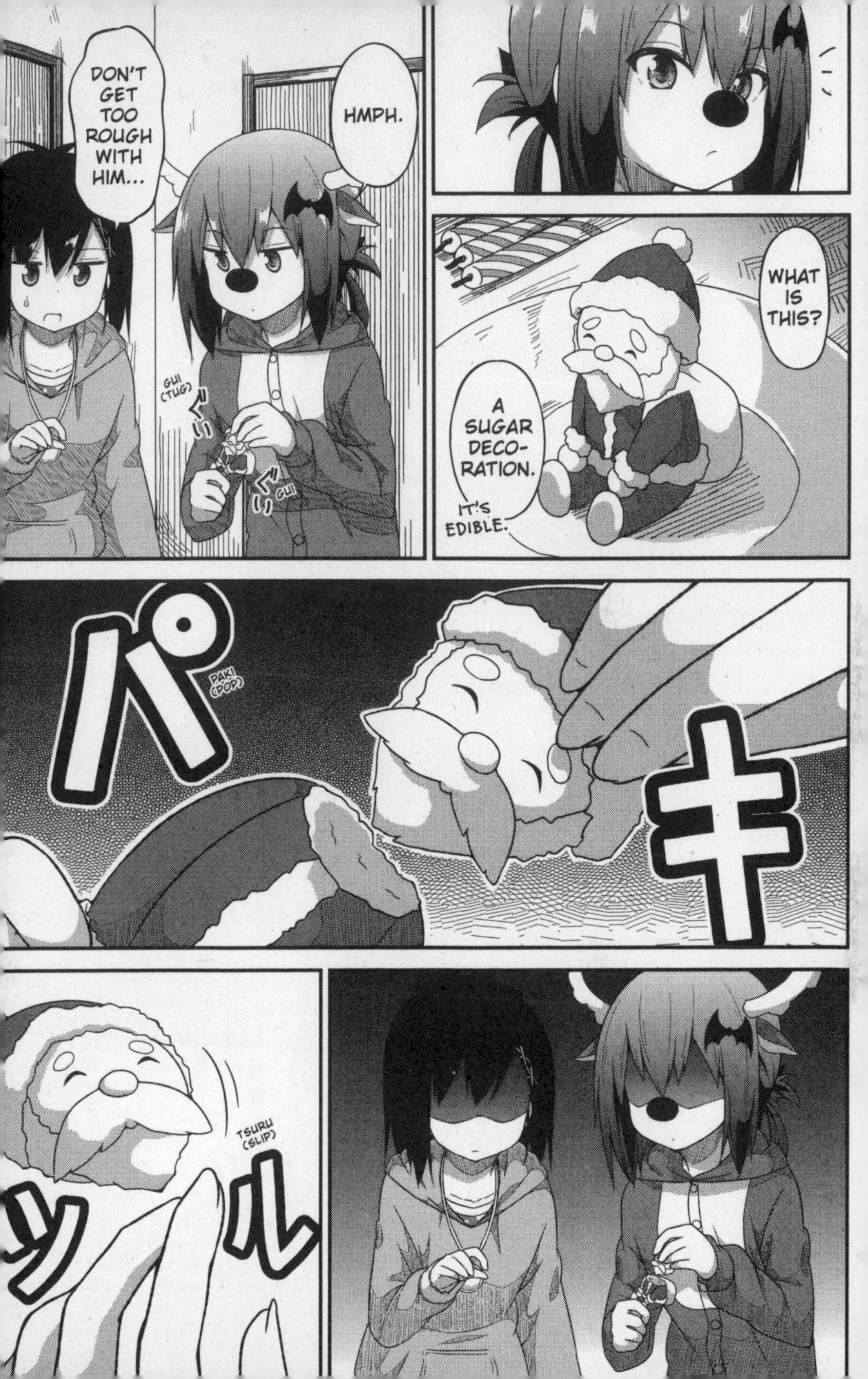
WHAT IS THIS?
A SUGAR DECO-RATION.
IT'S EDIBLE.
HMPH.
DON'T GET TOO ROUGH WITH HIM...
ぐい GUI (TUG)
ぐい GUI
パキ
PAKI (POP)
ツル
TSURU (SLIP)

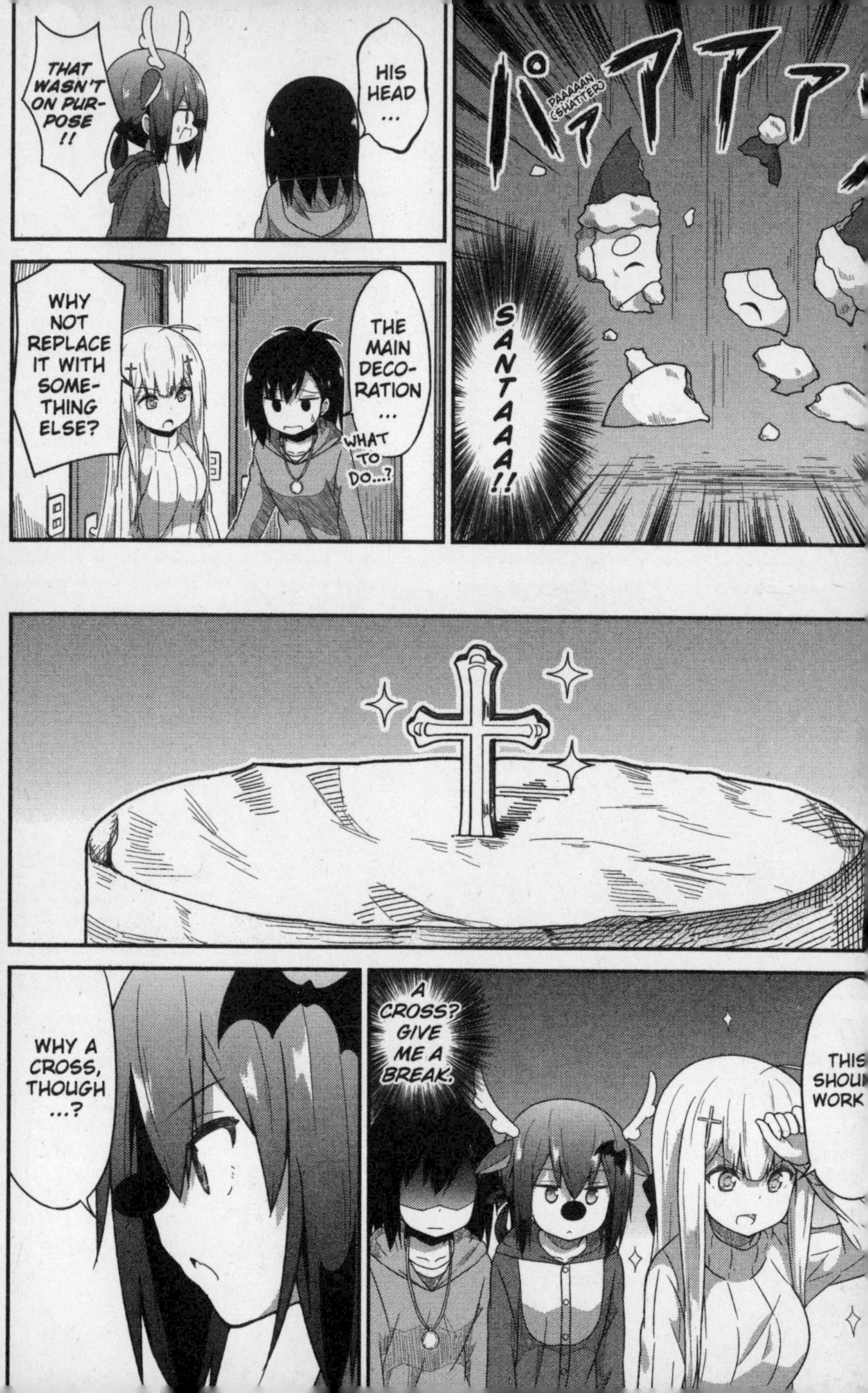
パアアアア
PAAAAAN (SHATTER)
SANTAAAA!!
HIS HEAD ...
THAT WASN'T ON PURPOSE !!
THE MAIN DECORATION ...
WHAT TO DO...?
WHY NOT REPLACE IT WITH SOMETHING ELSE?
THIS SHOUL WORK
A CROSS? GIVE ME A BREAK.
WHY A CROSS, THOUGH ...?

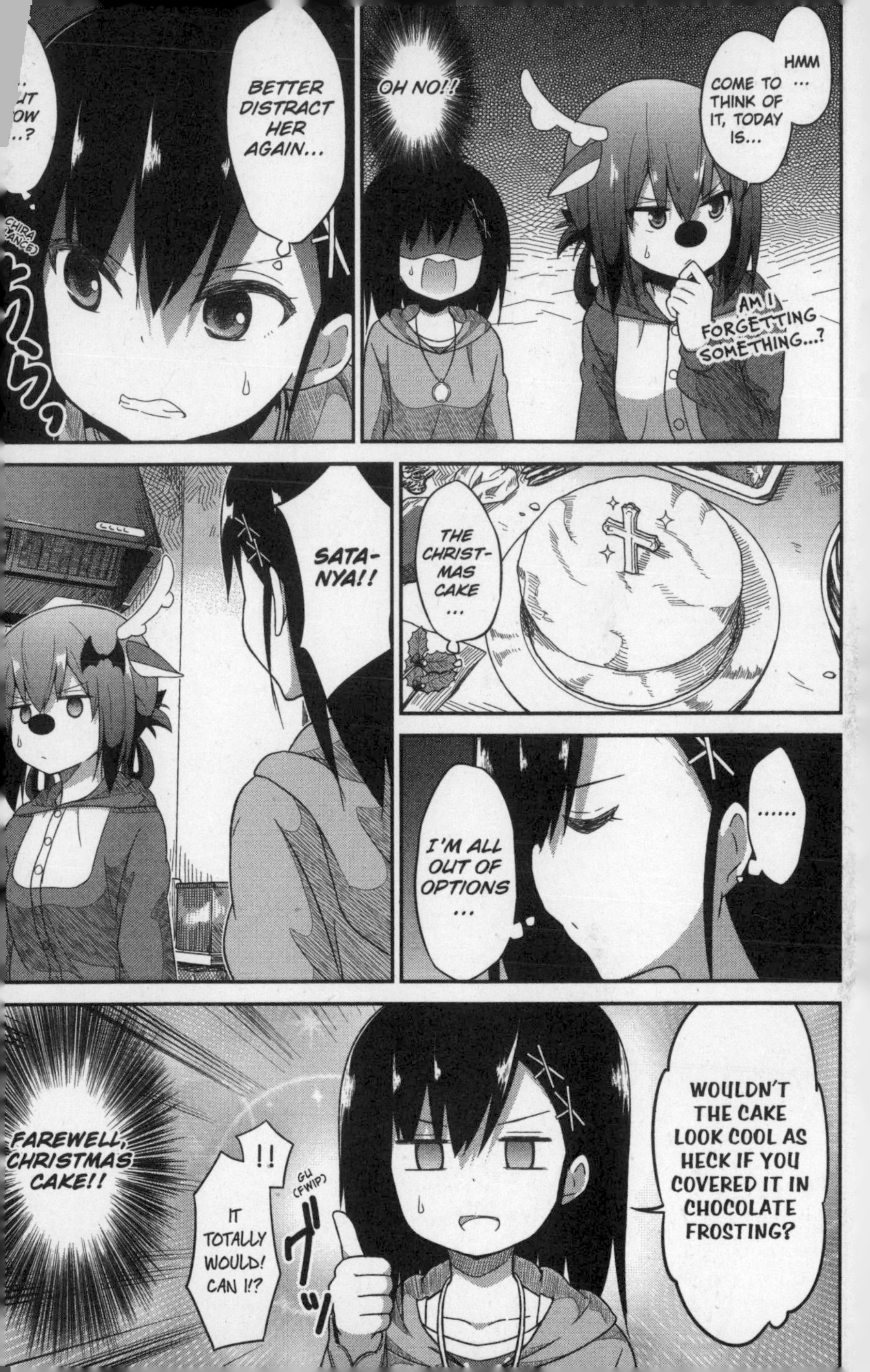
HMM ...
COME TO THINK OF IT, TODAY IS...
AM I FORGETTING SOMETHING...?
OH NO!!
BETTER DISTRACT HER AGAIN...
CHIRA
THE CHRISTMAS CAKE ...
......
I'M ALL OUT OF OPTIONS ...
SATANYA!!
WOULDN'T THE CAKE LOOK COOL AS HECK IF YOU COVERED IT IN CHOCOLATE FROSTING?
!!
GU (FWIP)
IT TOTALLY WOULD! CAN I!?
FAREWELL, CHRISTMAS CAKE!!

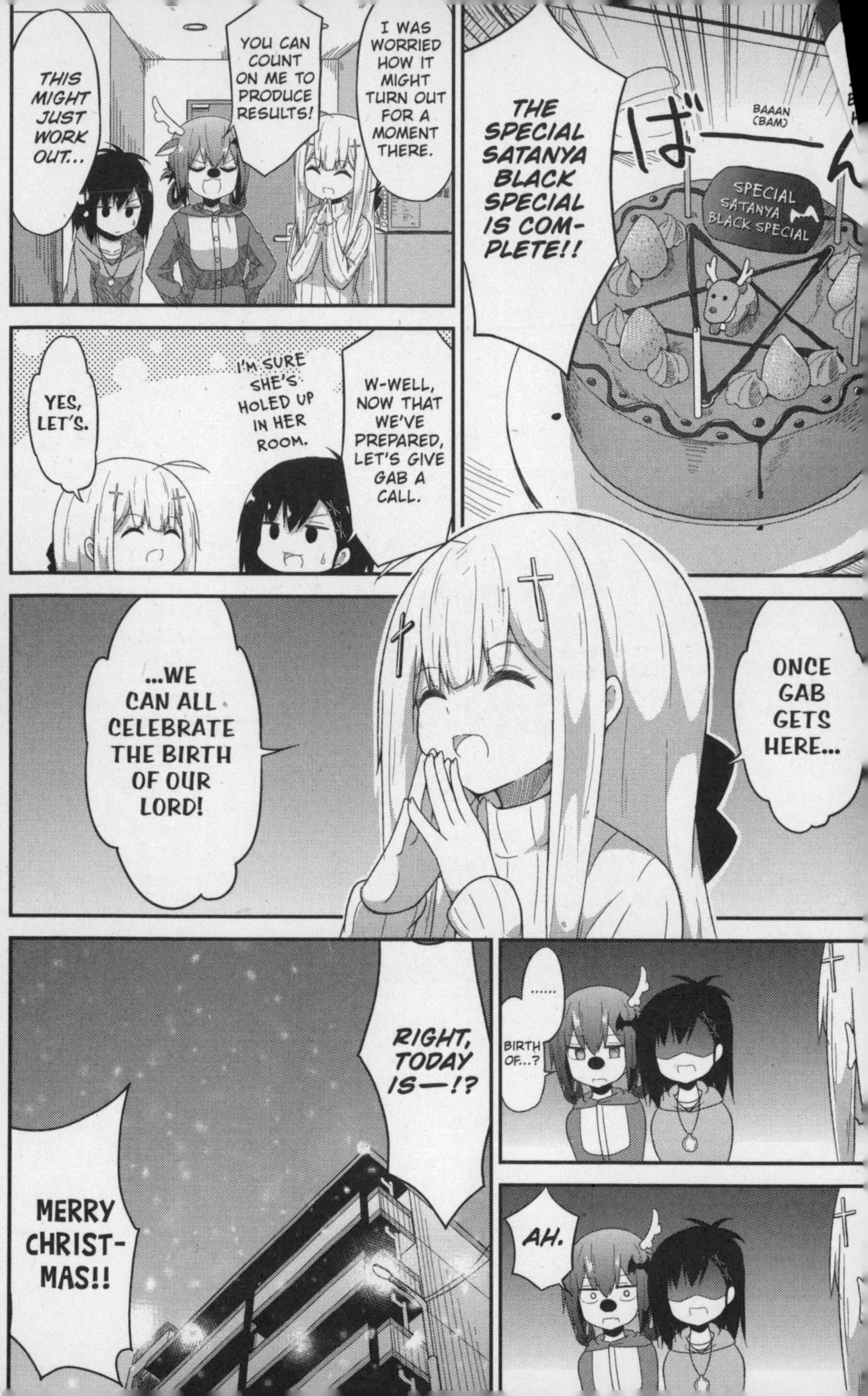
THE SPECIAL SATANYA BLACK SPECIAL IS COMPLETE!!
BAAAN (BAM)
SPECIAL SATANYA BLACK SPECIAL
I WAS WORRIED HOW IT MIGHT TURN OUT FOR A MOMENT THERE.
YOU CAN COUNT ON ME TO PRODUCE RESULTS!
THIS MIGHT JUST WORK OUT...
W-WELL, NOW THAT WE'VE PREPARED, LET'S GIVE GAB A CALL.
I'M SURE SHE'S HOLED UP IN HER ROOM.
YES, LET'S.
ONCE GAB GETS HERE...
...WE CAN ALL CELEBRATE THE BIRTH OF OUR LORD!
......
BIRTH OF...?
AH.
RIGHT, TODAY IS—!?
MERRY CHRISTMAS!!

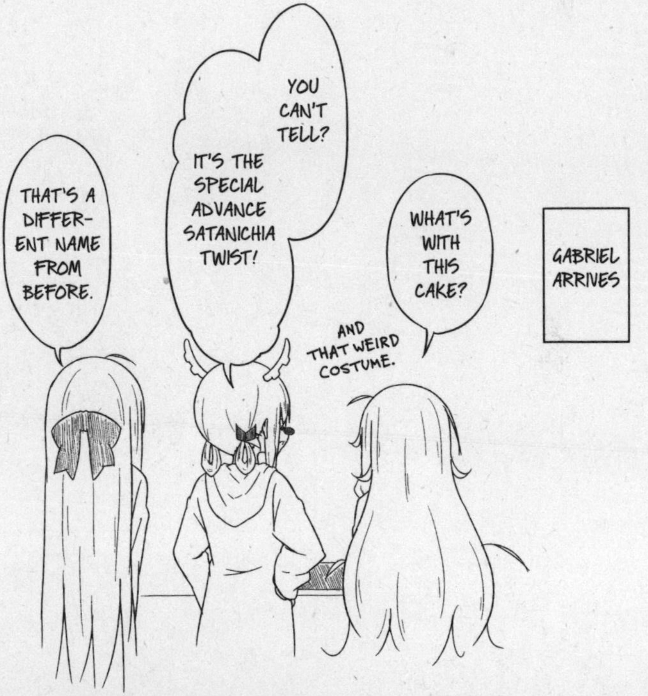
GABRIEL ARRIVES
WHAT'S WITH THIS CAKE?
AND THAT WEIRD COSTUME.
YOU CAN'T TELL?
IT'S THE SPECIAL ADVANCE SATANICHIA TWIST!
THAT'S A DIFFER-ENT NAME FROM BEFORE.

Gabriel Dropout

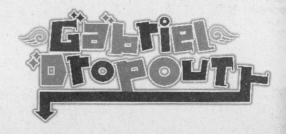

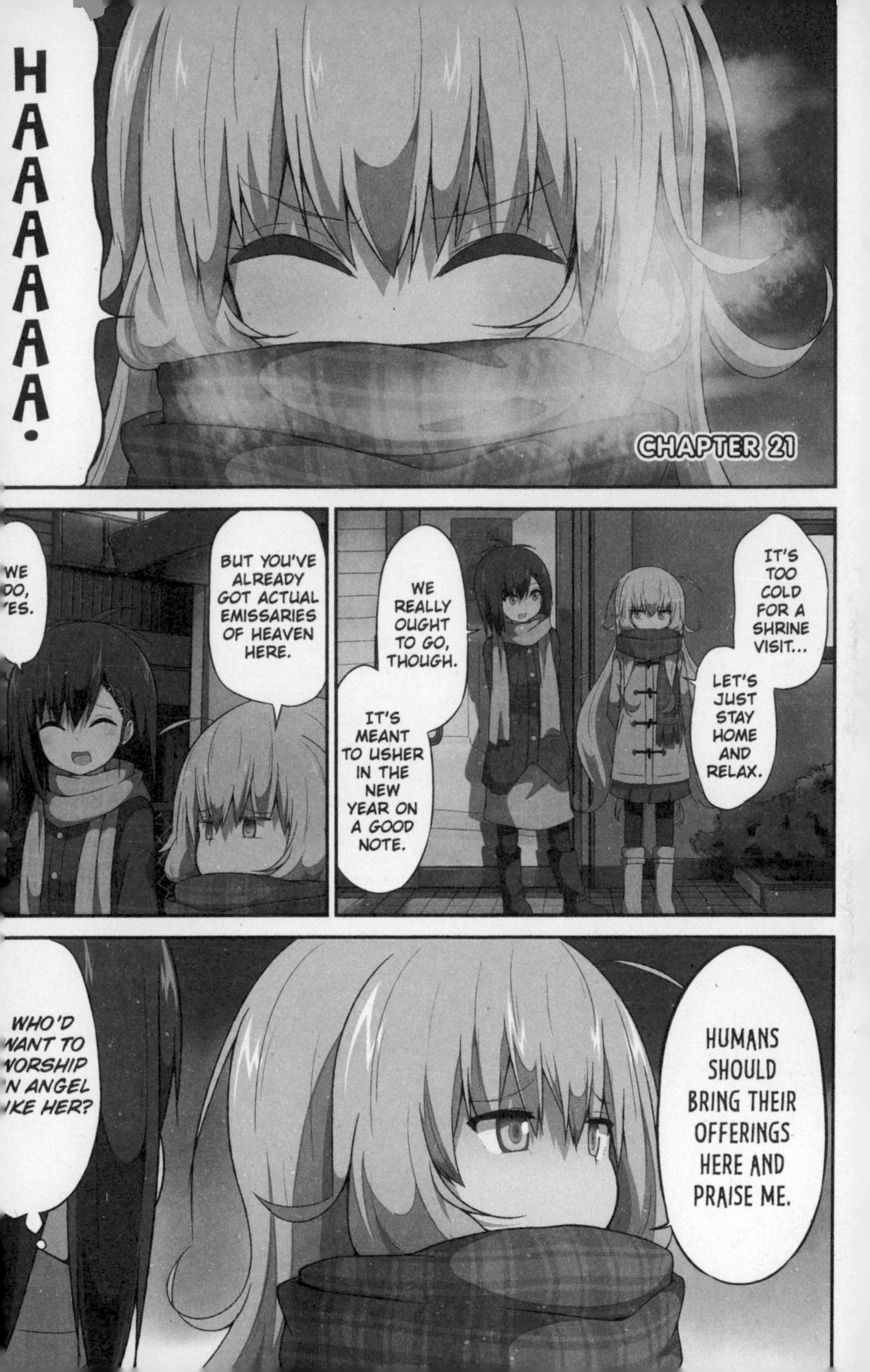
HAAAAAAA!
CHAPTER 21
IT'S TOO COLD FOR A SHRINE VISIT...
LET'S JUST STAY HOME AND RELAX.
WE REALLY OUGHT TO GO, THOUGH.
IT'S MEANT TO USHER IN THE NEW YEAR ON A GOOD NOTE.
BUT YOU'VE ALREADY GOT ACTUAL EMISSARIES OF HEAVEN HERE.
WE DO, YES.
HUMANS SHOULD BRING THEIR OFFERINGS HERE AND PRAISE ME.
WHO'D WANT TO WORSHIP AN ANGEL LIKE HER?

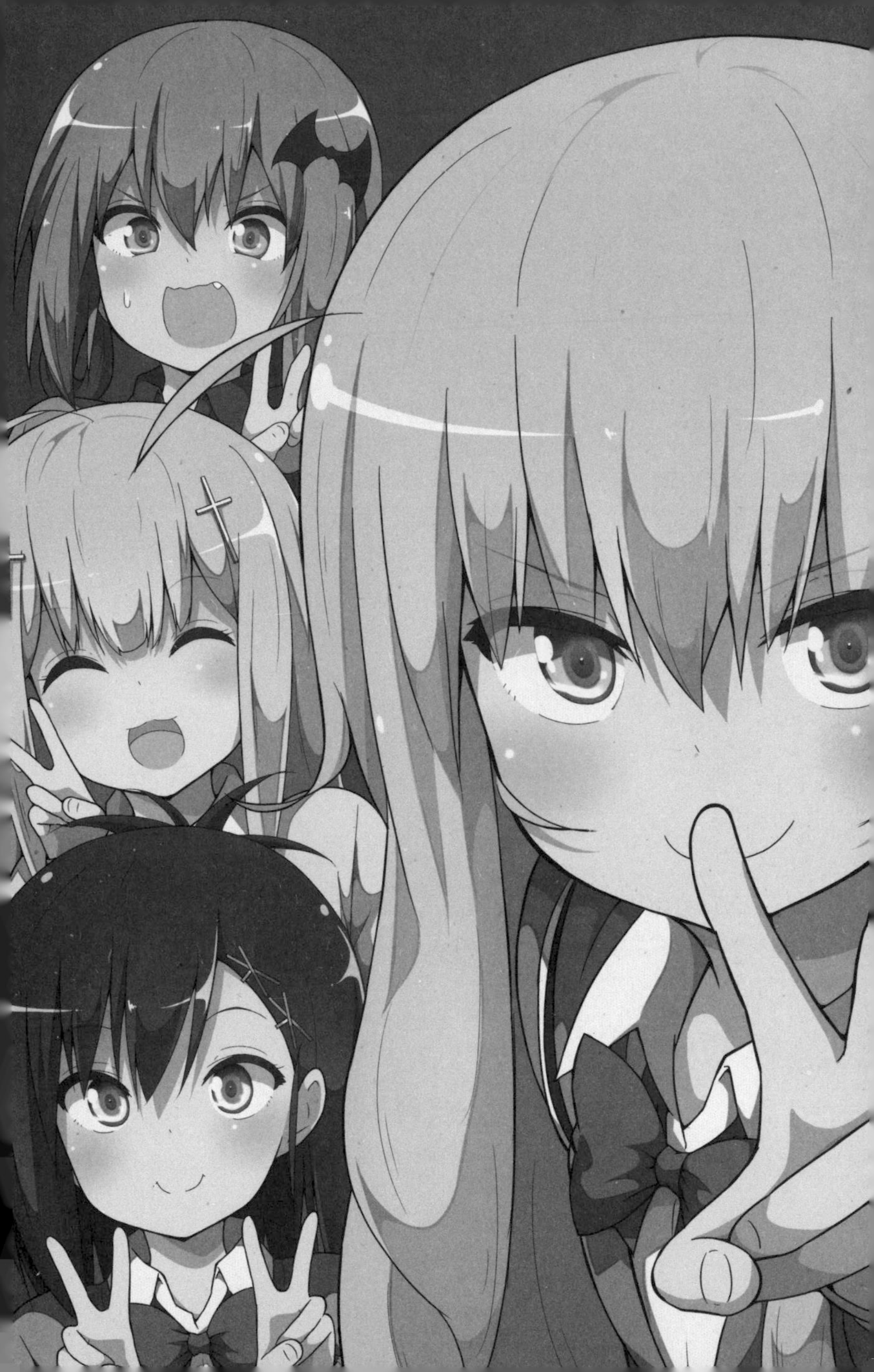

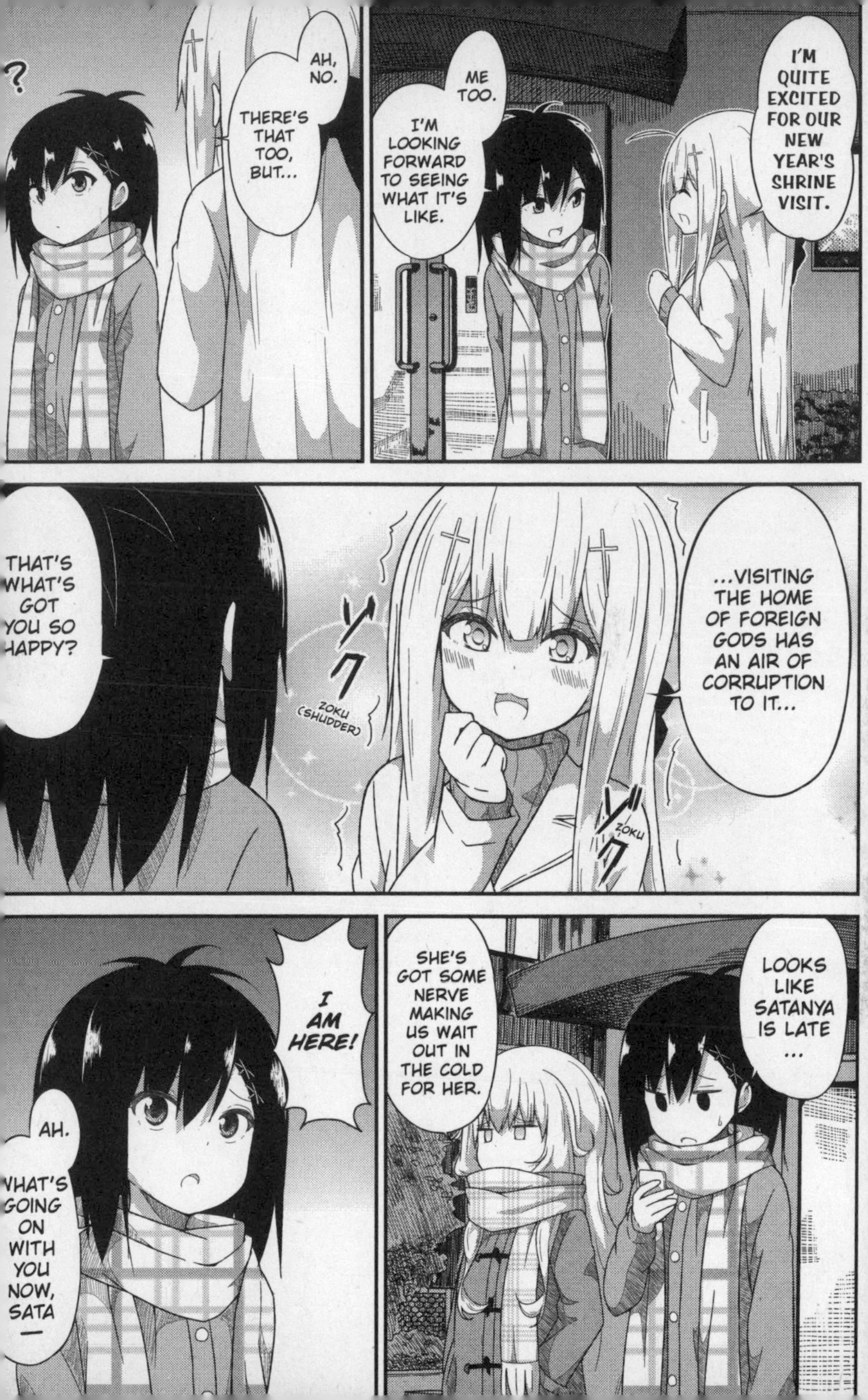
I'M QUITE EXCITED FOR OUR NEW YEAR'S SHRINE VISIT.
ME TOO.
I'M LOOKING FORWARD TO SEEING WHAT IT'S LIKE.
AH, NO.
THERE'S THAT TOO, BUT...
?
...VISITING THE HOME OF FOREIGN GODS HAS AN AIR OF CORRUPTION TO IT...
ゾク
ZOKU (SHUDDER)
ゾク
ZOKU
THAT'S WHAT'S GOT YOU SO HAPPY?
LOOKS LIKE SATANYA IS LATE ...
SHE'S GOT SOME NERVE MAKING US WAIT OUT IN THE COLD FOR HER.
I AM HERE!
AH.
WHAT'S GOING ON WITH YOU NOW, SATA—

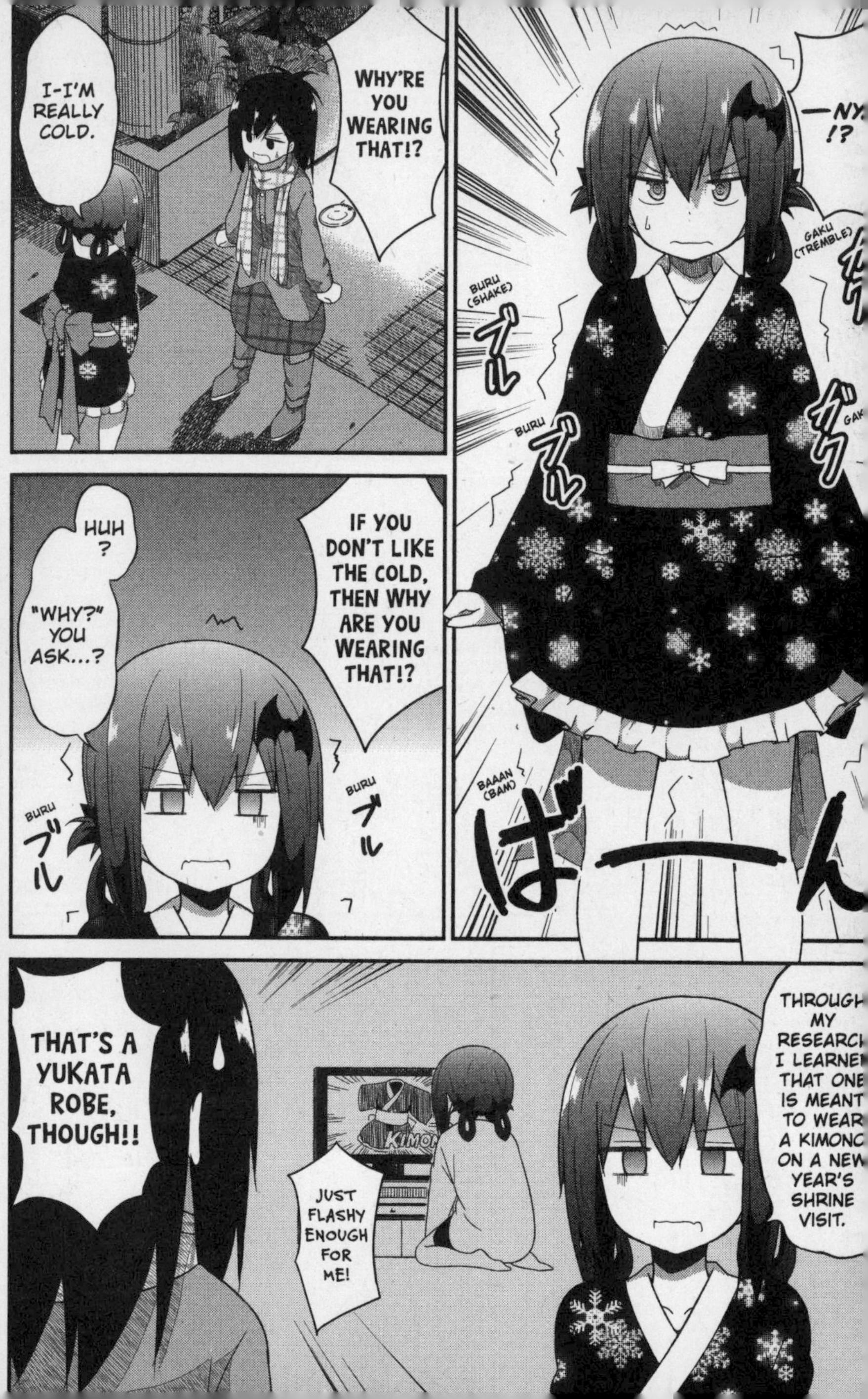
—NY
!?
GAKU (TREMBLE)
ガク
BURU (SHAKE)
ブル
BURU
ブル
GAK
BAAAN (BAM)
ばーん
WHY'RE YOU WEARING THAT!?
I-I'M REALLY COLD.
IF YOU DON'T LIKE THE COLD, THEN WHY ARE YOU WEARING THAT!?
BURU
ブル
HUH?
"WHY?" YOU ASK...?
BURU
ブル
THROUGH MY RESEARCH I LEARNED THAT ONE IS MEANT TO WEAR A KIMONO ON A NEW YEAR'S SHRINE VISIT.
KIMON
JUST FLASHY ENOUGH FOR ME!
THAT'S A YUKATA ROBE, THOUGH!!

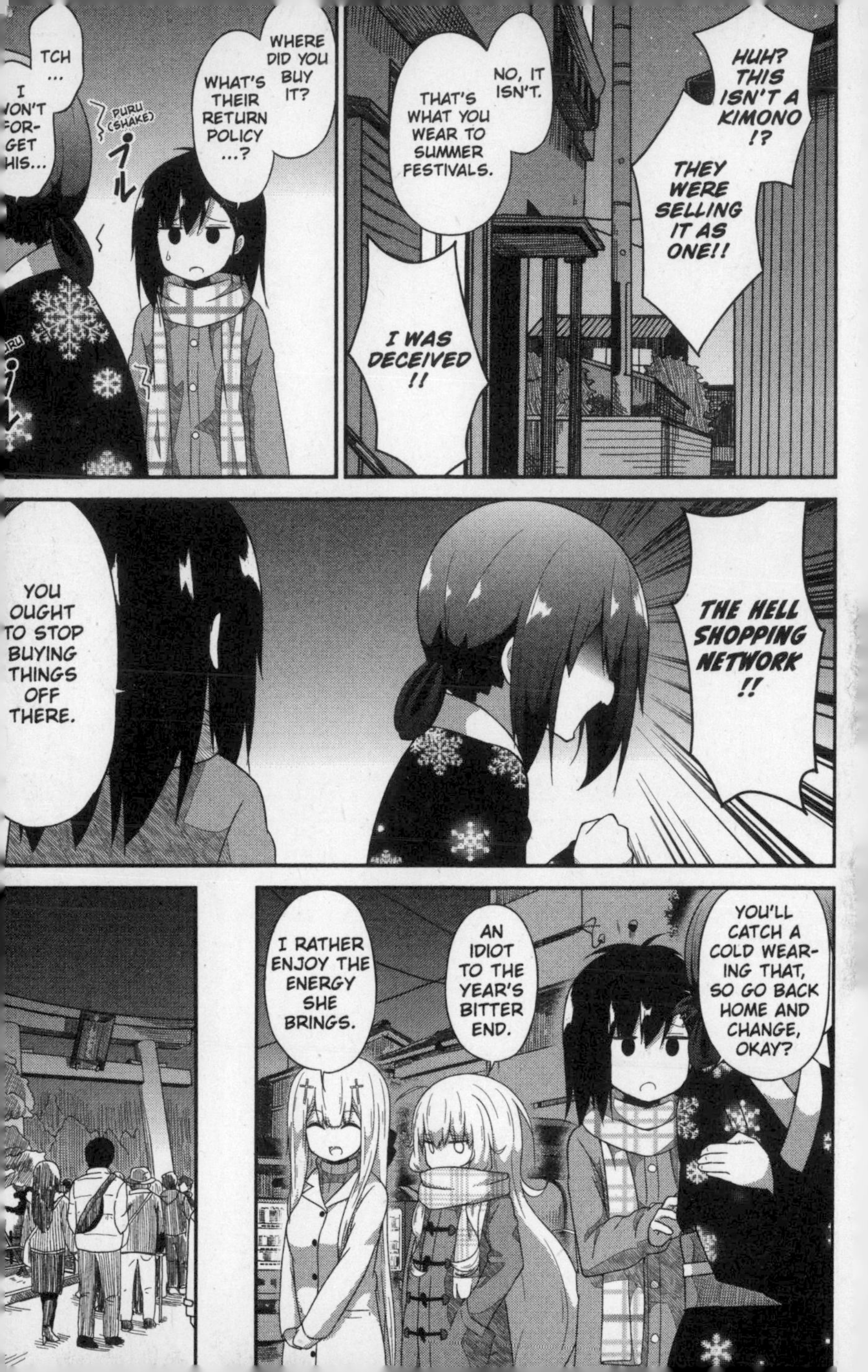
HUH? THIS ISN'T A KIMONO!? THEY WERE SELLING IT AS ONE!!
NO, IT ISN'T. THAT'S WHAT YOU WEAR TO SUMMER FESTIVALS.
I WAS DECEIVED!!
WHERE DID YOU BUY IT? WHAT'S THEIR RETURN POLICY...?
PURU (SHAKE)
TCH... I WON'T FORGET THIS...
PURU
THE HELL SHOPPING NETWORK!!
YOU OUGHT TO STOP BUYING THINGS OFF THERE.
YOU'LL CATCH A COLD WEARING THAT, SO GO BACK HOME AND CHANGE, OKAY?
AN IDIOT TO THE YEAR'S BITTER END.
I RATHER ENJOY THE ENERGY SHE BRINGS.

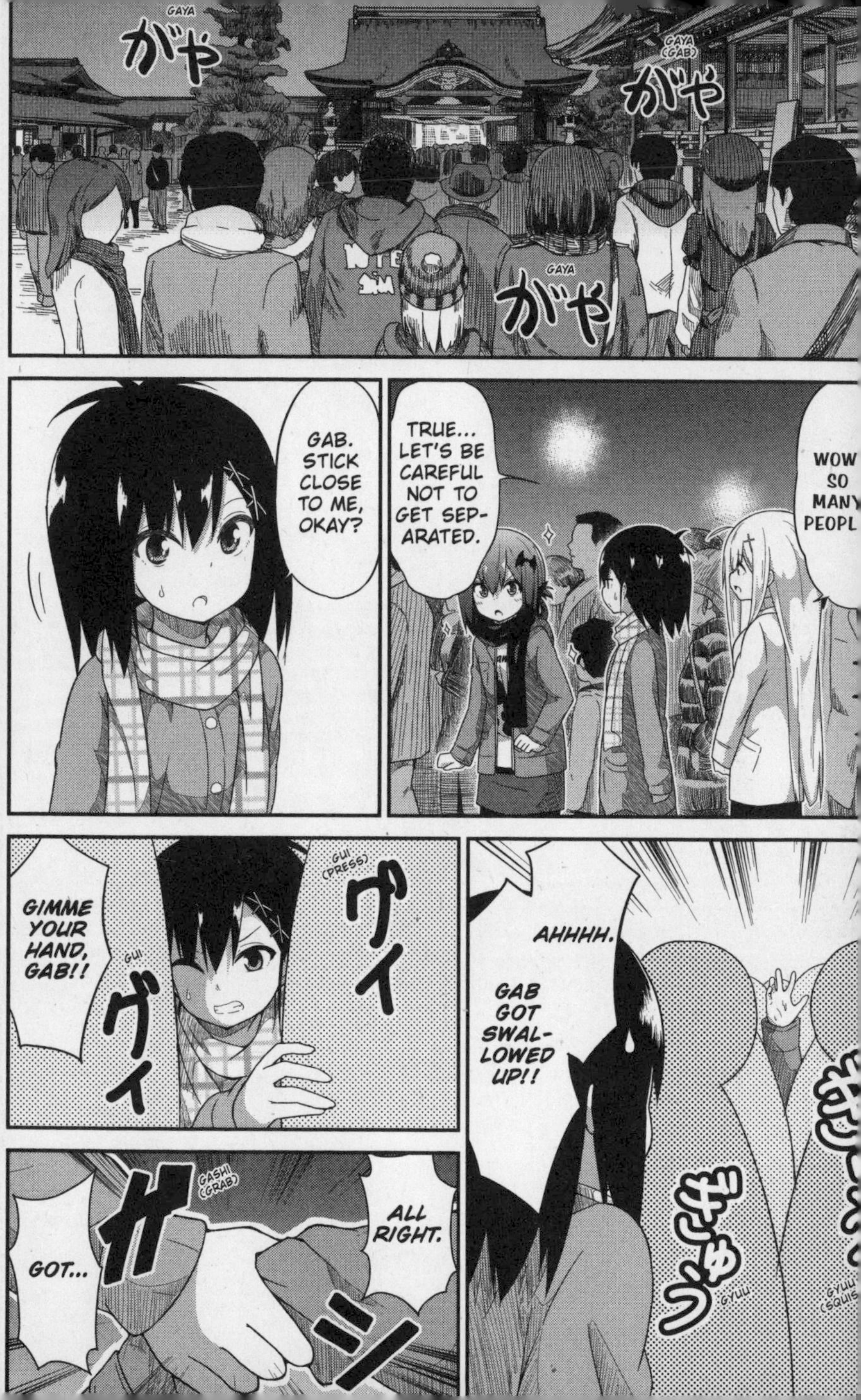
GAYA (GAB)
がや
GAYA
がや
GAYA
がや
WOW SO MANY PEOPL
TRUE... LET'S BE CAREFUL NOT TO GET SEP-ARATED.
GAB. STICK CLOSE TO ME, OKAY?
AHHHH.
GAB GOT SWAL-LOWED UP!!
GYUU (SQUIS
GYUU
ぎゅう
GUI (PRESS)
グイ
GUI
グイ
GIMME YOUR HAND, GAB!!
ALL RIGHT.
GASHI (GRAB)
ガシ
GOT...

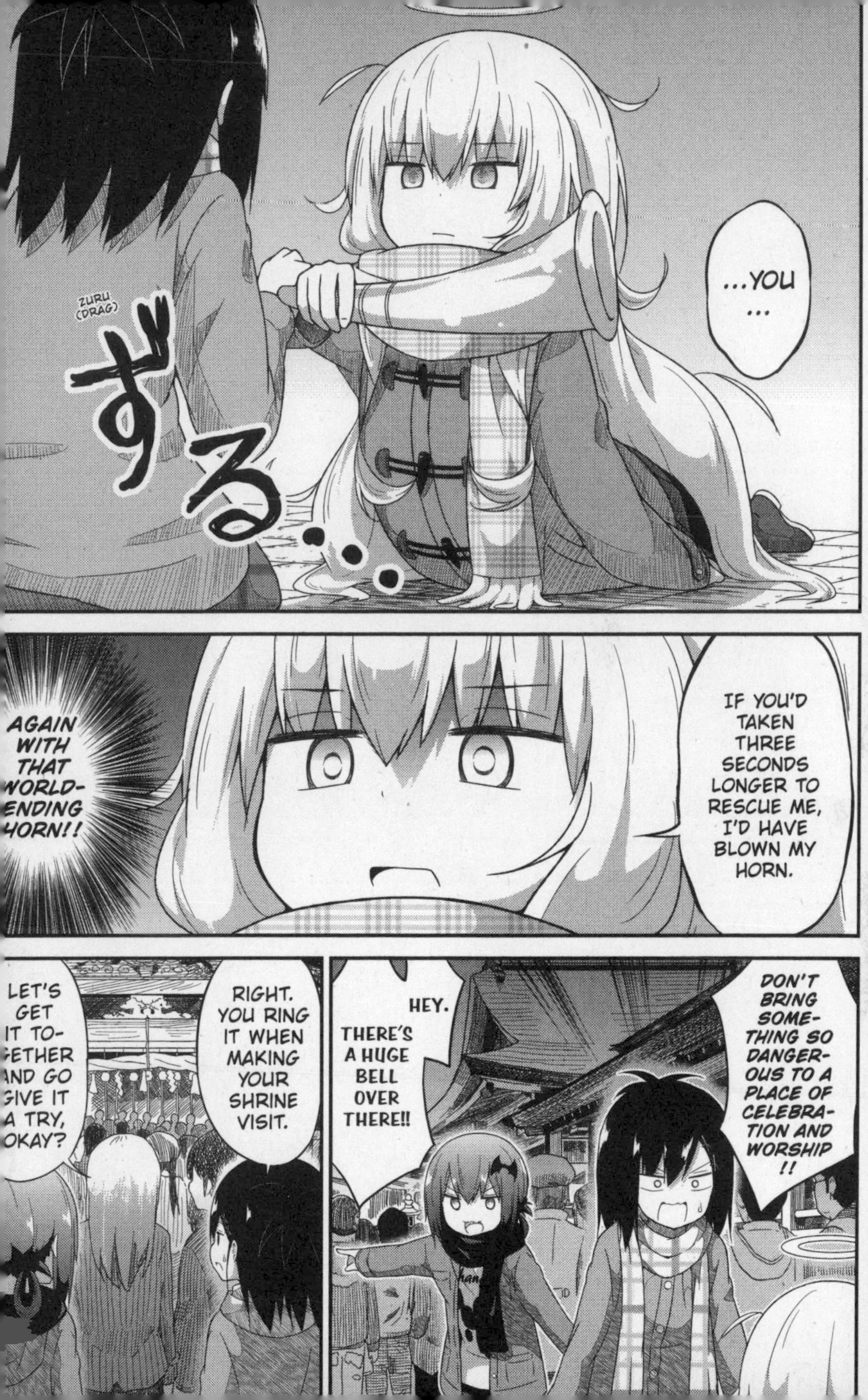
...YOU ...
ZURU (DRAG)
ずる...
IF YOU'D TAKEN THREE SECONDS LONGER TO RESCUE ME, I'D HAVE BLOWN MY HORN.
AGAIN WITH THAT WORLD-ENDING HORN!!
DON'T BRING SOME-THING SO DANGER-OUS TO A PLACE OF CELEBRA-TION AND WORSHIP !!
HEY. THERE'S A HUGE BELL OVER THERE!!
RIGHT. YOU RING IT WHEN MAKING YOUR SHRINE VISIT.
LET'S GET IT TO-GETHER AND GO GIVE IT A TRY, OKAY?

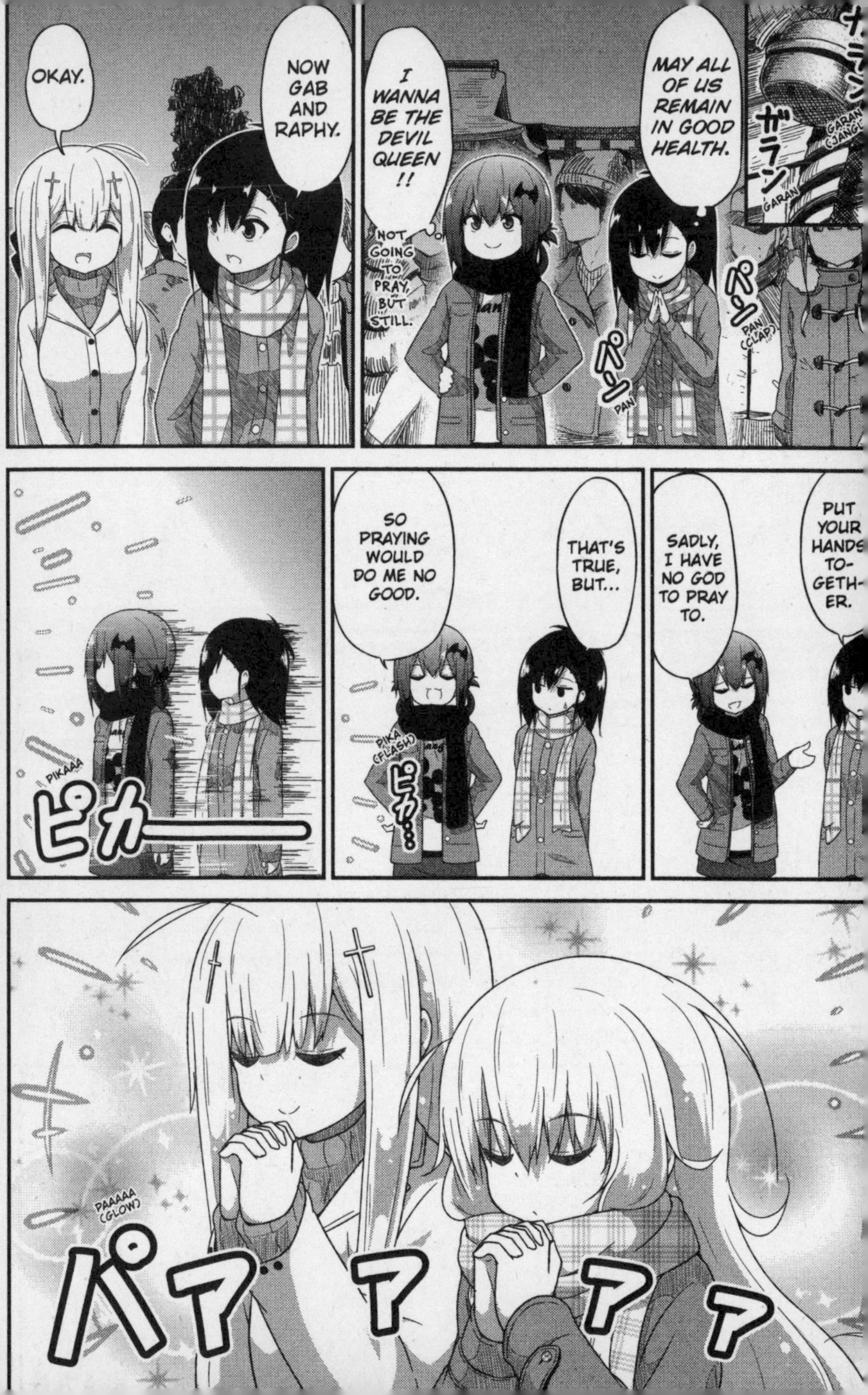
ガラン
GARAN (JANGLE)
ガラン
GARAN
MAY ALL OF US REMAIN IN GOOD HEALTH.
パン
PAN (CLAP)
パン
PAN
I WANNA BE THE DEVIL QUEEN!!
NOT GOING TO PRAY, BUT STILL.
NOW GAB AND RAPHY.
OKAY.
PUT YOUR HANDS TO-GETH-ER.
SADLY, I HAVE NO GOD TO PRAY TO.
THAT'S TRUE, BUT...
SO PRAYING WOULD DO ME NO GOOD.
PIKA (FLASH)
ピカ…
PIKAAA
ピカー
PAAAAA (GLOW)
パァァァァ

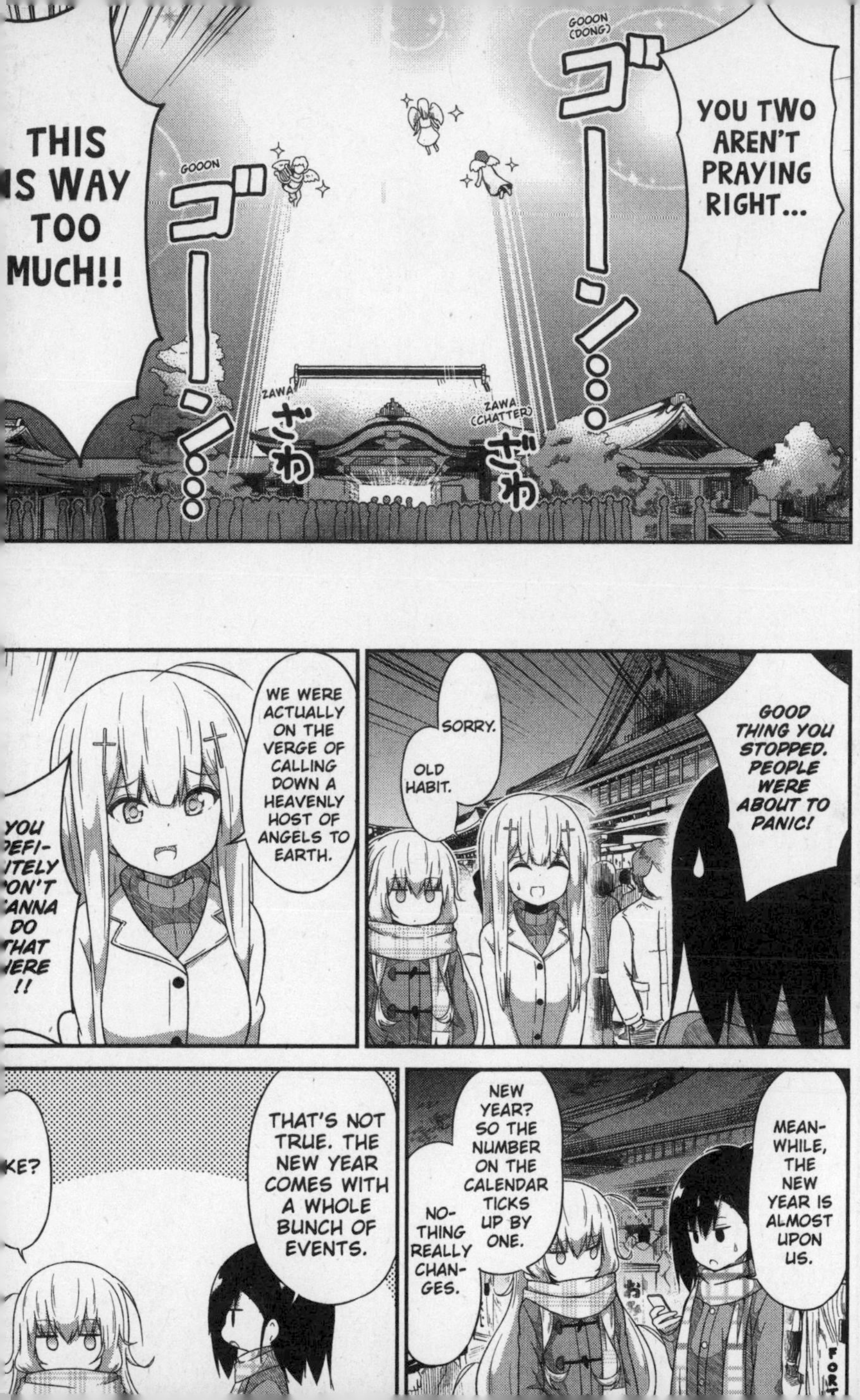
YOU TWO AREN'T PRAYING RIGHT...
GOOON (DONG)
ゴーン…
GOOON
ゴーン…
ZAWA (CHATTER)
ざわ
ZAWA
ざわ
THIS IS WAY TOO MUCH!!
GOOD THING YOU STOPPED. PEOPLE WERE ABOUT TO PANIC!
SORRY.
OLD HABIT.
WE WERE ACTUALLY ON THE VERGE OF CALLING DOWN A HEAVENLY HOST OF ANGELS TO EARTH.
YOU EFI- ITELY ON'T ANNA DO THAT ERE !!
MEAN-WHILE, THE NEW YEAR IS ALMOST UPON US.
NEW YEAR? SO THE NUMBER ON THE CALENDAR TICKS UP BY ONE.
NO-THING REALLY CHANGES.
THAT'S NOT TRUE. THE NEW YEAR COMES WITH A WHOLE BUNCH OF EVENTS.
KE?

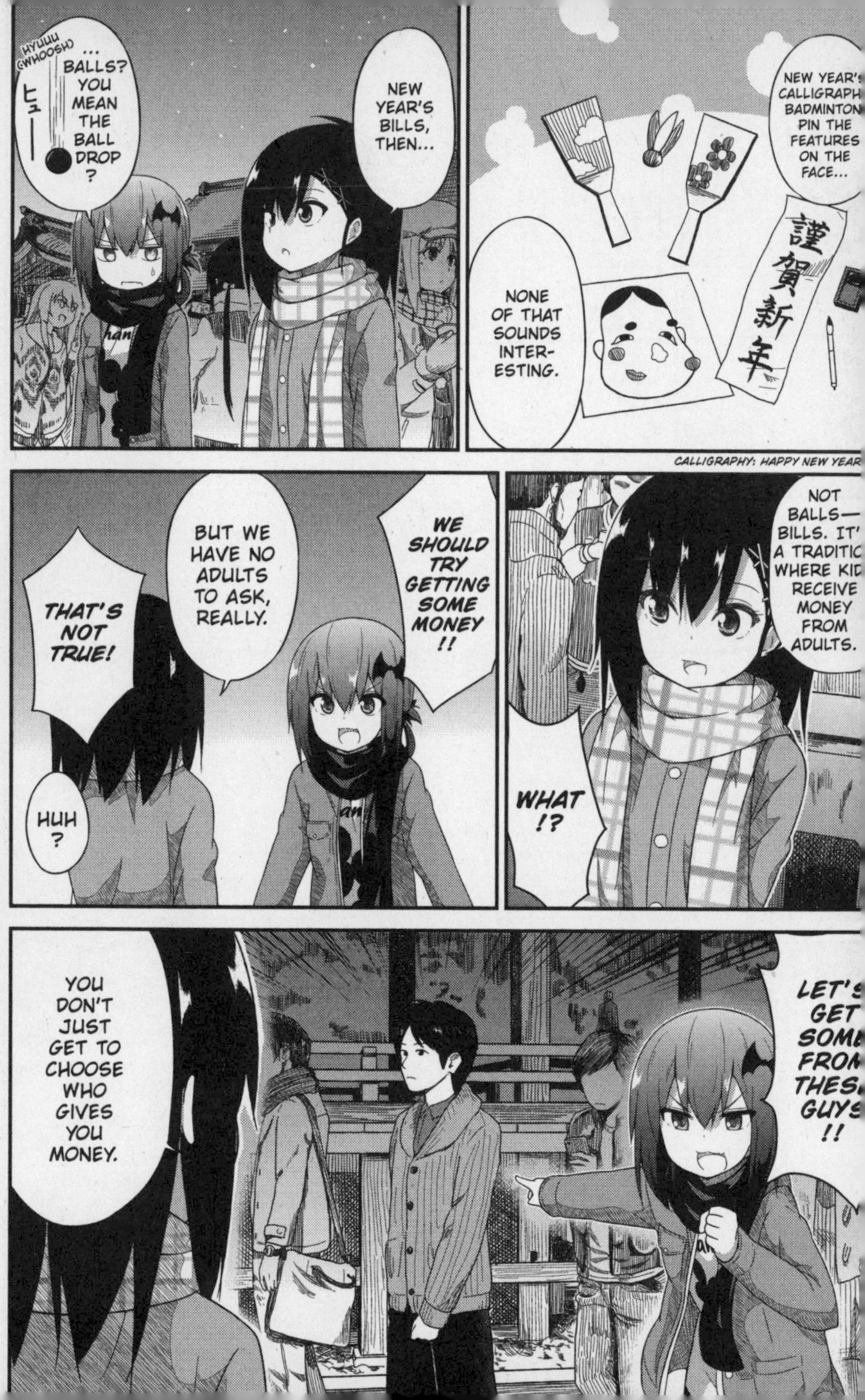
NEW YEAR'S CALLIGRAPH BADMINTON PIN THE FEATURES ON THE FACE...
謹賀新年
NONE OF THAT SOUNDS INTER-ESTING.
CALLIGRAPHY: HAPPY NEW YEAR
NEW YEAR'S BILLS, THEN...
HYUUU (WHOOSH)
ヒュー
...BALLS? YOU MEAN THE BALL DROP?
NOT BALLS—BILLS. IT' A TRADITIC WHERE KID RECEIVE MONEY FROM ADULTS.
WHAT!?
WE SHOULD TRY GETTING SOME MONEY!!
BUT WE HAVE NO ADULTS TO ASK, REALLY.
THAT'S NOT TRUE!
HUH?
LET'S GET SOME FROM THESE GUYS!!
YOU DON'T JUST GET TO CHOOSE WHO GIVES YOU MONEY.

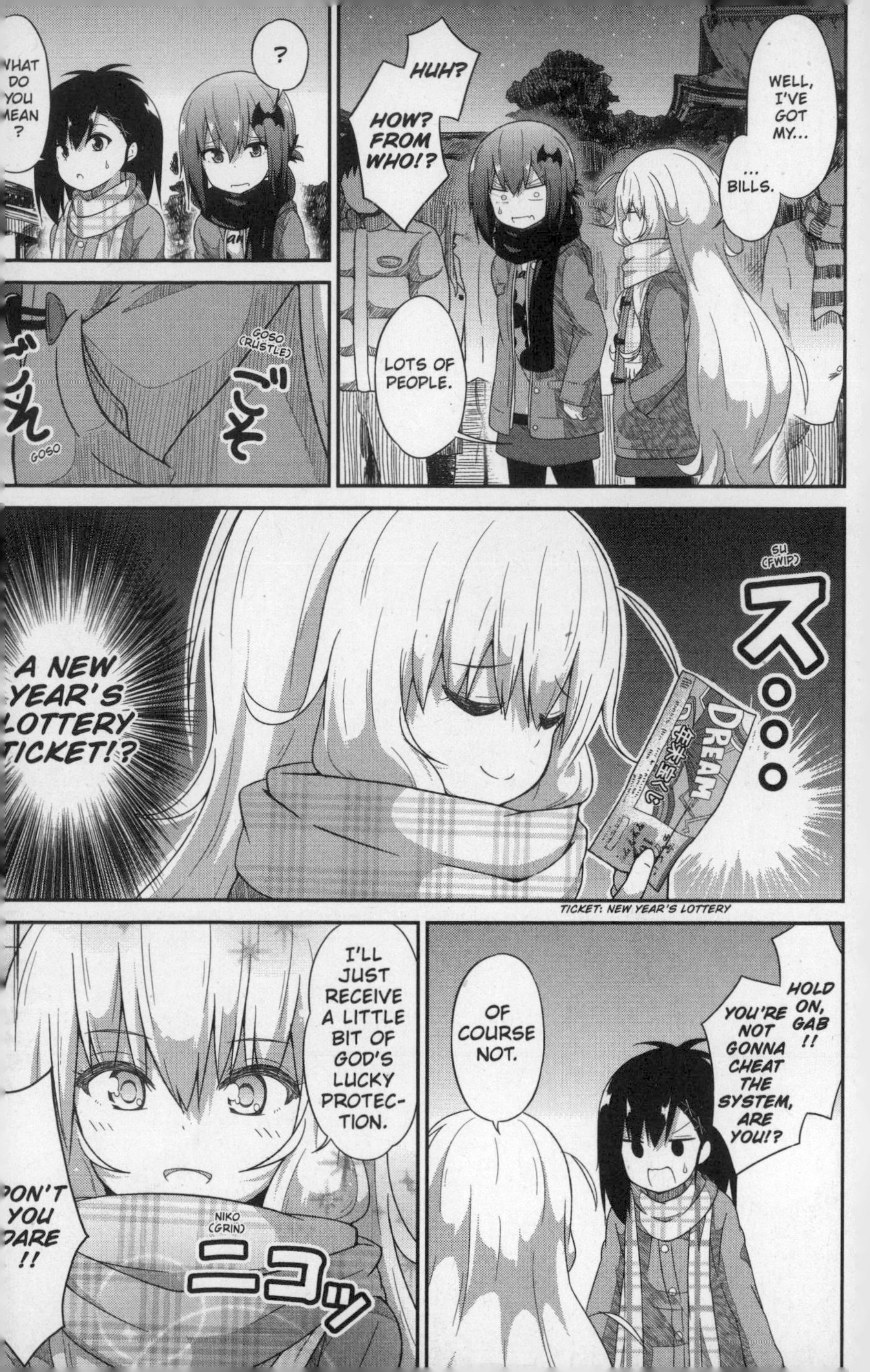
WELL, I'VE GOT MY...
... BILLS.
HUH?
HOW? FROM WHO!?
LOTS OF PEOPLE.
?
WHAT DO YOU MEAN ?
GOSO (RUSTLE)
ごそ
ごそ
GOSO
SU (FWIP)
ス…
A NEW YEAR'S LOTTERY TICKET!?
DREAM
年末宝くじ
TICKET: NEW YEAR'S LOTTERY
HOLD ON, GAB !!
YOU'RE NOT GONNA CHEAT THE SYSTEM, ARE YOU!?
OF COURSE NOT.
I'LL JUST RECEIVE A LITTLE BIT OF GOD'S LUCKY PROTECTION.
NIKO (GRIN)
ニコッ
DON'T YOU DARE !!

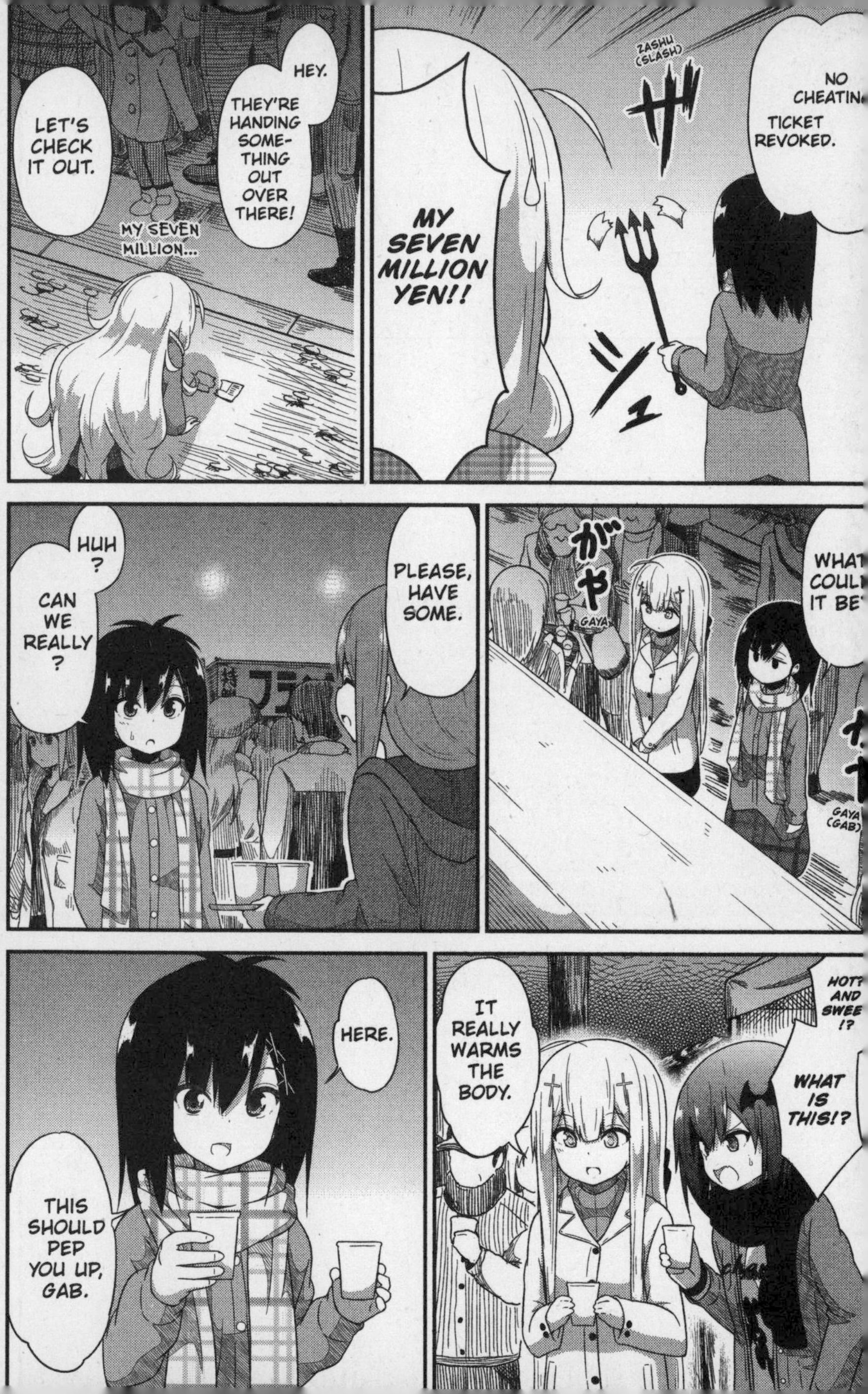
NO CHEATIN
TICKET REVOKED.
ZASHU (SLASH)
MY SEVEN MILLION YEN!!
HEY.
THEY'RE HANDING SOME-THING OUT OVER THERE!
LET'S CHECK IT OUT.
MY SEVEN MILLION...
WHAT COUL IT BE
がや
GAYA
GAYA (GAB)
PLEASE, HAVE SOME.
HUH? CAN WE REALLY?
HOT AND SWEE !?
WHAT IS THIS!?
IT REALLY WARMS THE BODY.
HERE.
THIS SHOULD PEP YOU UP, GAB.

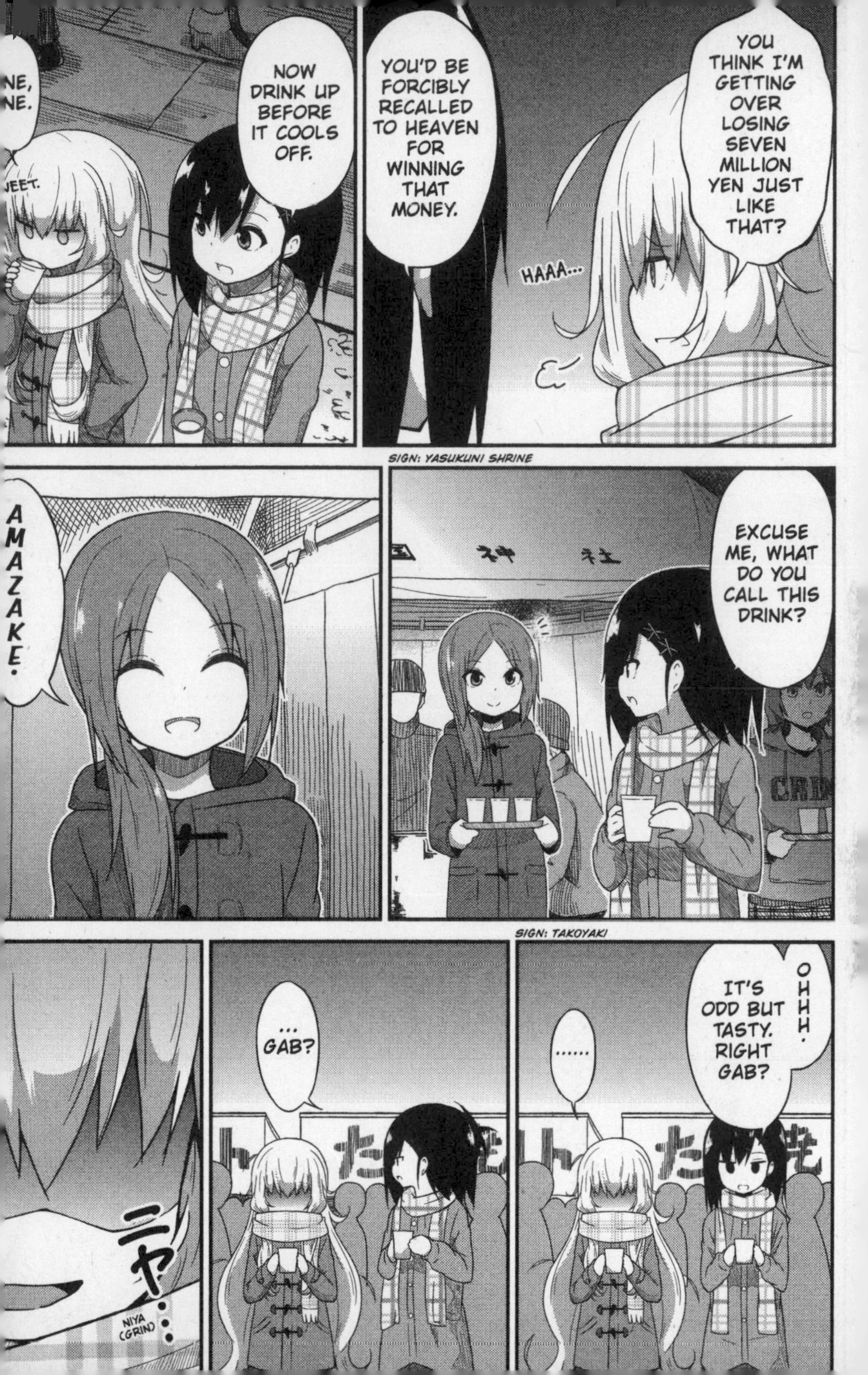
YOU THINK I'M GETTING OVER LOSING SEVEN MILLION YEN JUST LIKE THAT?
HAAA...
YOU'D BE FORCIBLY RECALLED TO HEAVEN FOR WINNING THAT MONEY.
NOW DRINK UP BEFORE IT COOLS OFF.
SIGN: YASUKUNI SHRINE
EXCUSE ME, WHAT DO YOU CALL THIS DRINK?
AMAZAKE.
SIGN: TAKOYAKI
OHHH.
IT'S ODD BUT TASTY. RIGHT GAB?
......
... GAB?
ニヤ
NIYA (GRIN)

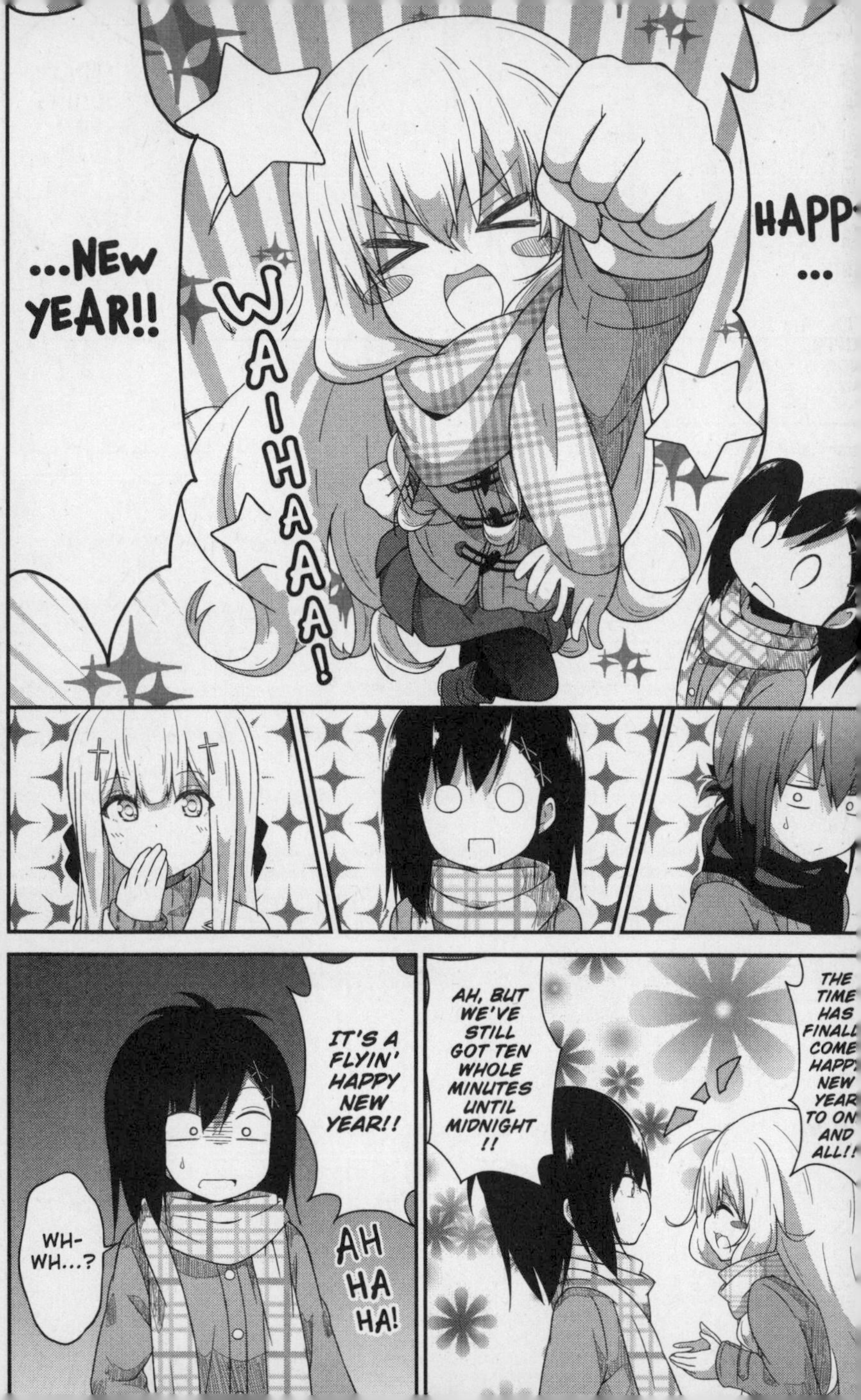
HAPP-...
WAIHAAAA!
...NEW YEAR!!
THE TIME HAS FINALL COME HAPP NEW YEAR TO ON AND ALL!!
AH, BUT WE'VE STILL GOT TEN WHOLE MINUTES UNTIL MIDNIGHT!!
IT'S A FLYIN' HAPPY NEW YEAR!!
AH HA HA HA!
WH-WH...?

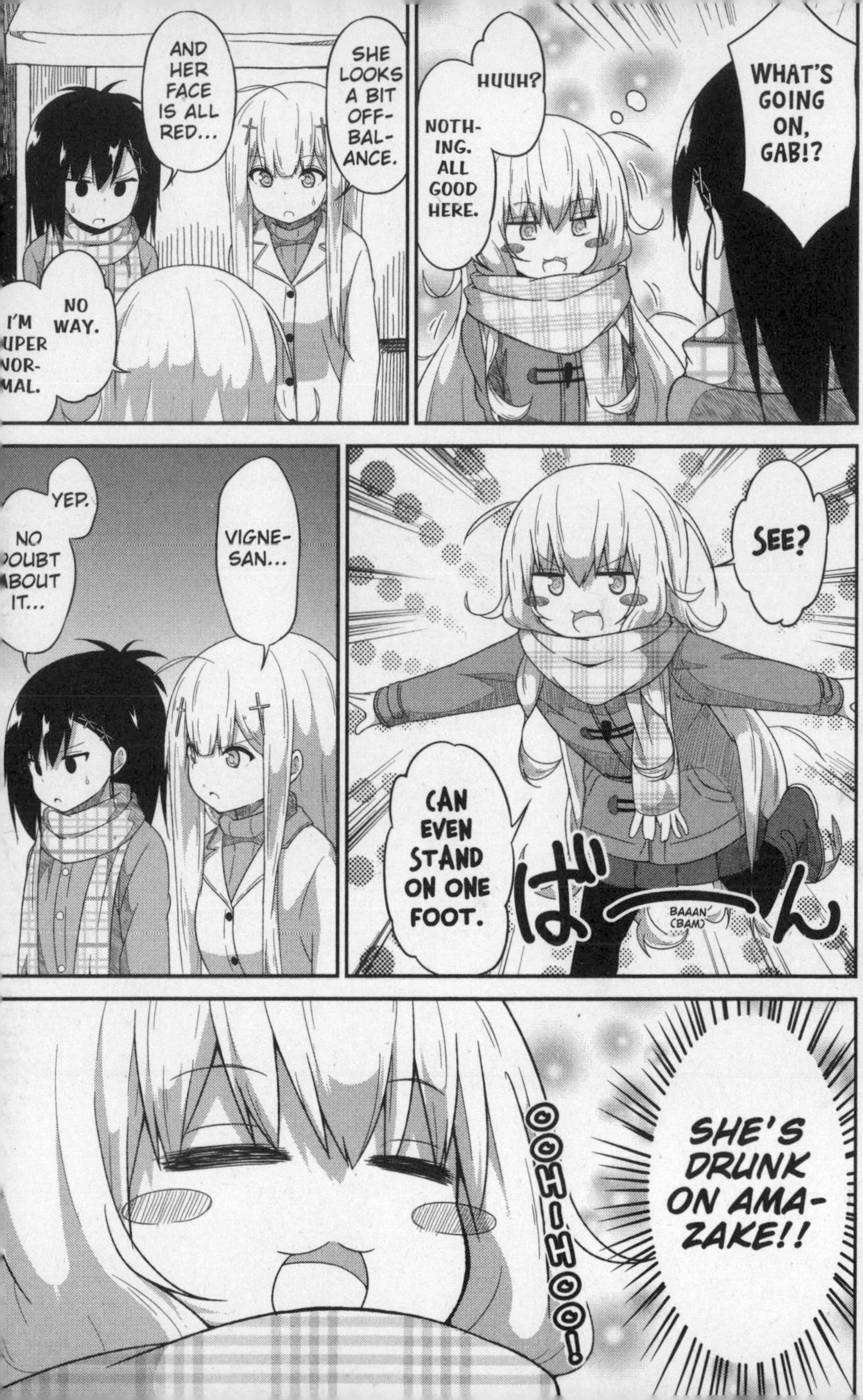
WHAT'S GOING ON, GAB!?
HUUH?
NOTHING. ALL GOOD HERE.
SHE LOOKS A BIT OFF-BALANCE.
AND HER FACE IS ALL RED...
NO WAY.
I'M UPER NORMAL.
SEE?
CAN EVEN STAND ON ONE FOOT.
ばーん
BAAAN (BAM)
VIGNE-SAN...
YEP.
NO OUBT BOUT IT...
SHE'S DRUNK ON AMAZAKE!!
OOHI-HOOO!

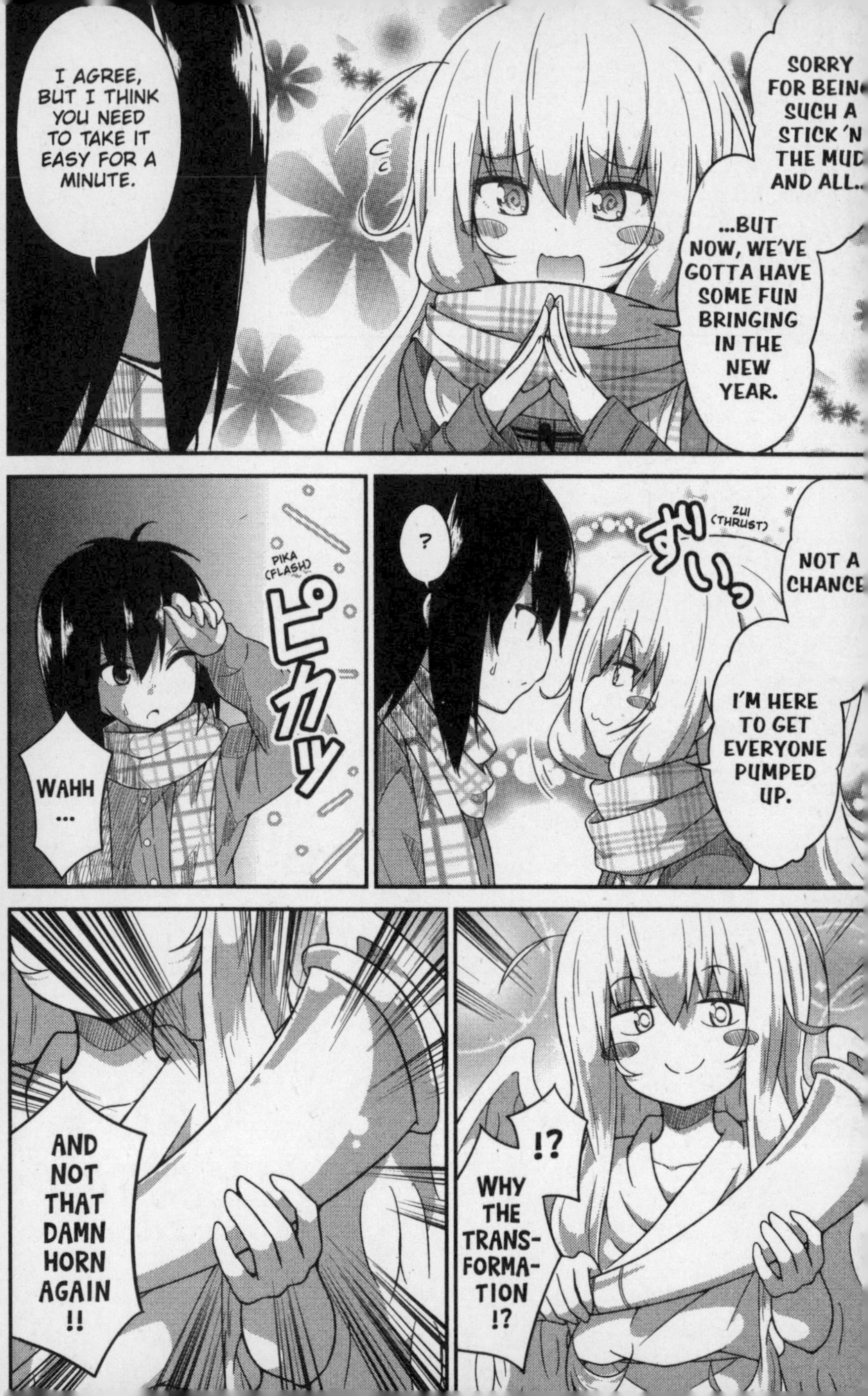
SORRY FOR BEIN SUCH A STICK 'N THE MUD AND ALL..
...BUT NOW, WE'VE GOTTA HAVE SOME FUN BRINGING IN THE NEW YEAR.
I AGREE, BUT I THINK YOU NEED TO TAKE IT EASY FOR A MINUTE.
ZUI (THRUST)
ずいっ
NOT A CHANCE
I'M HERE TO GET EVERYONE PUMPED UP.
?
PIKA (FLASH)
ピカッ
WAHH ...
!?
WHY THE TRANS-FORMA-TION !?
AND NOT THAT DAMN HORN AGAIN !!

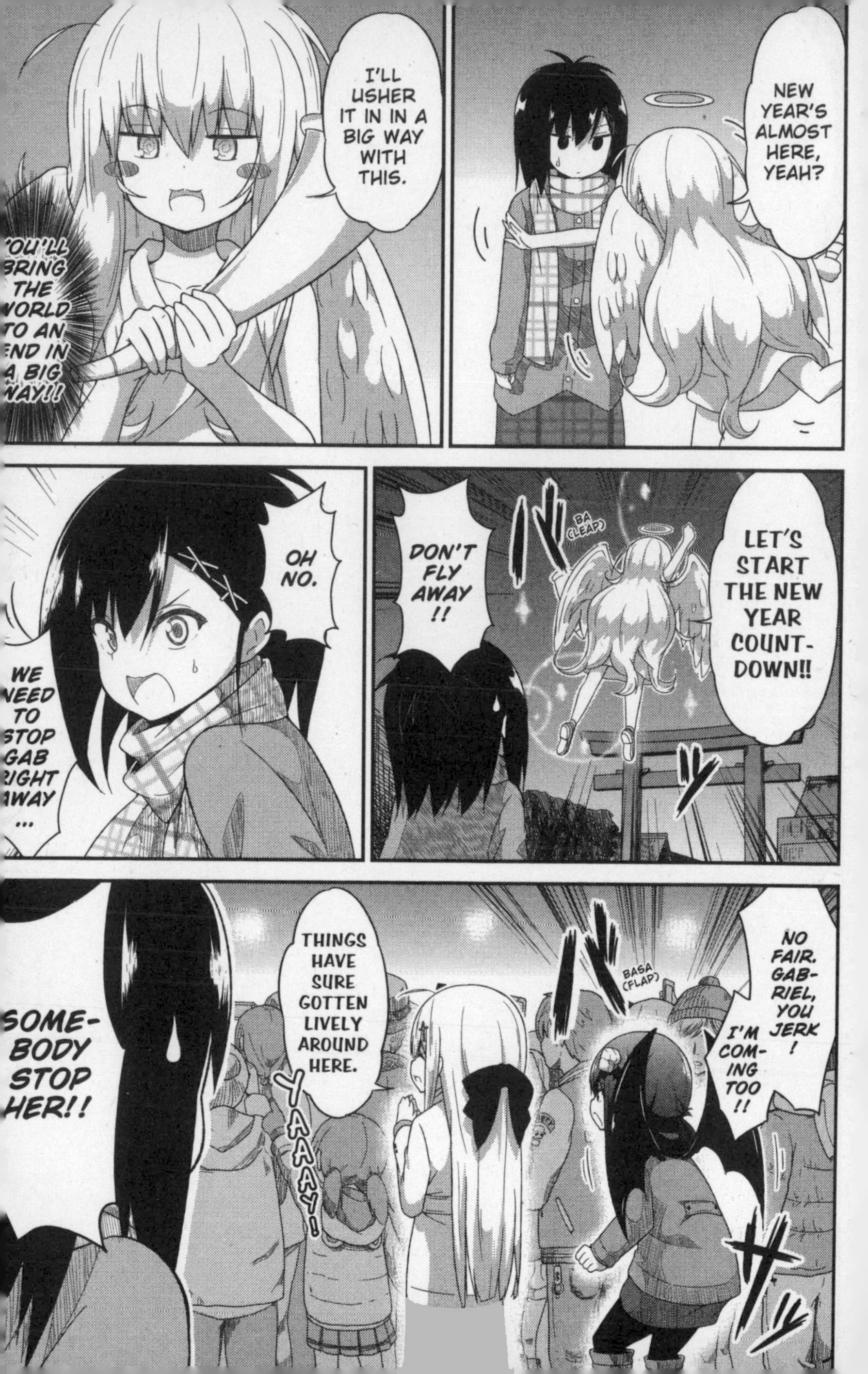
NEW YEAR'S ALMOST HERE, YEAH?
I'LL USHER IT IN IN A BIG WAY WITH THIS.
YOU'LL BRING THE WORLD TO AN END IN A BIG WAY!!
LET'S START THE NEW YEAR COUNT-DOWN!!
BA (LEAP)
DON'T FLY AWAY!!
OH NO.
WE NEED TO STOP GAB RIGHT AWAY...
NO FAIR. GAB-RIEL, YOU JERK!
I'M COM-ING TOO!!
BASA (FLAP)
THINGS HAVE SURE GOTTEN LIVELY AROUND HERE.
YAAAAY!
SOME-BODY STOP HER!!

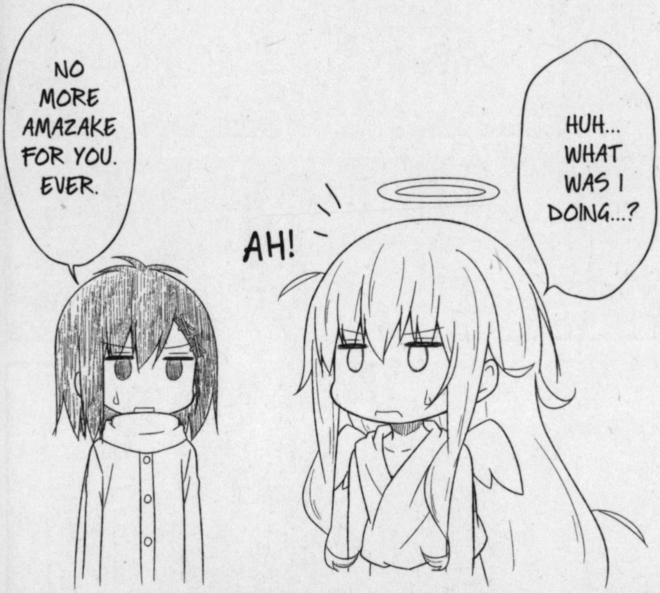
HUH... WHAT WAS I DOING...?
AH!
NO MORE AMAZAKE FOR YOU. EVER.

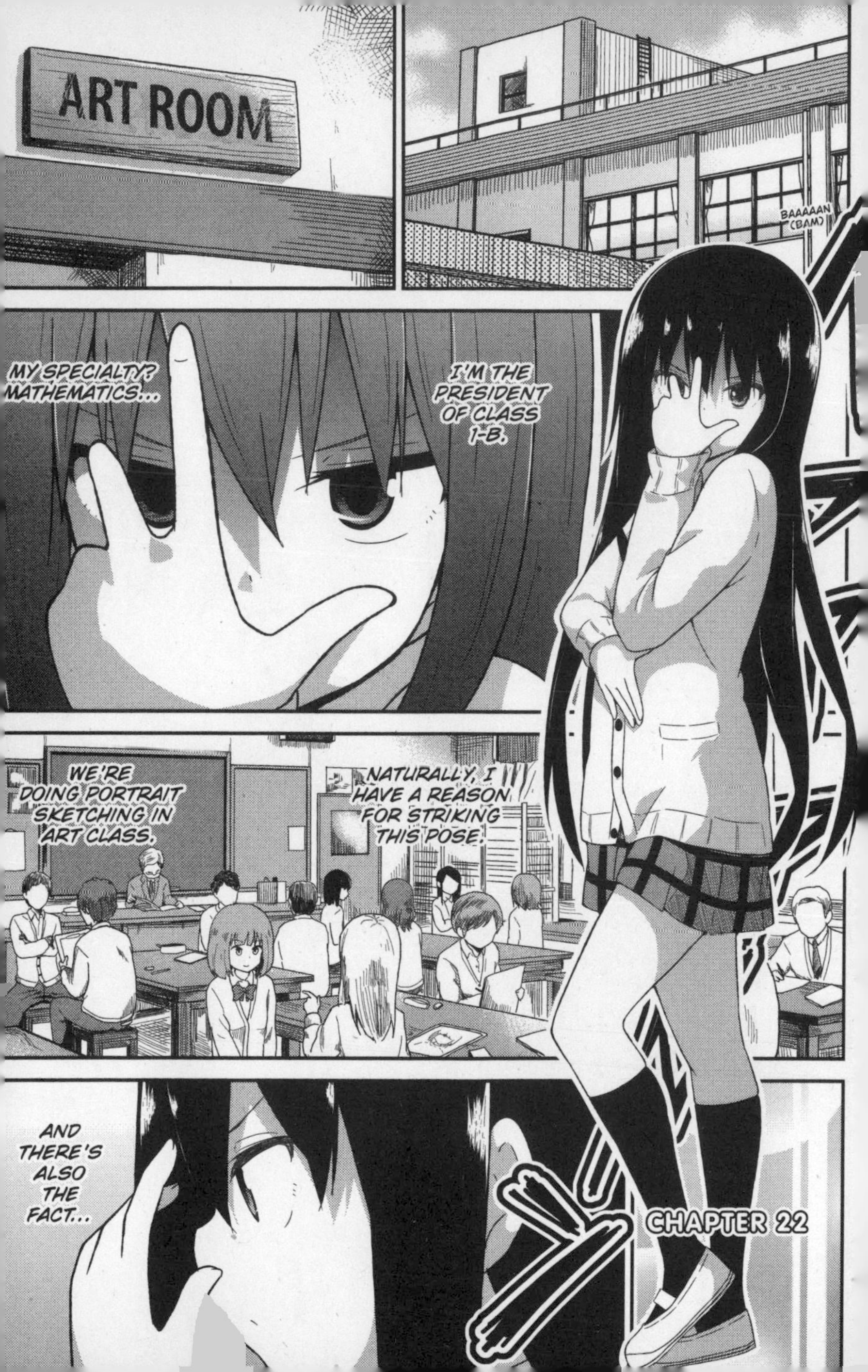
ART ROOM
BAAAAAN (BAM)
CHAPTER 22
I'M THE PRESIDENT OF CLASS 1-B.
MY SPECIALTY? MATHEMATICS...
NATURALLY, I HAVE A REASON FOR STRIKING THIS POSE.
WE'RE DOING PORTRAIT SKETCHING IN ART CLASS.
AND THERE'S ALSO THE FACT...

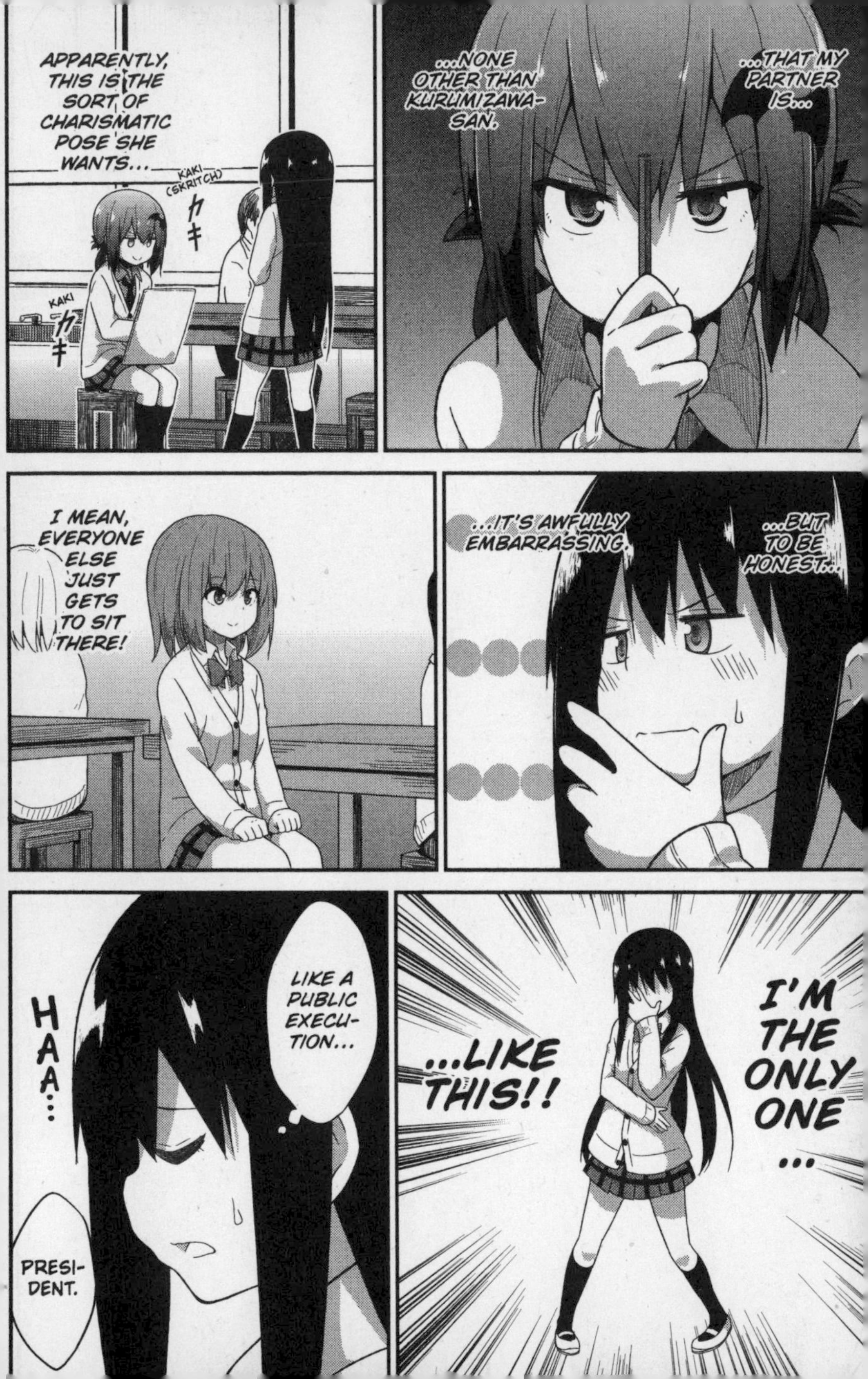
...THAT MY PARTNER IS...
...NONE OTHER THAN KURUMIZAWA-SAN.
APPARENTLY, THIS IS THE SORT OF CHARISMATIC POSE SHE WANTS...
KAKI (SKRITCH)
カキ
KAKI
カキ
...BUT TO BE HONEST...
...IT'S AWFULLY EMBARRASSING.
I MEAN, EVERYONE ELSE JUST GETS TO SIT THERE!
I'M THE ONLY ONE...
...LIKE THIS!!
LIKE A PUBLIC EXECUTION...
HAA...
PRESIDENT.

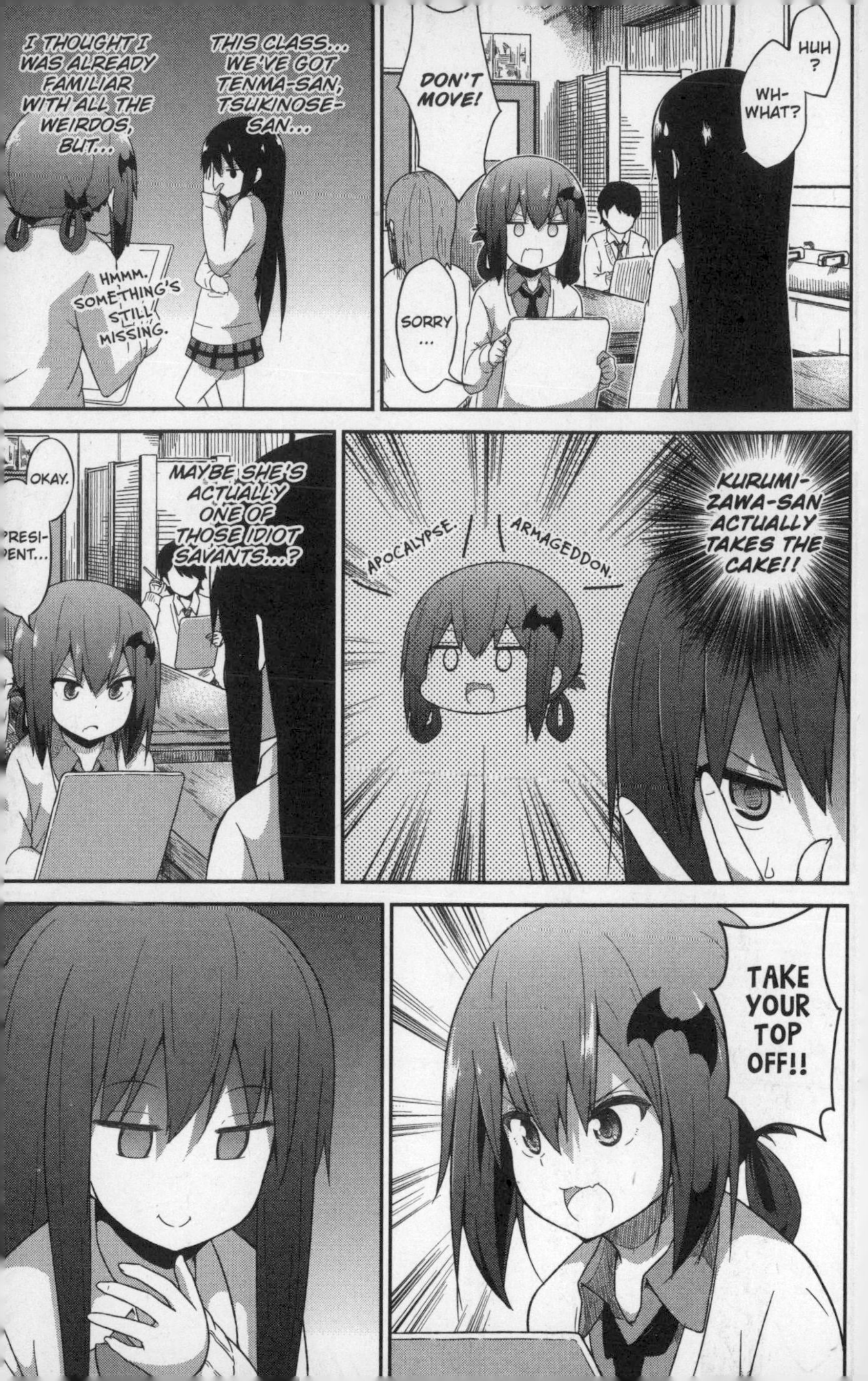
HUH?
WH-WHAT?
DON'T MOVE!
SORRY...
THIS CLASS... WE'VE GOT TENMA-SAN, TSUKINOSE-SAN...
I THOUGHT I WAS ALREADY FAMILIAR WITH ALL THE WEIRDOS, BUT...
HMMM. SOMETHING'S STILL MISSING.
KURUMI-ZAWA-SAN ACTUALLY TAKES THE CAKE!!
ARMAGEDDON.
APOCALYPSE.
MAYBE SHE'S ACTUALLY ONE OF THOSE IDIOT SAVANTS...?
OKAY.
PRESI-DENT...
TAKE YOUR TOP OFF!!

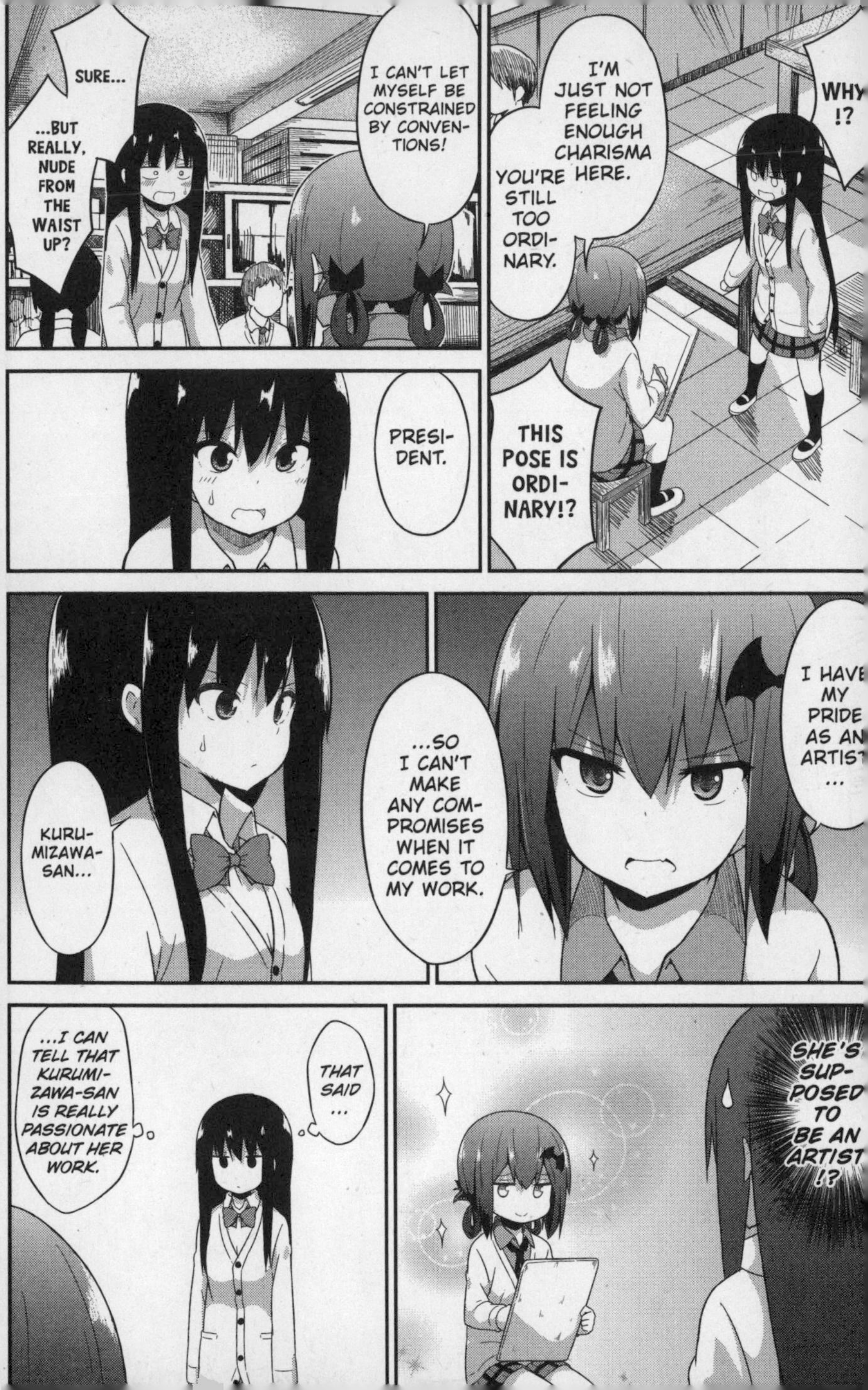
WHY!?
I'M JUST NOT FEELING ENOUGH CHARISMA HERE.
YOU'RE STILL TOO ORDINARY.
THIS POSE IS ORDINARY!?
I CAN'T LET MYSELF BE CONSTRAINED BY CONVENTIONS!
SURE...
...BUT REALLY, NUDE FROM THE WAIST UP?
PRESIDENT.
I HAVE MY PRIDE AS AN ARTIST...
...SO I CAN'T MAKE ANY COMPROMISES WHEN IT COMES TO MY WORK.
KURUMIZAWA-SAN...
SHE'S SUPPOSED TO BE AN ARTIST!?
THAT SAID...
...I CAN TELL THAT KURUMIZAWA-SAN IS REALLY PASSIONATE ABOUT HER WORK.

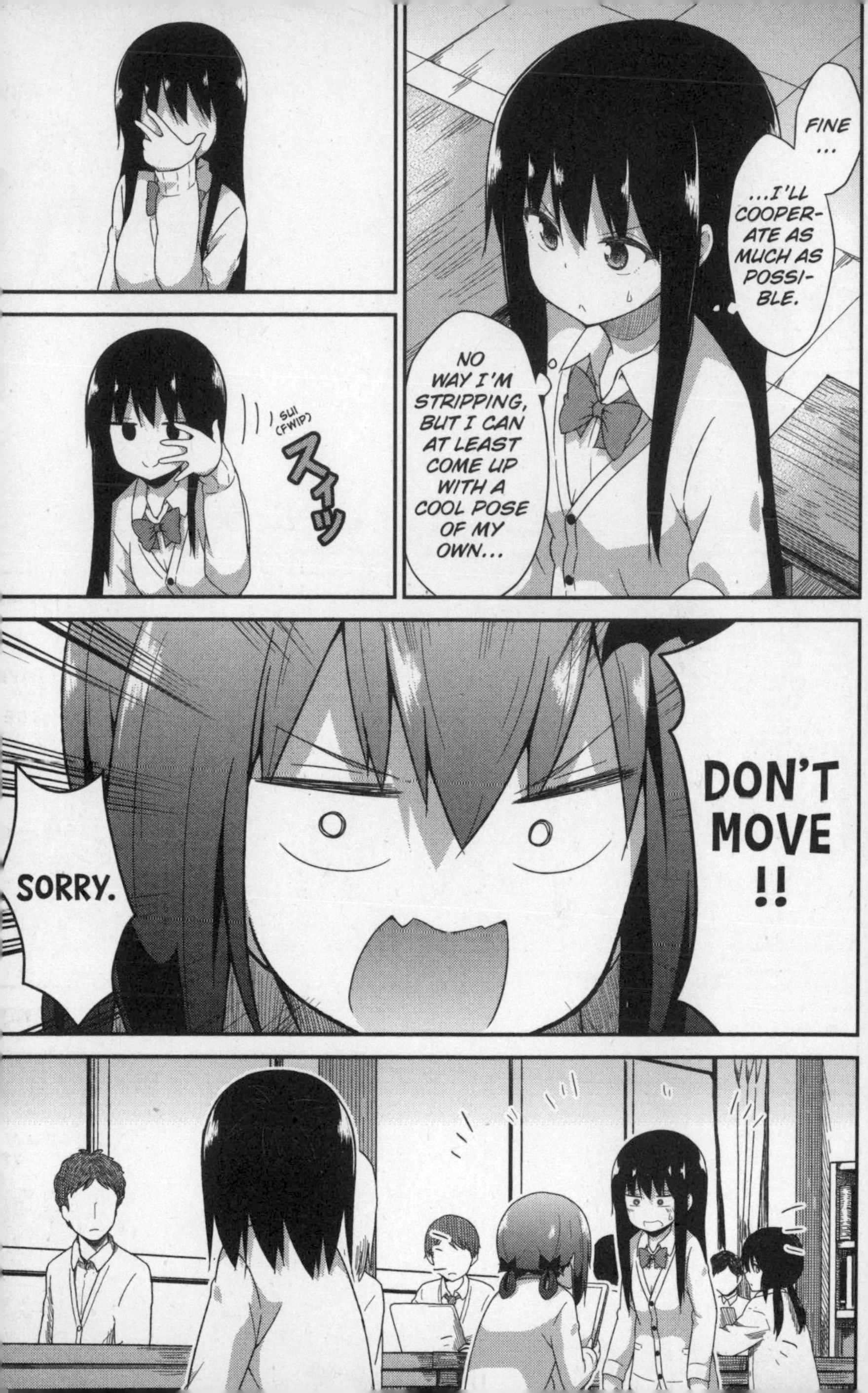
FINE ...
...I'LL COOPER-ATE AS MUCH AS POSSI-BLE.
NO WAY I'M STRIPPING, BUT I CAN AT LEAST COME UP WITH A COOL POSE OF MY OWN...
SUI (FWIP)
スイッ
DON'T MOVE !!
SORRY.

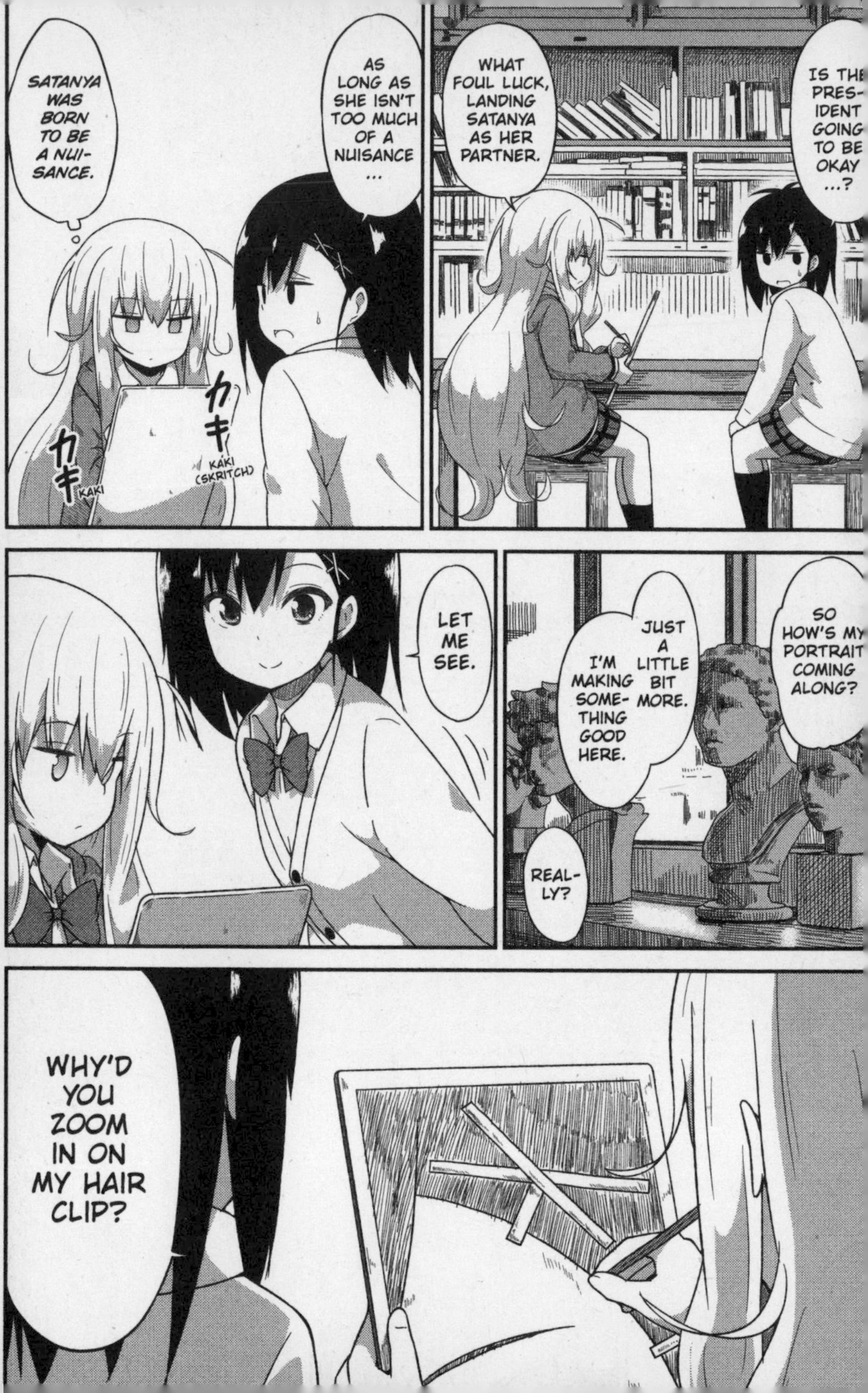
IS THE PRESIDENT GOING TO BE OKAY ...?
WHAT FOUL LUCK, LANDING SATANYA AS HER PARTNER.
AS LONG AS SHE ISN'T TOO MUCH OF A NUISANCE ...
SATANYA WAS BORN TO BE A NUISANCE.
カキ KAKI (SKRITCH)
カキ KAKI
SO HOW'S MY PORTRAIT COMING ALONG?
JUST A LITTLE BIT MORE.
I'M MAKING SOMETHING GOOD HERE.
REALLY?
LET ME SEE.
WHY'D YOU ZOOM IN ON MY HAIR CLIP?

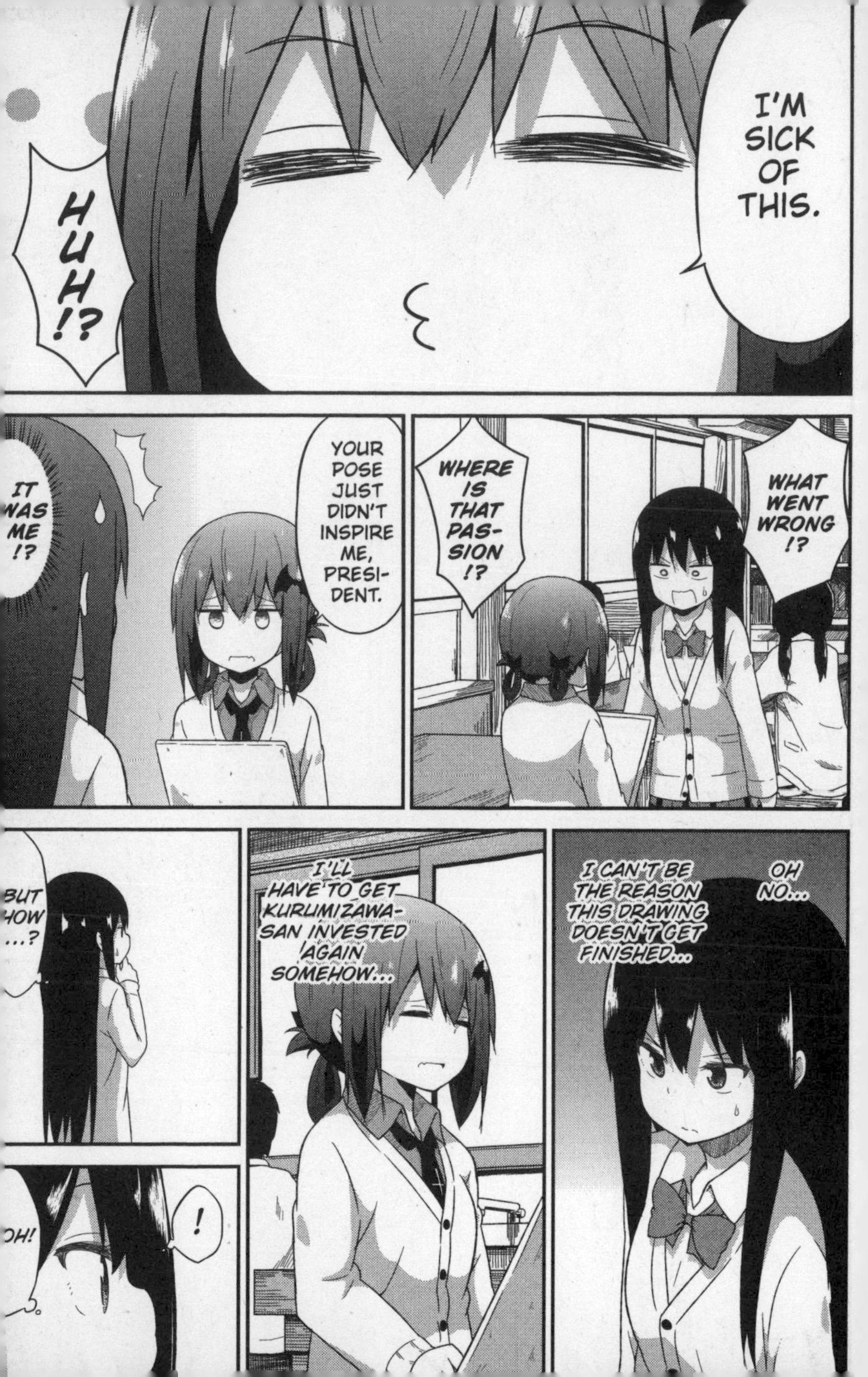
I'M SICK OF THIS.
HUH!?
WHAT WENT WRONG!?
WHERE IS THAT PASSION!?
YOUR POSE JUST DIDN'T INSPIRE ME, PRESIDENT.
IT WAS ME!?
OH NO...
I CAN'T BE THE REASON THIS DRAWING DOESN'T GET FINISHED...
I'LL HAVE TO GET KURUMIZAWA-SAN INVESTED AGAIN SOMEHOW...
BUT HOW...?
!
OH!

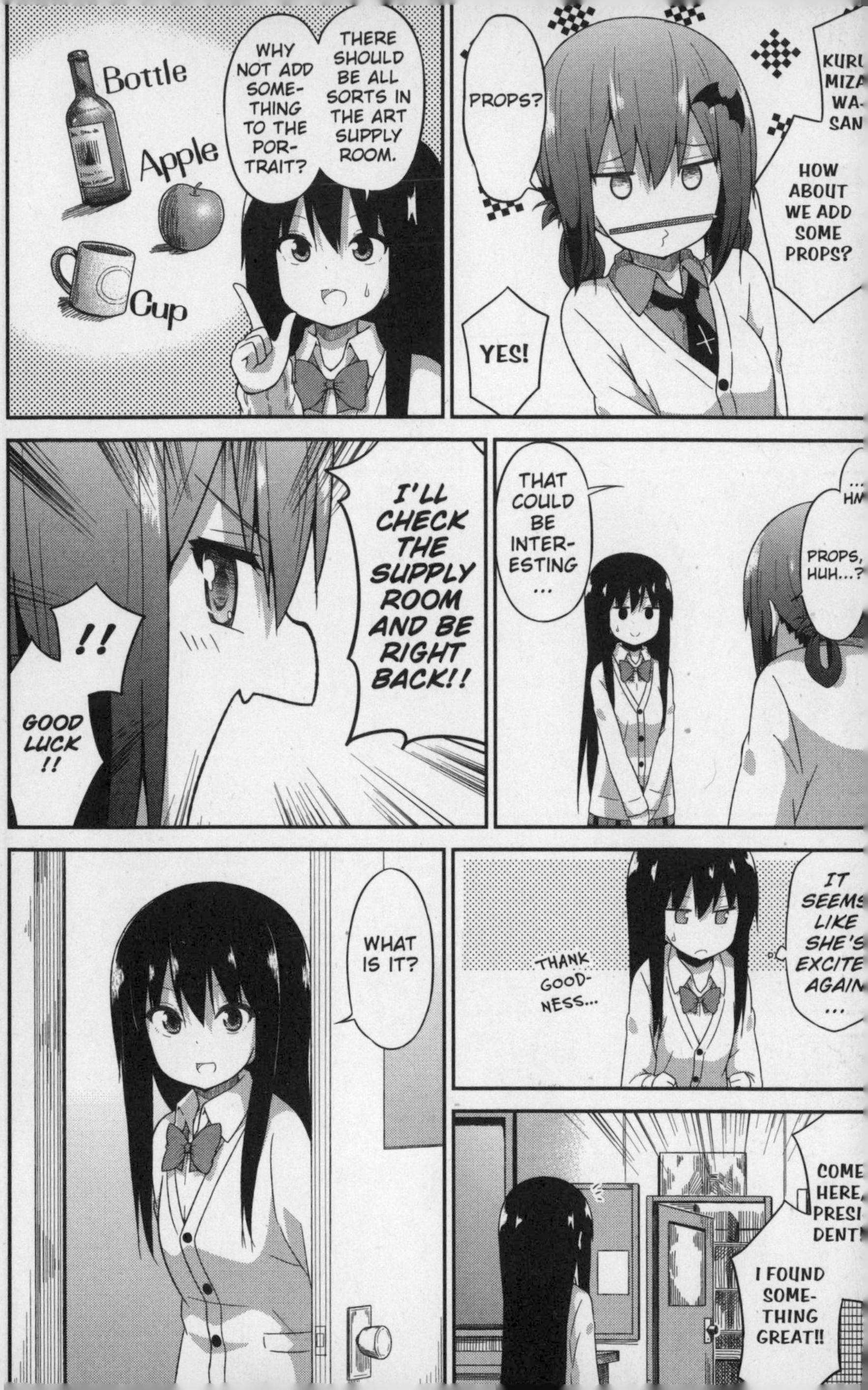
KURU MIZA WA- SAN
HOW ABOUT WE ADD SOME PROPS?
PROPS?
YES!
THERE SHOULD BE ALL SORTS IN THE ART SUPPLY ROOM.
WHY NOT ADD SOME-THING TO THE POR-TRAIT?
Bottle
Apple
Cup
... HM
PROPS, HUH...?
THAT COULD BE INTER-ESTING ...
I'LL CHECK THE SUPPLY ROOM AND BE RIGHT BACK!!
!!
GOOD LUCK !!
IT SEEMS LIKE SHE'S EXCITE AGAIN ...
THANK GOOD-NESS...
COME HERE, PRESI DENT
I FOUND SOME-THING GREAT!!
WHAT IS IT?

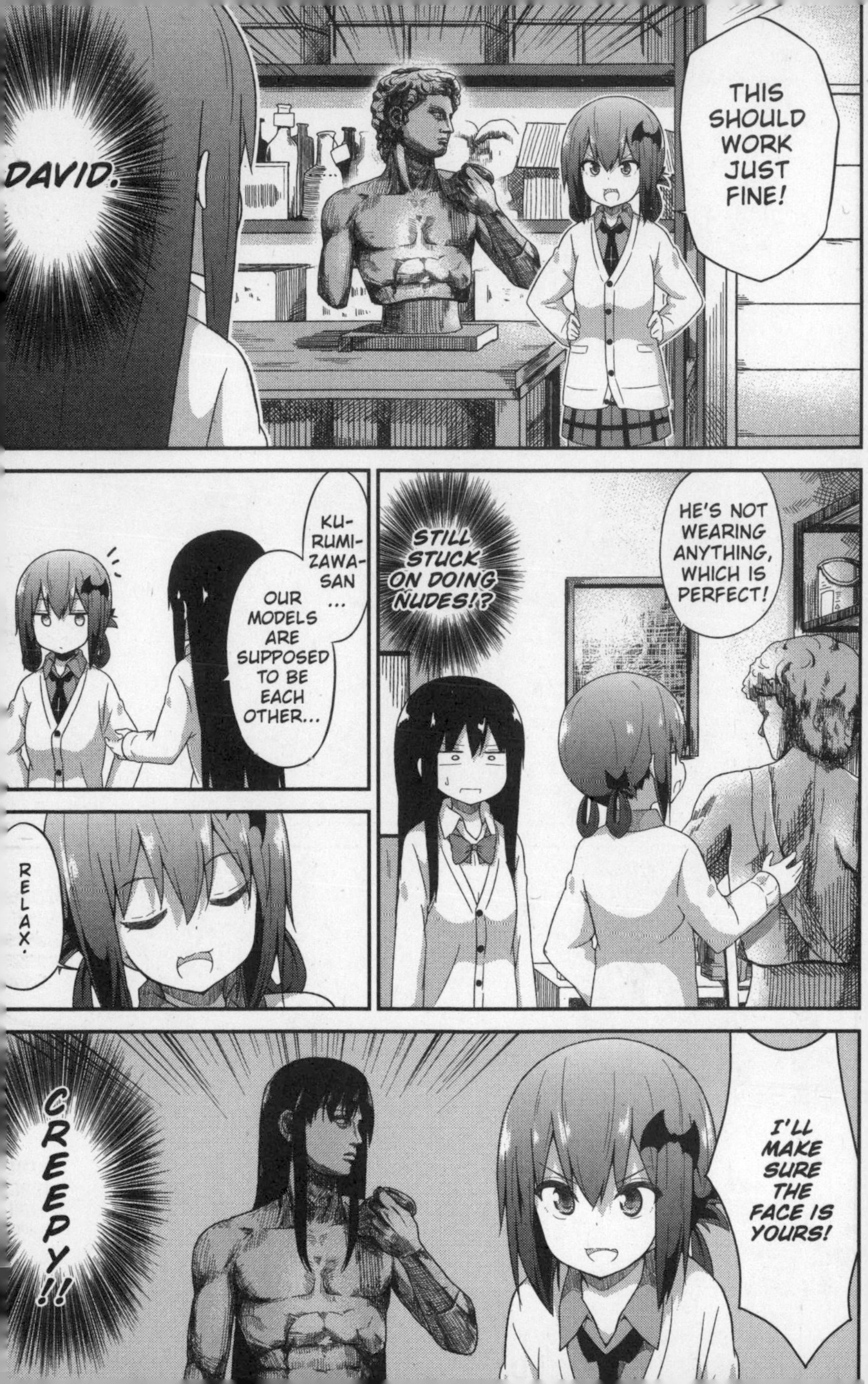
THIS SHOULD WORK JUST FINE!
DAVID.
HE'S NOT WEARING ANYTHING, WHICH IS PERFECT!
STILL STUCK ON DOING NUDES!?
KU-RUMI-ZAWA-SAN ...
OUR MODELS ARE SUPPOSED TO BE EACH OTHER...
RELAX.
I'LL MAKE SURE THE FACE IS YOURS!
CREEPY!!

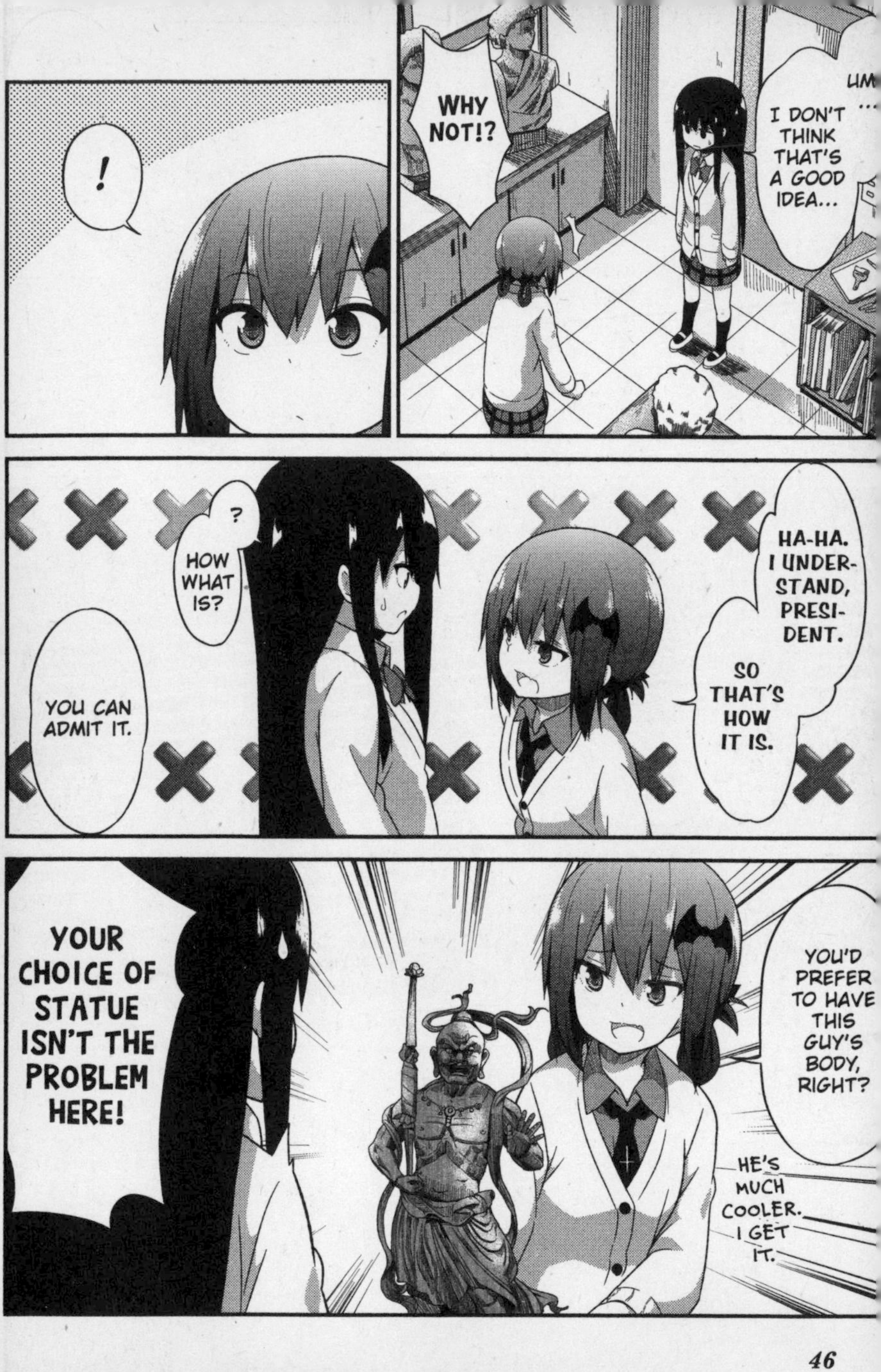
UM...
I DON'T THINK THAT'S A GOOD IDEA...
WHY NOT!?
!
HA-HA. I UNDERSTAND, PRESIDENT.
SO THAT'S HOW IT IS.
?
HOW WHAT IS?
YOU CAN ADMIT IT.
YOU'D PREFER TO HAVE THIS GUY'S BODY, RIGHT?
HE'S MUCH COOLER. I GET IT.
YOUR CHOICE OF STATUE ISN'T THE PROBLEM HERE!

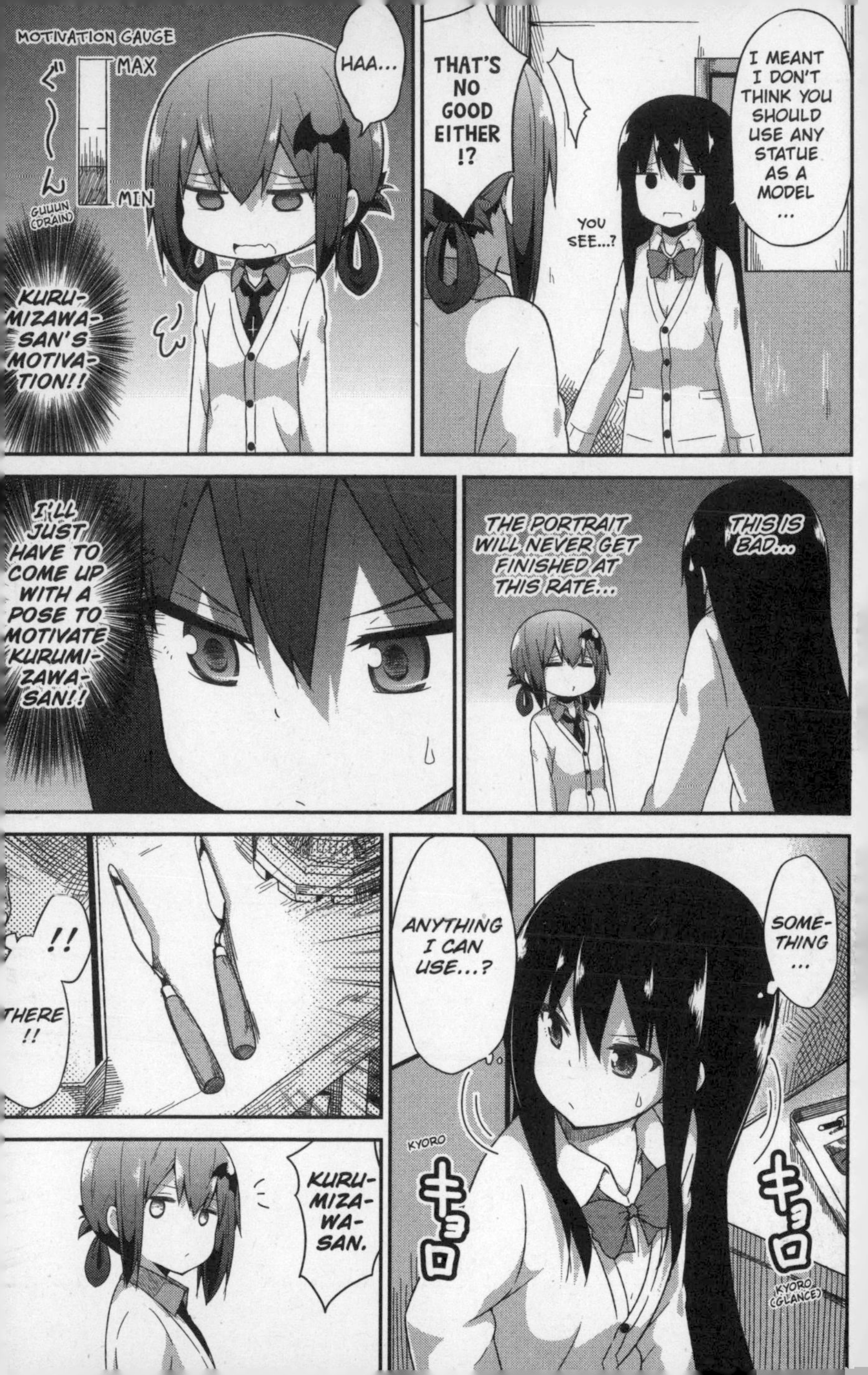
I MEANT I DON'T THINK YOU SHOULD USE ANY STATUE AS A MODEL ...
YOU SEE...?
THAT'S NO GOOD EITHER !?
HAA...
MOTIVATION GAUGE
MAX
MIN
ぐ〜〜ん
GUUUN (DRAIN)
KURUMIZAWA-SAN'S MOTIVATION!!
THIS IS BAD...
THE PORTRAIT WILL NEVER GET FINISHED AT THIS RATE...
I'LL JUST HAVE TO COME UP WITH A POSE TO MOTIVATE KURUMIZAWA-SAN!!
SOME-THING ...
ANYTHING I CAN USE...?
キョロ
KYORO (GLANCE)
キョロ
KYORO
!!
THERE !!
KURU-MIZA-WA-SAN.

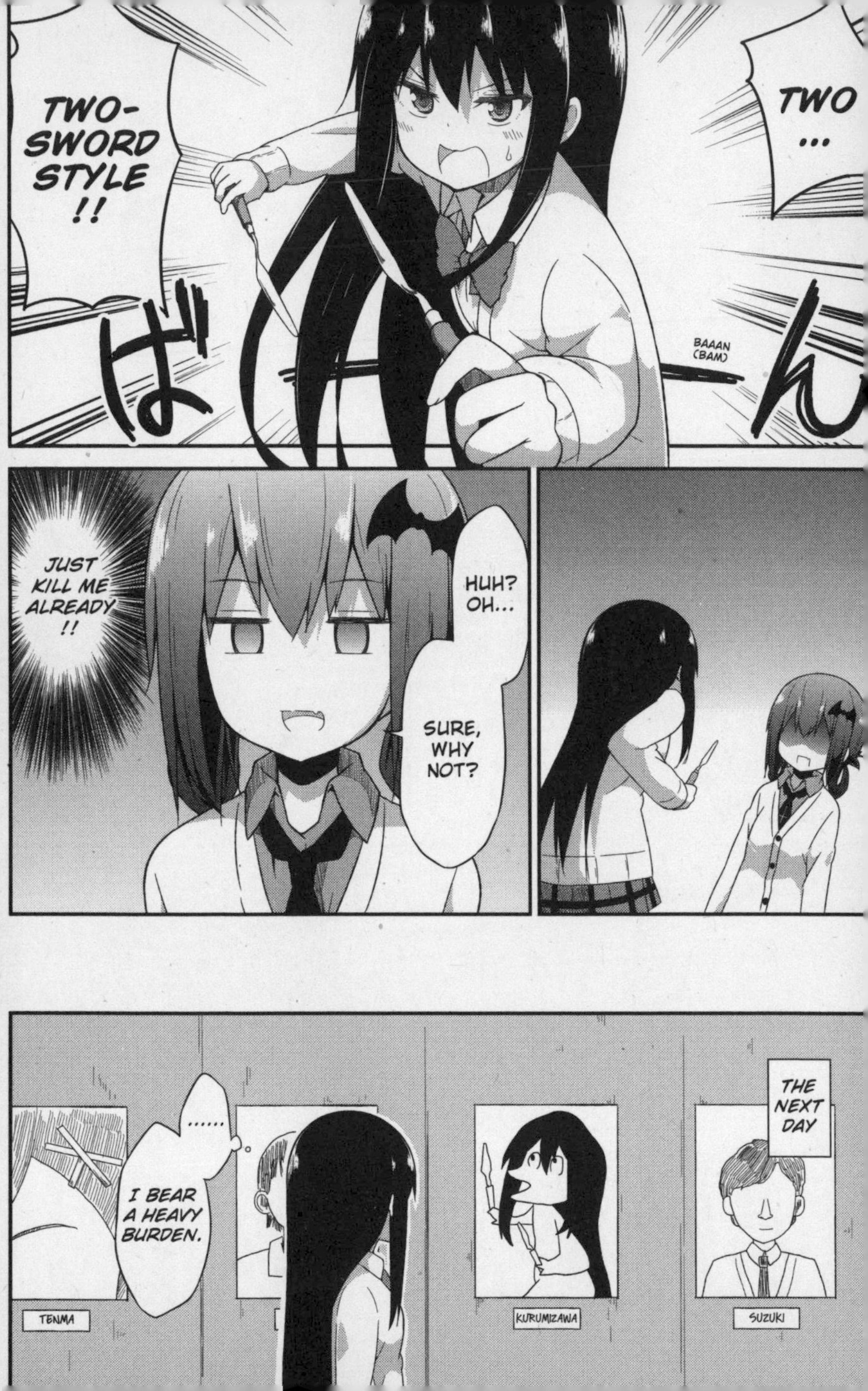
TWO ...
TWO-SWORD STYLE !!
ばーん
BAAAN (BAM)
HUH? OH...
SURE, WHY NOT?
JUST KILL ME ALREADY !!
THE NEXT DAY
SUZUKI
KURUMIZAWA
......
I BEAR A HEAVY BURDEN.
TENMA

POR-
TRAIT
BY THE
CLASS
PRESI-
DENT

Gabriel DropOut

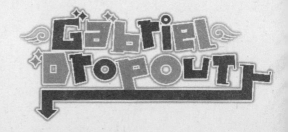

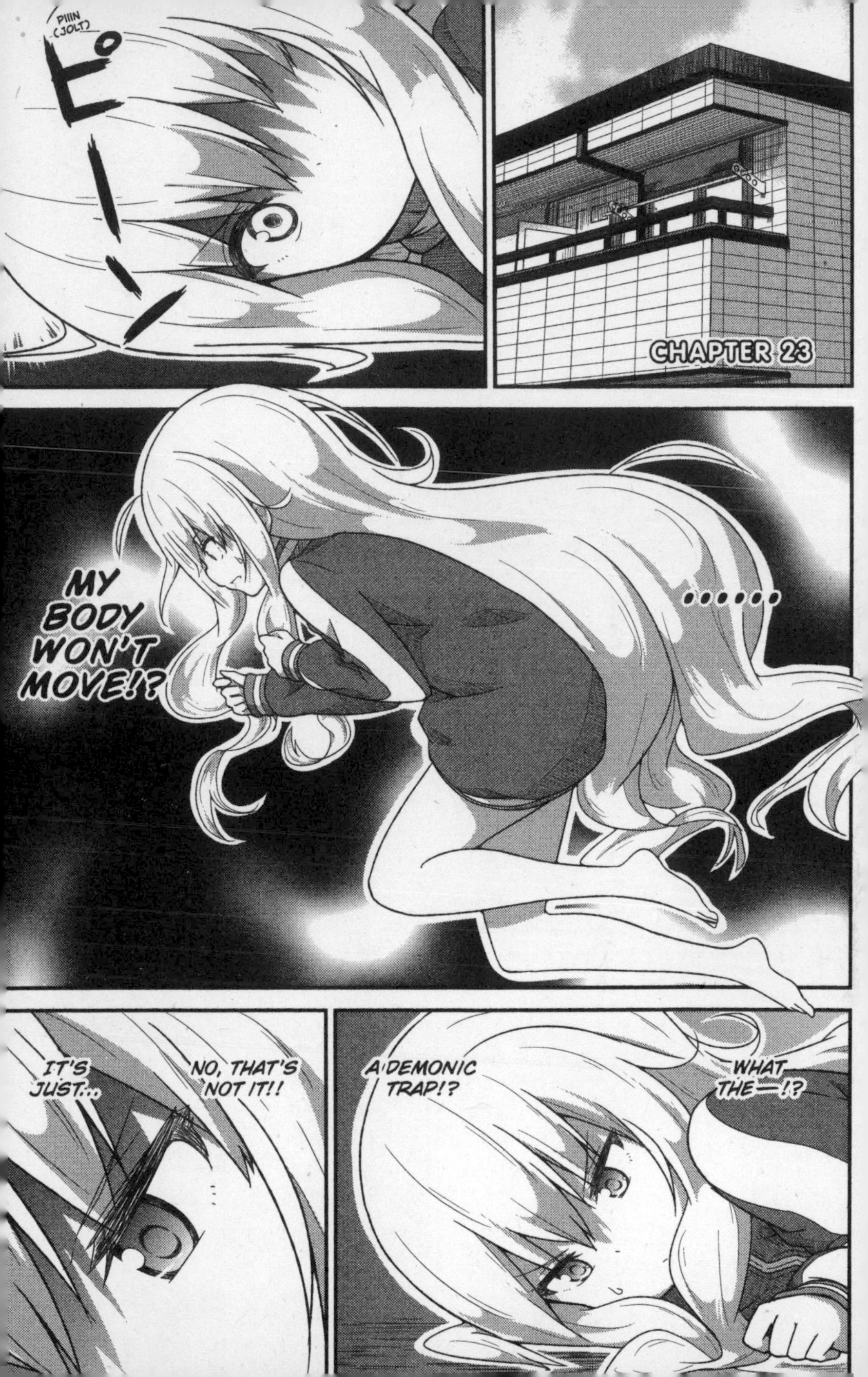
CHAPTER 23
PIIIN (JOLT)
......
MY BODY WON'T MOVE!?
WHAT THE—!?
A DEMONIC TRAP!?
NO, THAT'S NOT IT!!
IT'S JUST...

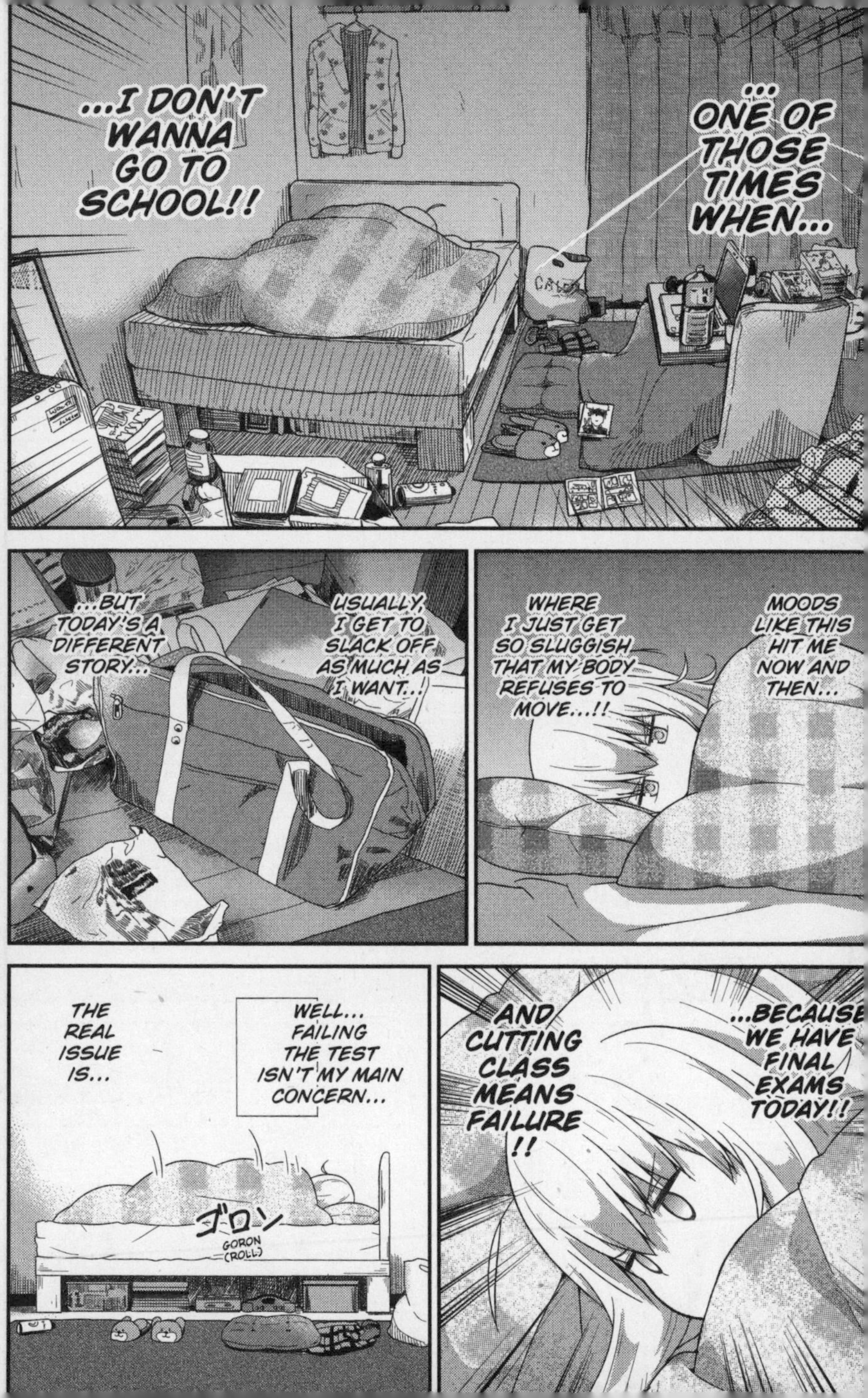
...ONE OF THOSE TIMES WHEN...
...I DON'T WANNA GO TO SCHOOL!!
MOODS LIKE THIS HIT ME NOW AND THEN...
WHERE I JUST GET SO SLUGGISH THAT MY BODY REFUSES TO MOVE...!!
USUALLY, I GET TO SLACK OFF AS MUCH AS I WANT...
...BUT TODAY'S A DIFFERENT STORY...
...BECAUSE WE HAVE FINAL EXAMS TODAY!!
AND CUTTING CLASS MEANS FAILURE!!
WELL... FAILING THE TEST ISN'T MY MAIN CONCERN...
THE REAL ISSUE IS...
ゴロン
GORON (ROLL)

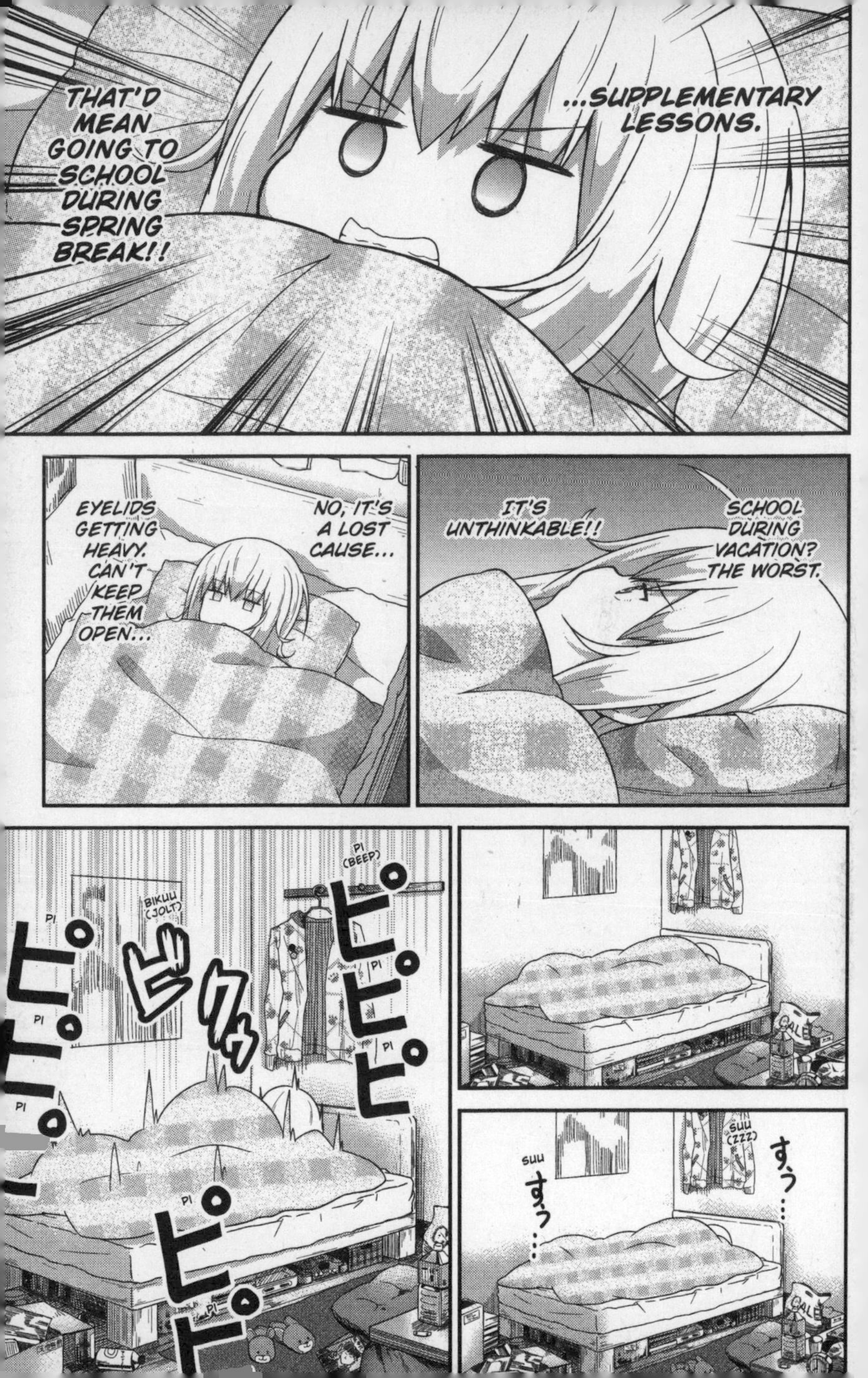
...SUPPLEMENTARY LESSONS.
THAT'D MEAN GOING TO SCHOOL DURING SPRING BREAK!!
SCHOOL DURING VACATION? THE WORST.
IT'S UNTHINKABLE!!
NO, IT'S A LOST CAUSE...
EYELIDS GETTING HEAVY. CAN'T KEEP THEM OPEN...
SUU (ZZZ)
すぅ…
SUU
すぅ…
PI (BEEP)
ピピピ
PI
PI
BIKUU (JOLT)
ビクゥ
PI
ピピ
PI
PI
ピピ
PI
PI

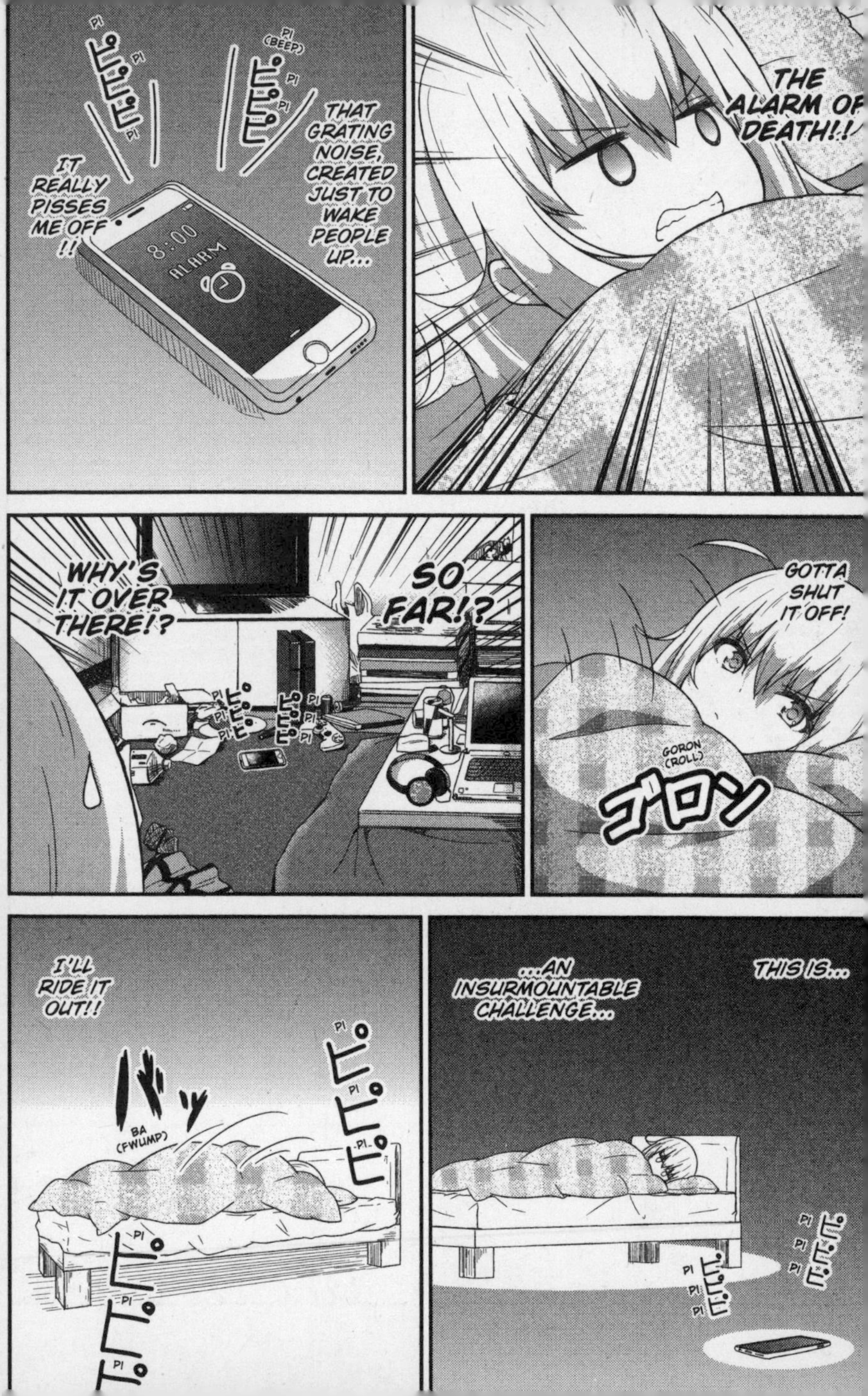
THE ALARM OF DEATH!!
PI (BEEP) PI PI
PI PI PI
THAT GRATING NOISE, CREATED JUST TO WAKE PEOPLE UP...
IT REALLY PISSES ME OFF!!
8:00
ALARM
GOTTA SHUT IT OFF!
GORON (ROLL)
SO FAR!?
WHY'S IT OVER THERE!?
PI PI PI
PI PI PI
THIS IS...
...AN INSURMOUNTABLE CHALLENGE...
PI PI PI
PI PI PI
I'LL RIDE IT OUT!!
PI PI PI
BA (FWUMP)
PI PI PI

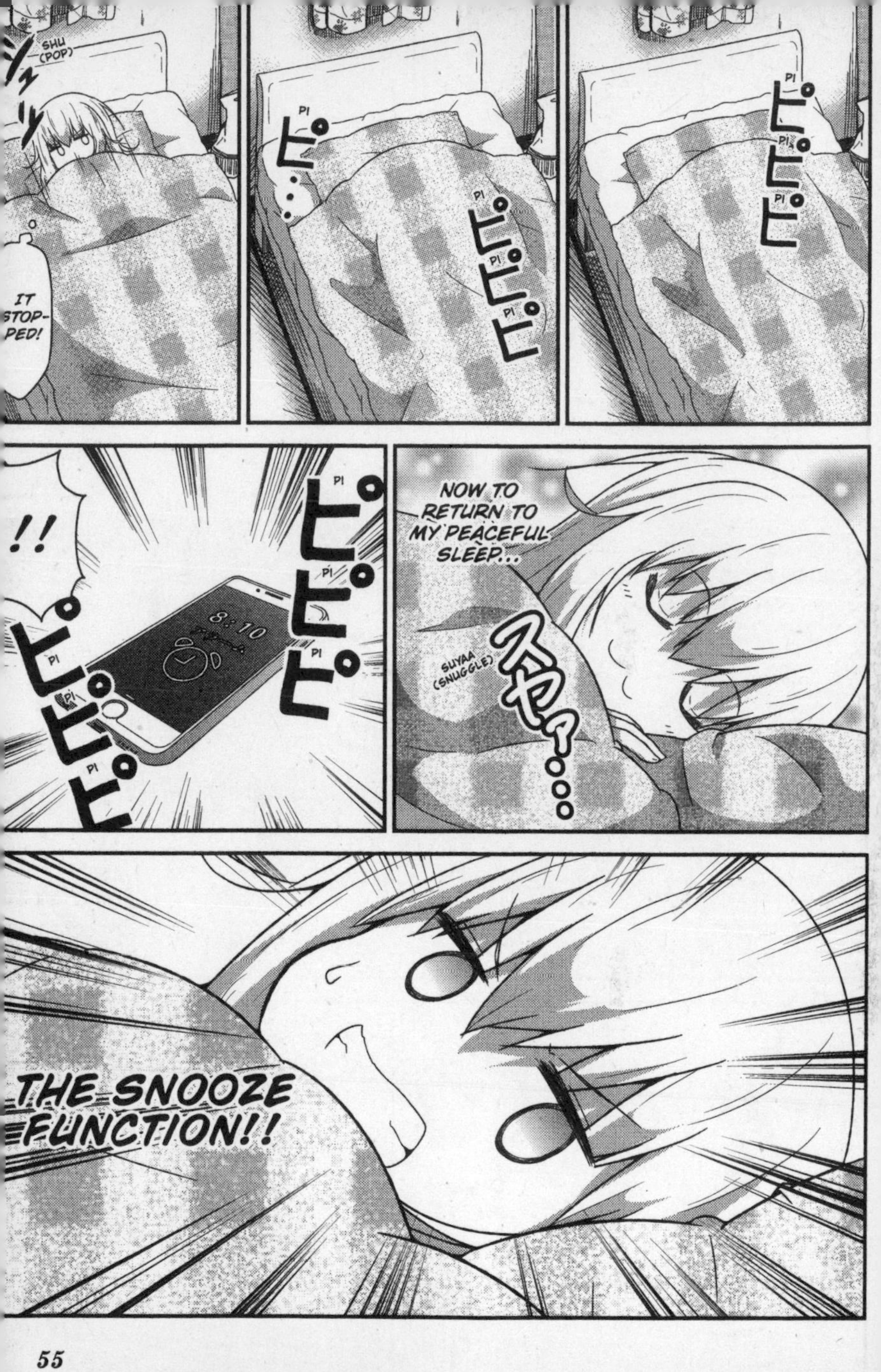
PI PI PI
ピピピ
PI
ピ…
PI PI PI
ピピピ
SHU (POP)
IT STOPPED!
NOW TO RETURN TO MY PEACEFUL SLEEP…
SUYAA (SNUGGLE)
スヤァ…
PI PI PI
ピピピ
PI PI PI
ピピピ
!!
8:10
THE SNOOZE FUNCTION!!

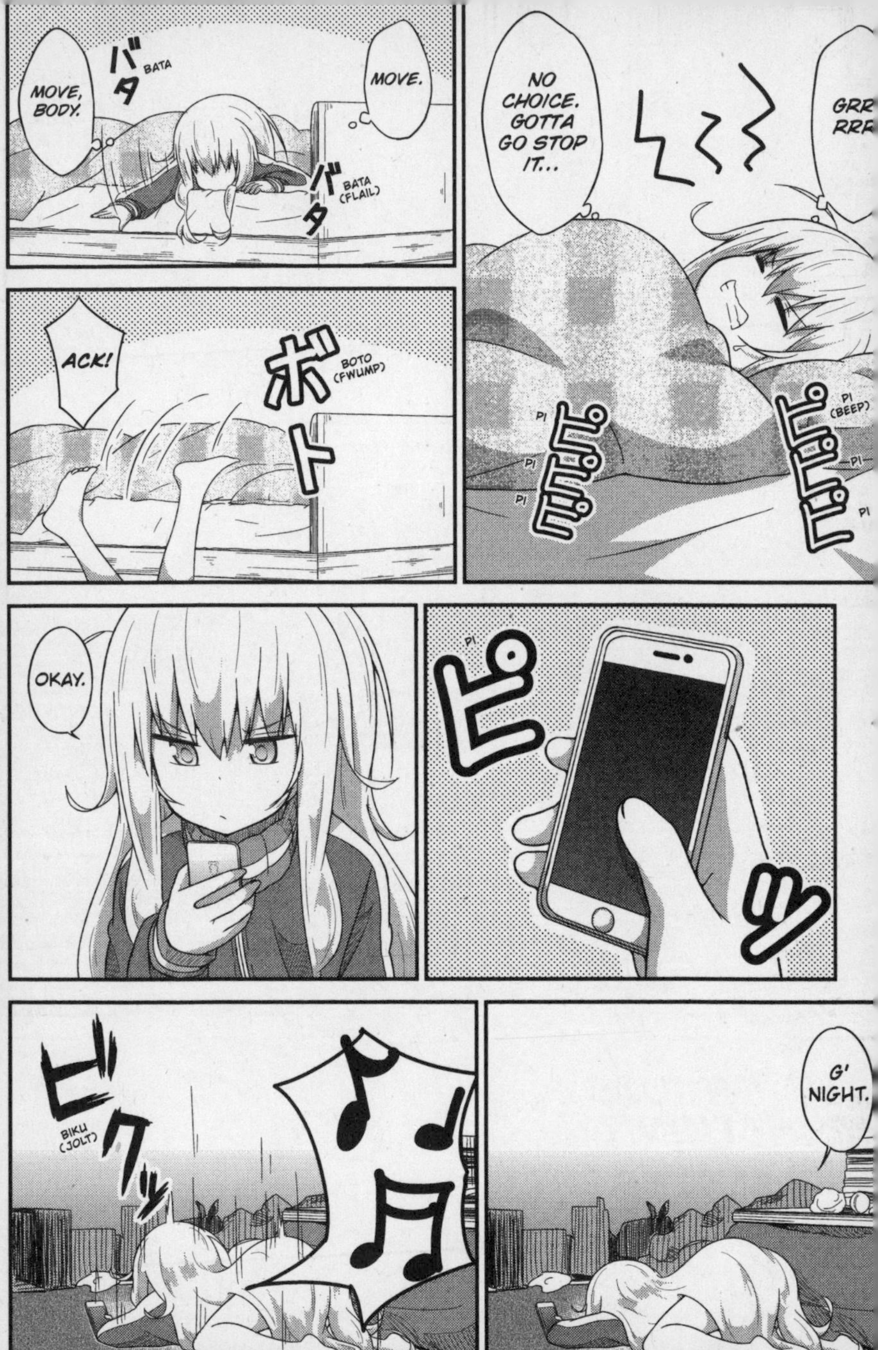
GRR RRR
NO CHOICE. GOTTA GO STOP IT...
ピピピ
PI (BEEP)
PI
PI
ピピピ
PI
PI
PI
MOVE.
バタ
BATA (FLAIL)
MOVE, BODY.
バタ
BATA
ボト
BOTO (FWUMP)
ACK!
ピッ
PI
OKAY.
G' NIGHT.
ビクッ
BIKU (JOLT)

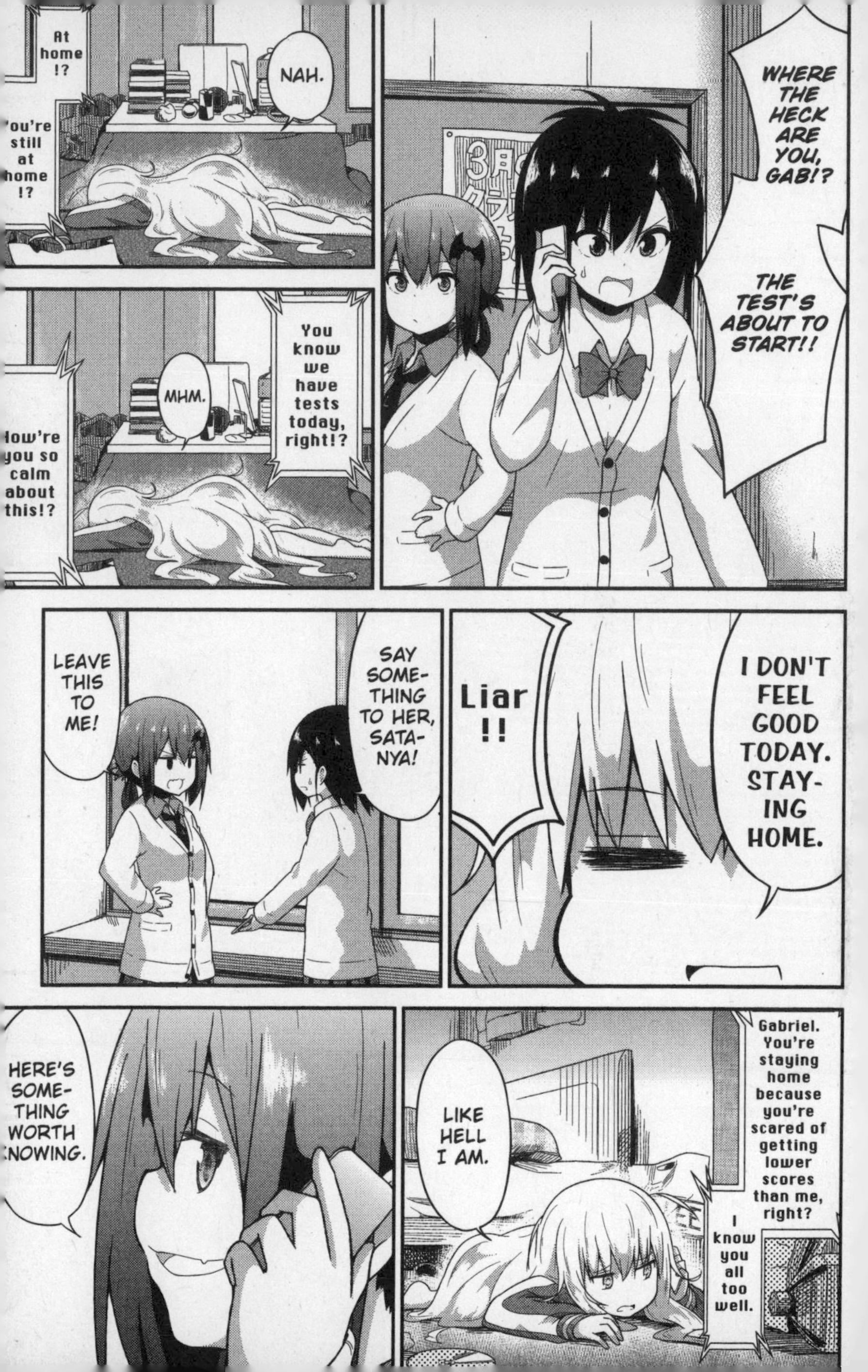
WHERE THE HECK ARE YOU, GAB!?
THE TEST'S ABOUT TO START!!
NAH.
At home !?
ou're still at home !?
You know we have tests today, right!?
MHM.
ow're you so calm about this!?
I DON'T FEEL GOOD TODAY. STAYING HOME.
Liar !!
SAY SOME-THING TO HER, SATA-NYA!
LEAVE THIS TO ME!
Gabriel. You're staying home because you're scared of getting lower scores than me, right?
I know you all too well.
LIKE HELL I AM.
HERE'S SOME-THING WORTH NOWING.

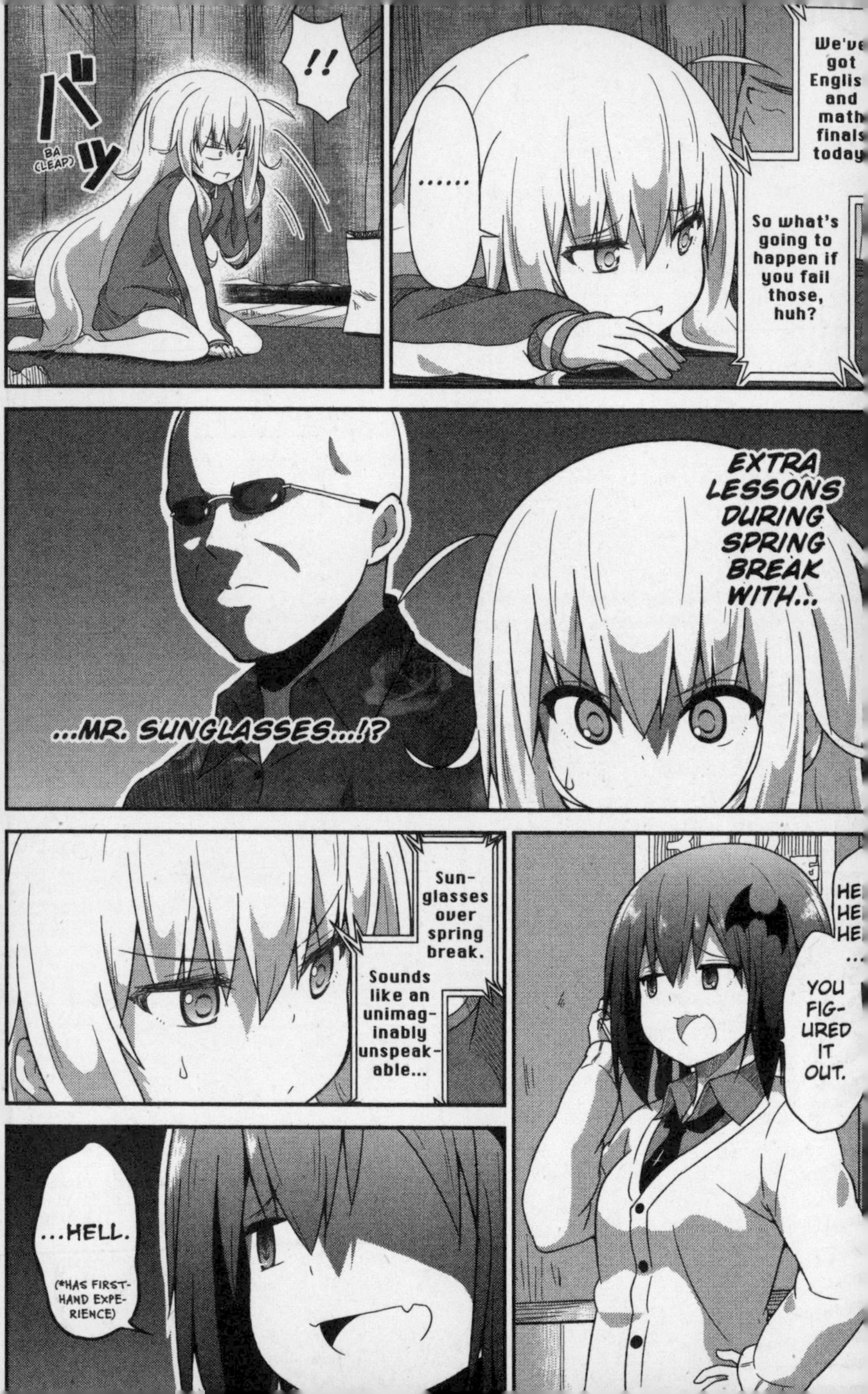
We've got Englis and math finals today
So what's going to happen if you fail those, huh?
......
!!
バッ
BA (LEAP)
EXTRA LESSONS DURING SPRING BREAK WITH...
...MR. SUNGLASSES...!?
HE HE HE... YOU FIG-URED IT OUT.
Sun-glasses over spring break.
Sounds like an unimag-inably unspeak-able...
...HELL.
(*HAS FIRST-HAND EXPE-RIENCE)

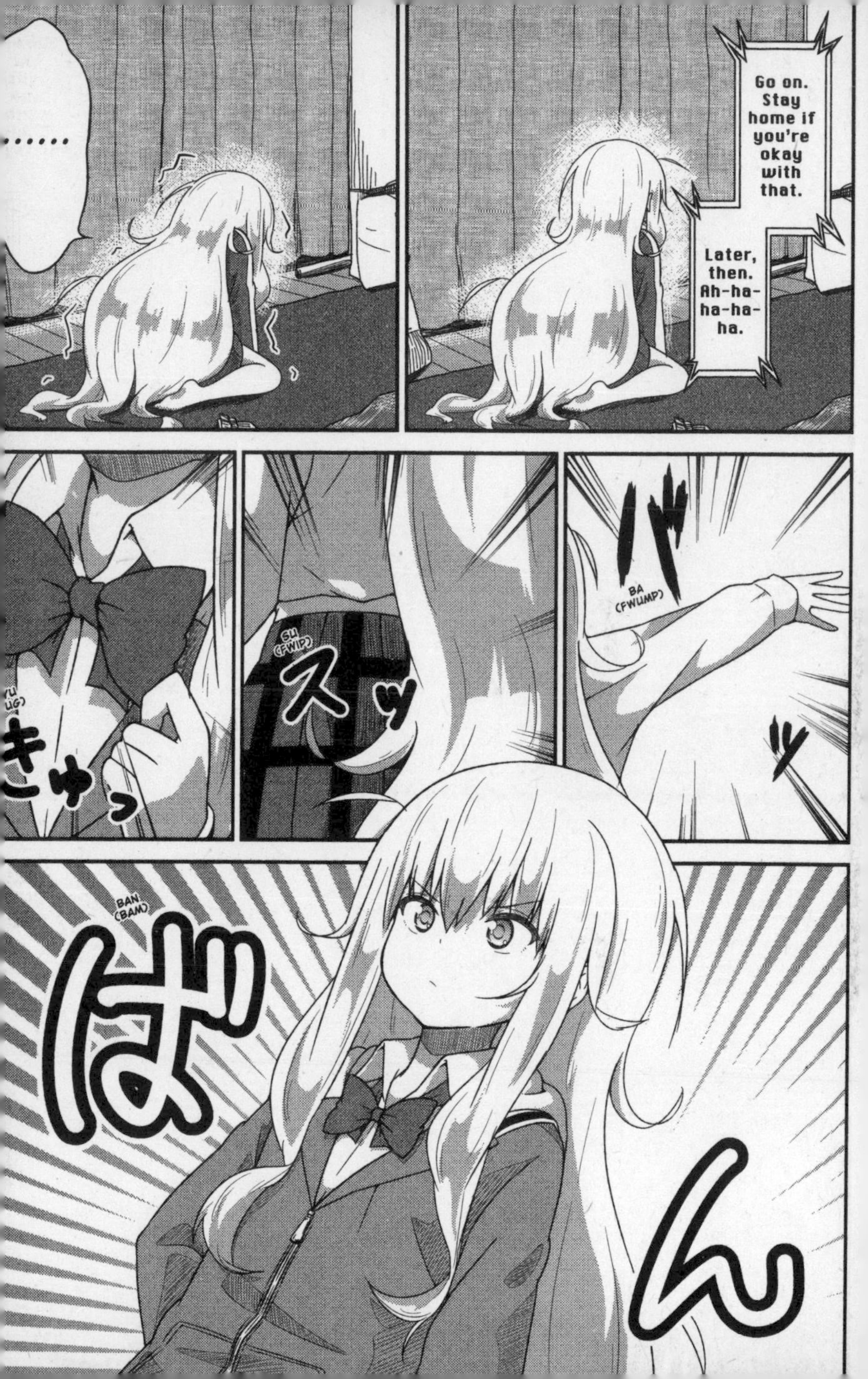
Go on. Stay home if you're okay with that.
Later, then. Ah-ha-ha-ha-ha.
......
バッ
BA (FWUMP)
スッ
SU (FWIP)
きゅっ
ばん
BAN (BAM)

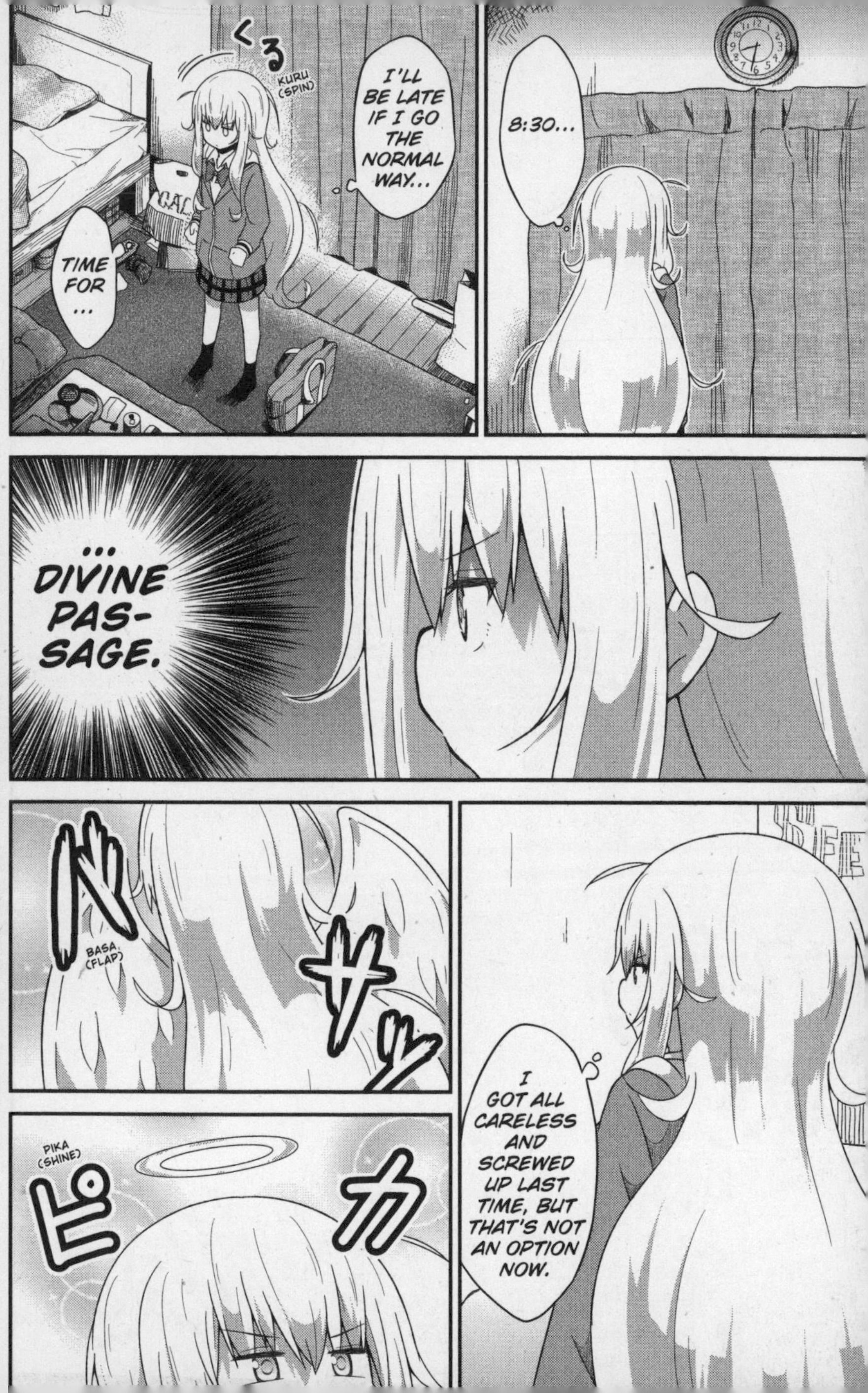
8:30...
くる
KURU (SPIN)
I'LL BE LATE IF I GO THE NORMAL WAY...
TIME FOR ...
... DIVINE PAS- SAGE.
I GOT ALL CARELESS AND SCREWED UP LAST TIME, BUT THAT'S NOT AN OPTION NOW.
バサッ
BASA (FLAP)
ピカ
PIKA (SHINE)

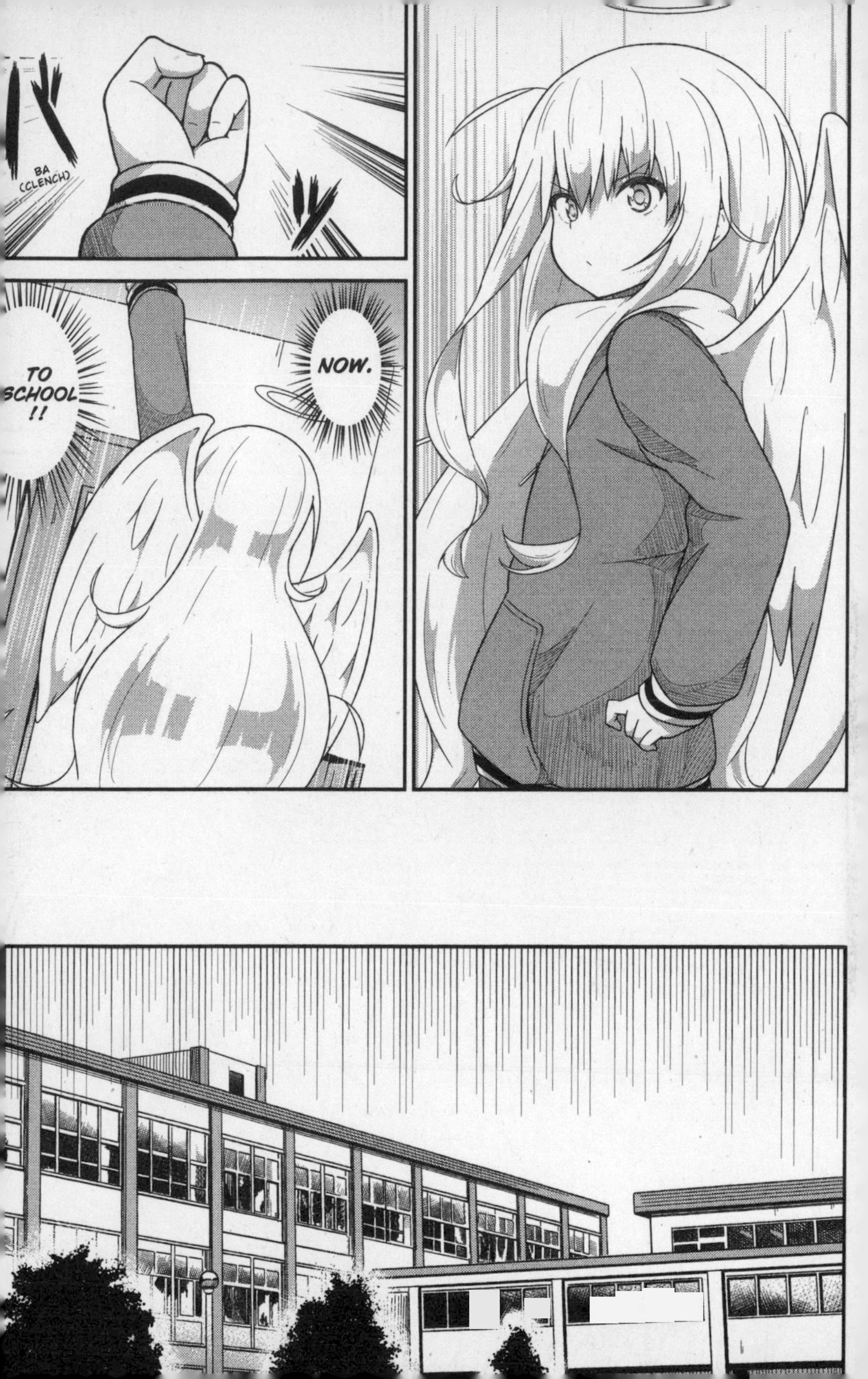
BA (CLENCH)
NOW.
TO SCHOOL !!

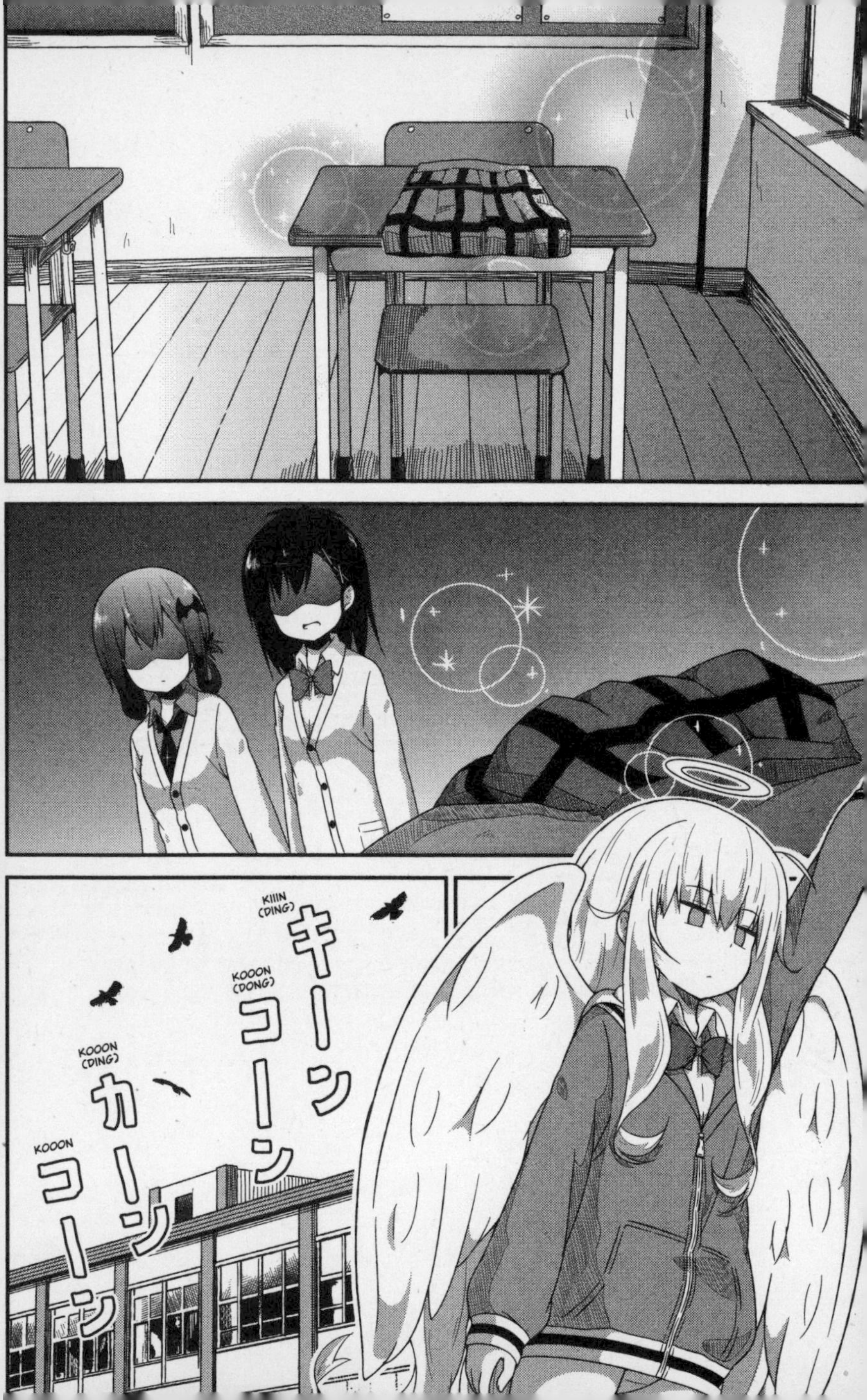
KIIIN (DING)
キーン
KOOON (DONG)
コーン
KOOON (DING)
カーン
KOOON
コーン

THIS BELONGS TO YOU, GABRIEL!
※ SATANYA
イラッ
IRA (IRK)

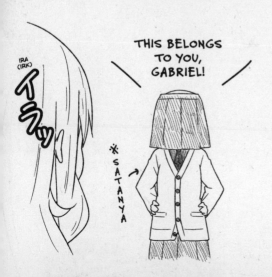

Gabriel Dropout

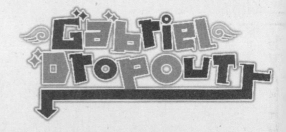

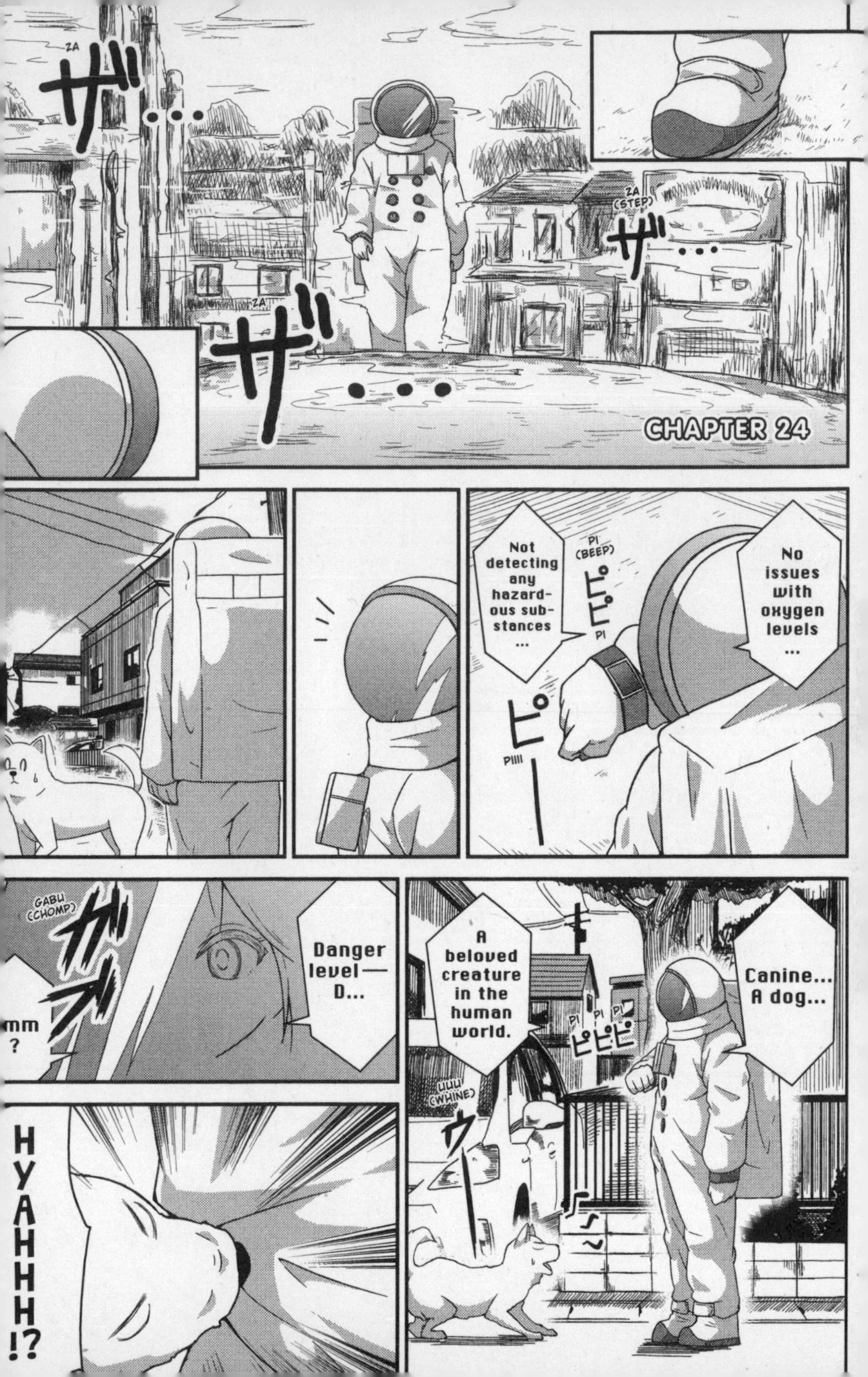
ZA (STEP)
ザ・・・
ZA
ザ・・・
ZA
ザ・・・
CHAPTER 24
No issues with oxygen levels ...
PI (BEEP)
ピピ
PI
Not detecting any hazard-ous sub-stances ...
ピー
PIIII
Canine... A dog...
A beloved creature in the human world.
PI PI PI
ピピピ
UUU (WHINE)
Danger level— D...
GABU (CHOMP)
mm ?
HYAHHHH!?

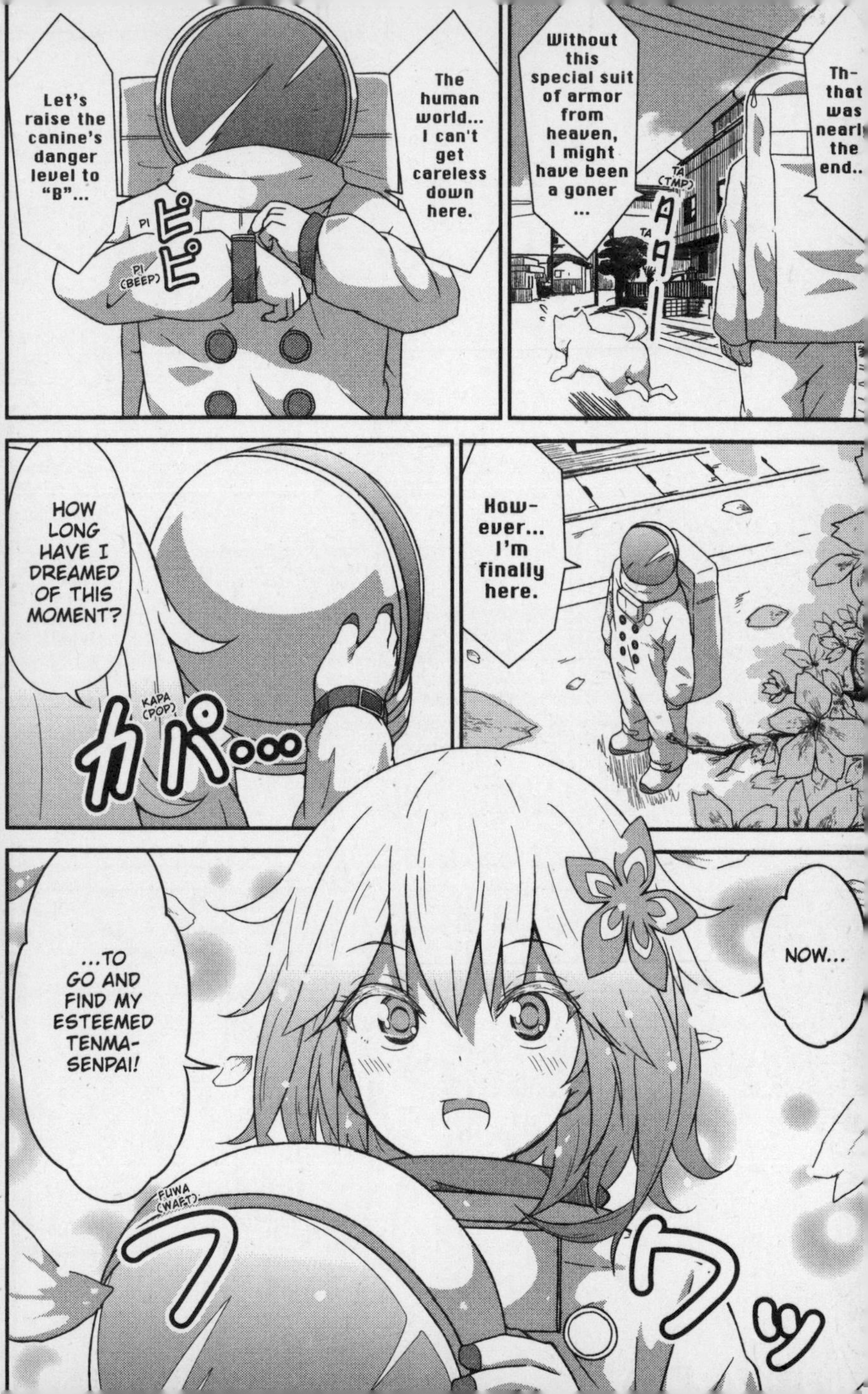
Th- that was nearl the end..
Without this special suit of armor from heaven, I might have been a goner ...
TA (TMP) TA
The human world... I can't get careless down here.
Let's raise the canine's danger level to "B"...
PI PI (BEEP)
How-ever... I'm finally here.
HOW LONG HAVE I DREAMED OF THIS MOMENT?
KAPA (POP)
カパ…
NOW...
...TO GO AND FIND MY ESTEEMED TENMA-SENPAI!
FUWA (WAFT)
フワッ

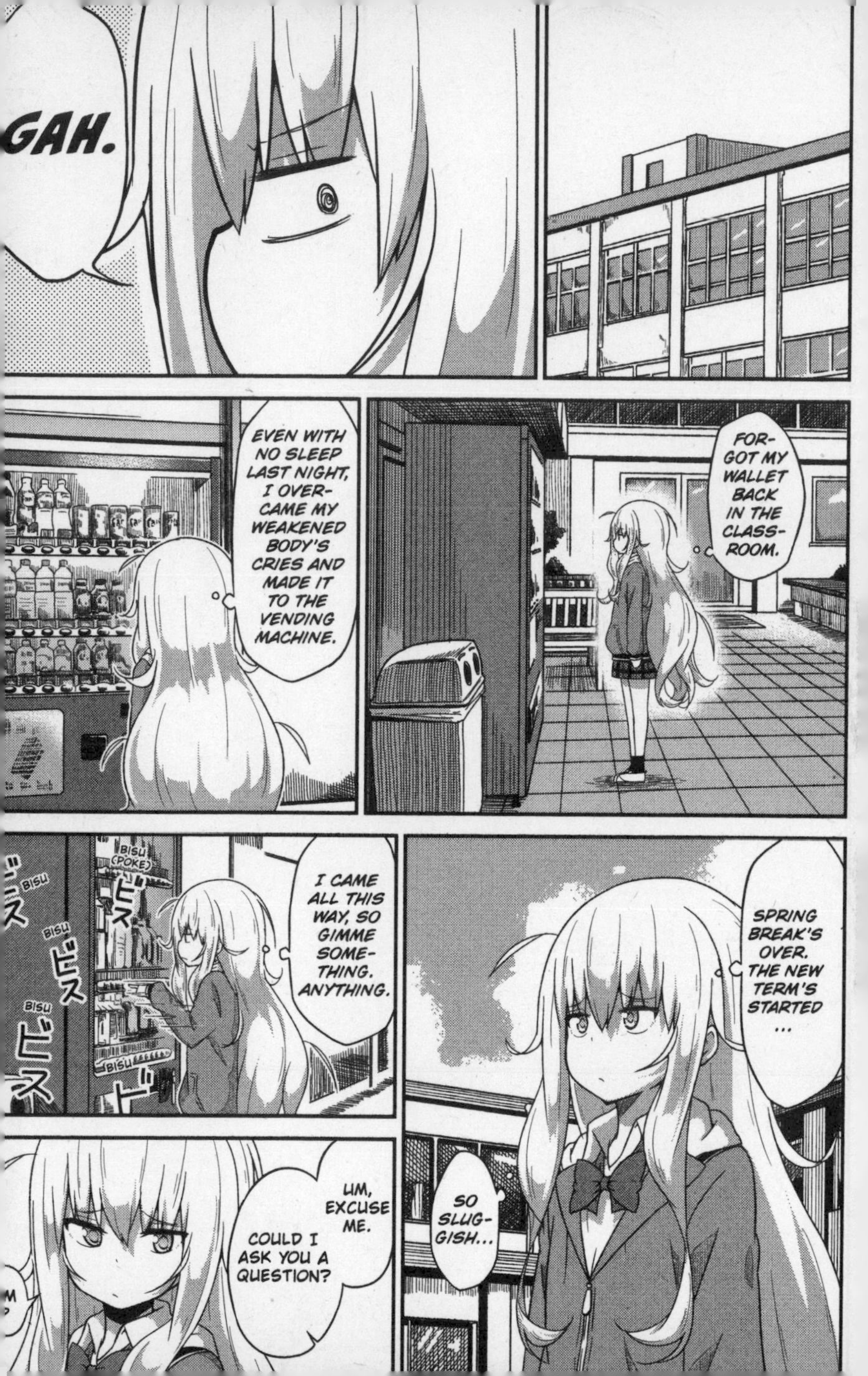
GAH.
FORGOT MY WALLET BACK IN THE CLASSROOM.
EVEN WITH NO SLEEP LAST NIGHT, I OVERCAME MY WEAKENED BODY'S CRIES AND MADE IT TO THE VENDING MACHINE.
SPRING BREAK'S OVER. THE NEW TERM'S STARTED...
SO SLUGGISH...
BISU (POKE)
ビス
BISU
ビス
BISU
ビス
BISU
ビス
BISU
I CAME ALL THIS WAY, SO GIMME SOMETHING. ANYTHING.
UM, EXCUSE ME.
COULD I ASK YOU A QUESTION?

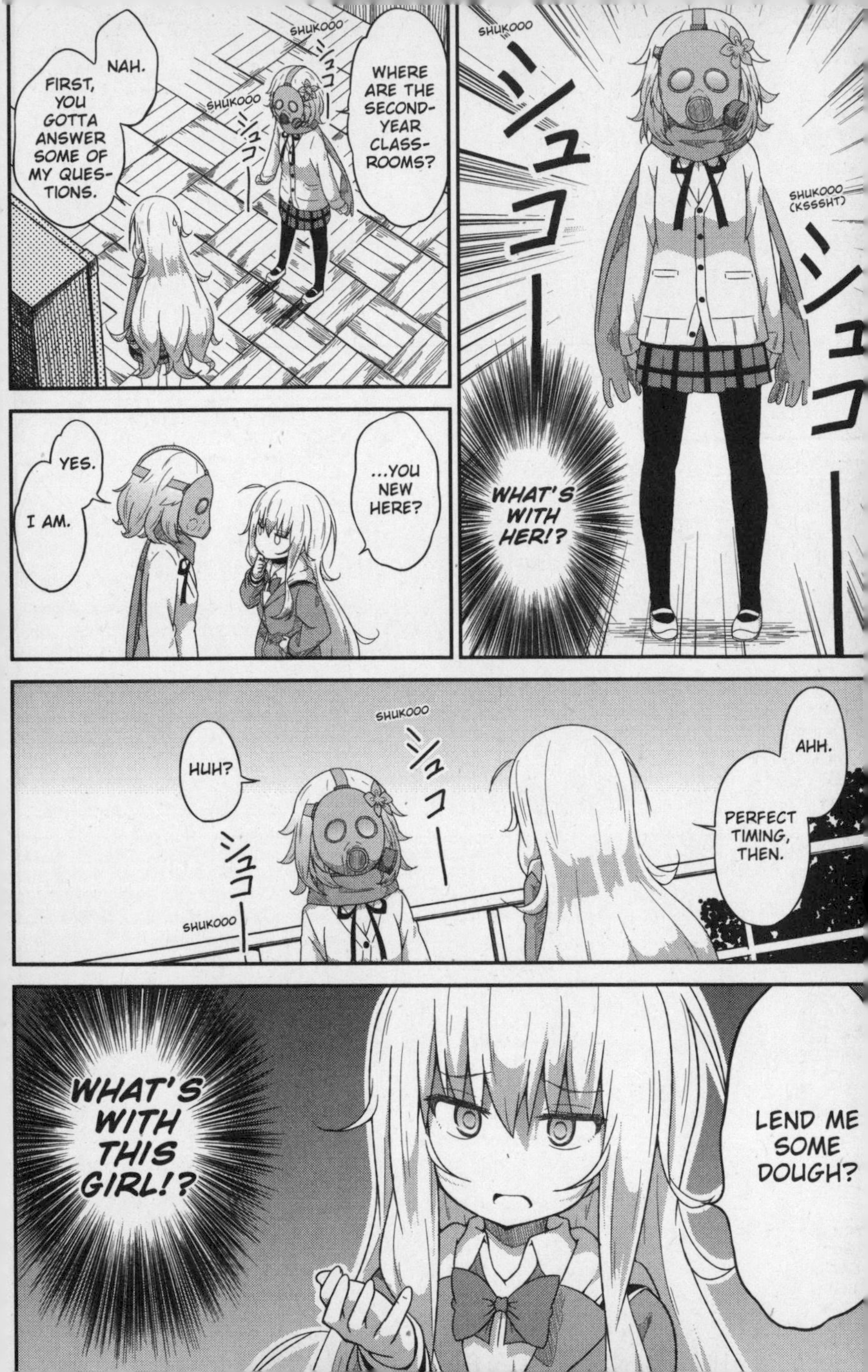
SHUKOOO
シュコー
SHUKOOO (KSSSHT)
シュコー
WHAT'S WITH HER!?
SHUKOOO
シュコー
WHERE ARE THE SECOND-YEAR CLASS-ROOMS?
SHUKOOO
シュコー
NAH.
FIRST, YOU GOTTA ANSWER SOME OF MY QUES-TIONS.
...YOU NEW HERE?
YES.
I AM.
AHH.
PERFECT TIMING, THEN.
SHUKOOO
シュコー
HUH?
シュコー
SHUKOOO
LEND ME SOME DOUGH?
WHAT'S WITH THIS GIRL!?

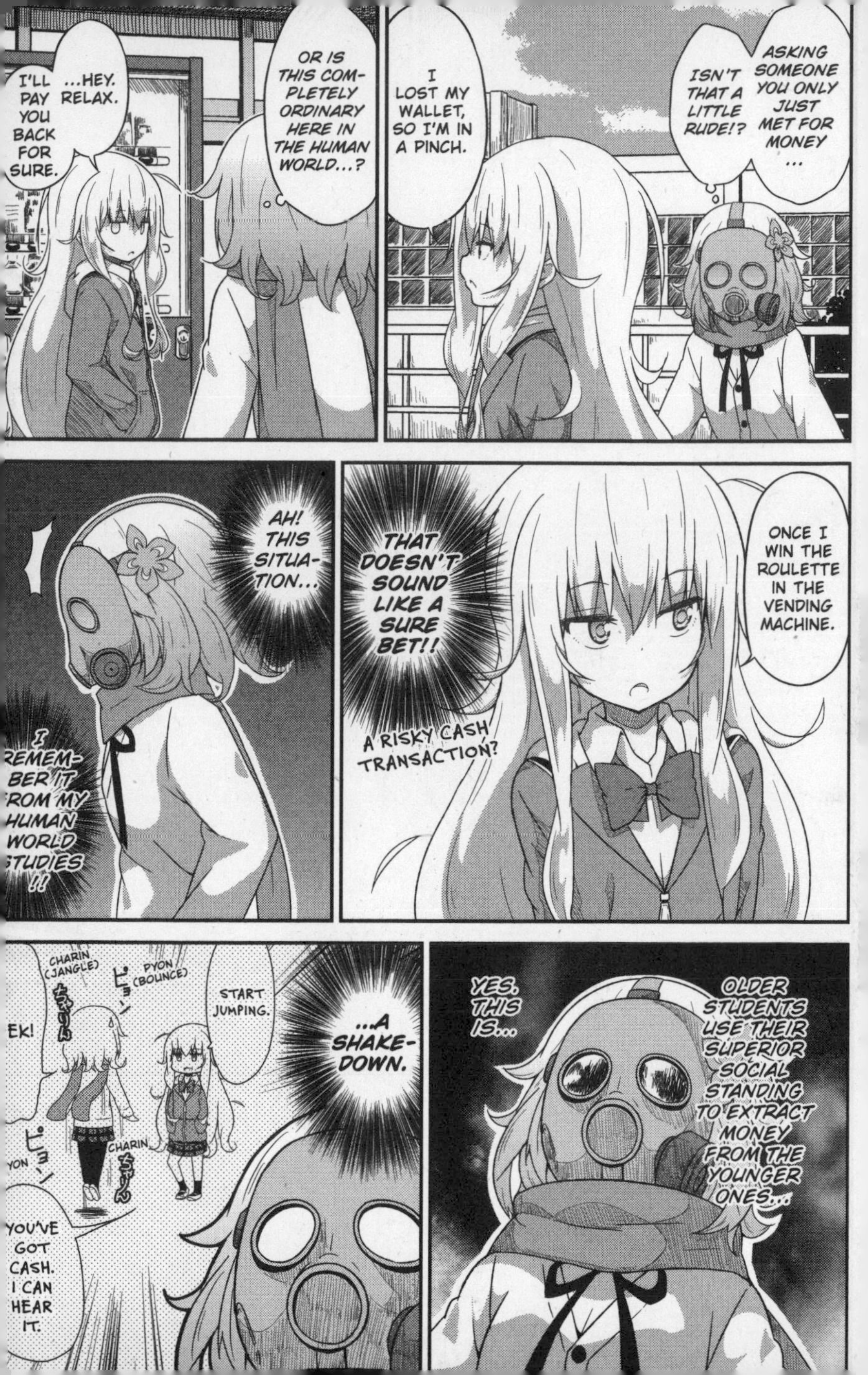

ASKING SOMEONE YOU ONLY JUST MET FOR MONEY...
ISN'T THAT A LITTLE RUDE!?
I LOST MY WALLET, SO I'M IN A PINCH.
OR IS THIS COMPLETELY ORDINARY HERE IN THE HUMAN WORLD...?
...HEY. RELAX.
I'LL PAY YOU BACK FOR SURE.
ONCE I WIN THE ROULETTE IN THE VENDING MACHINE.
THAT DOESN'T SOUND LIKE A SURE BET!!
A RISKY CASH TRANSACTION?
AH! THIS SITUATION...
I REMEMBER IT FROM MY HUMAN WORLD STUDIES!!
OLDER STUDENTS USE THEIR SUPERIOR SOCIAL STANDING TO EXTRACT MONEY FROM THE YOUNGER ONES...
YES. THIS IS...
...A SHAKEDOWN.
START JUMPING.
PYON (BOUNCE)
CHARIN (JANGLE)
EK!
CHARIN
YON
YOU'VE GOT CASH. I CAN HEAR IT.

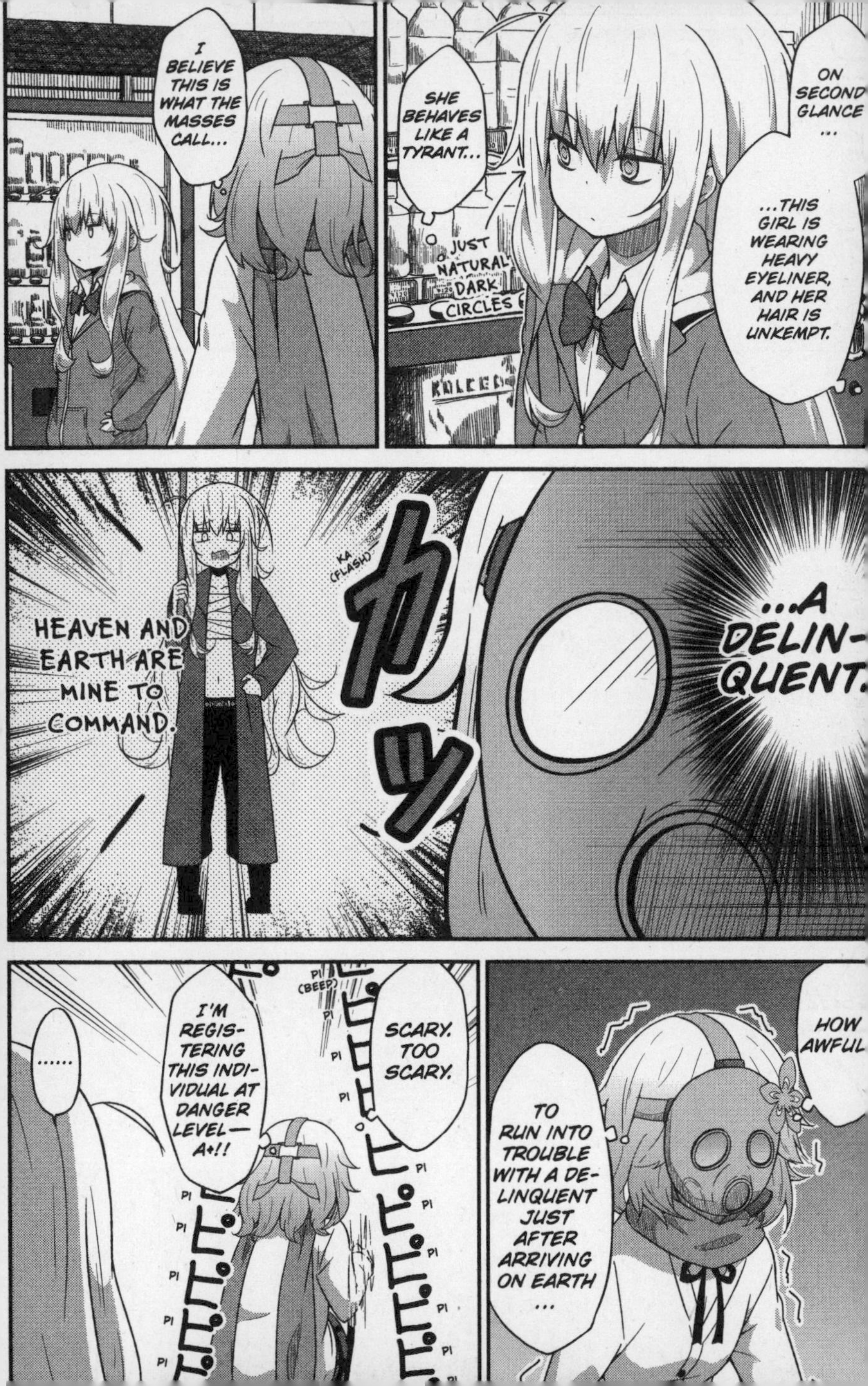

ON SECOND GLANCE ...
...THIS GIRL IS WEARING HEAVY EYELINER, AND HER HAIR IS UNKEMPT.
SHE BEHAVES LIKE A TYRANT...
JUST NATURAL DARK CIRCLES
I BELIEVE THIS IS WHAT THE MASSES CALL...
...A DELINQUENT.
KA (FLASH)
HEAVEN AND EARTH ARE MINE TO COMMAND.
HOW AWFUL
TO RUN INTO TROUBLE WITH A DELINQUENT JUST AFTER ARRIVING ON EARTH ...
SCARY. TOO SCARY.
PI (BEEP)
PI PI PI PI PI PI PI PI PI PI PI PI
I'M REGISTERING THIS INDIVIDUAL AT DANGER LEVEL—A+!!
......

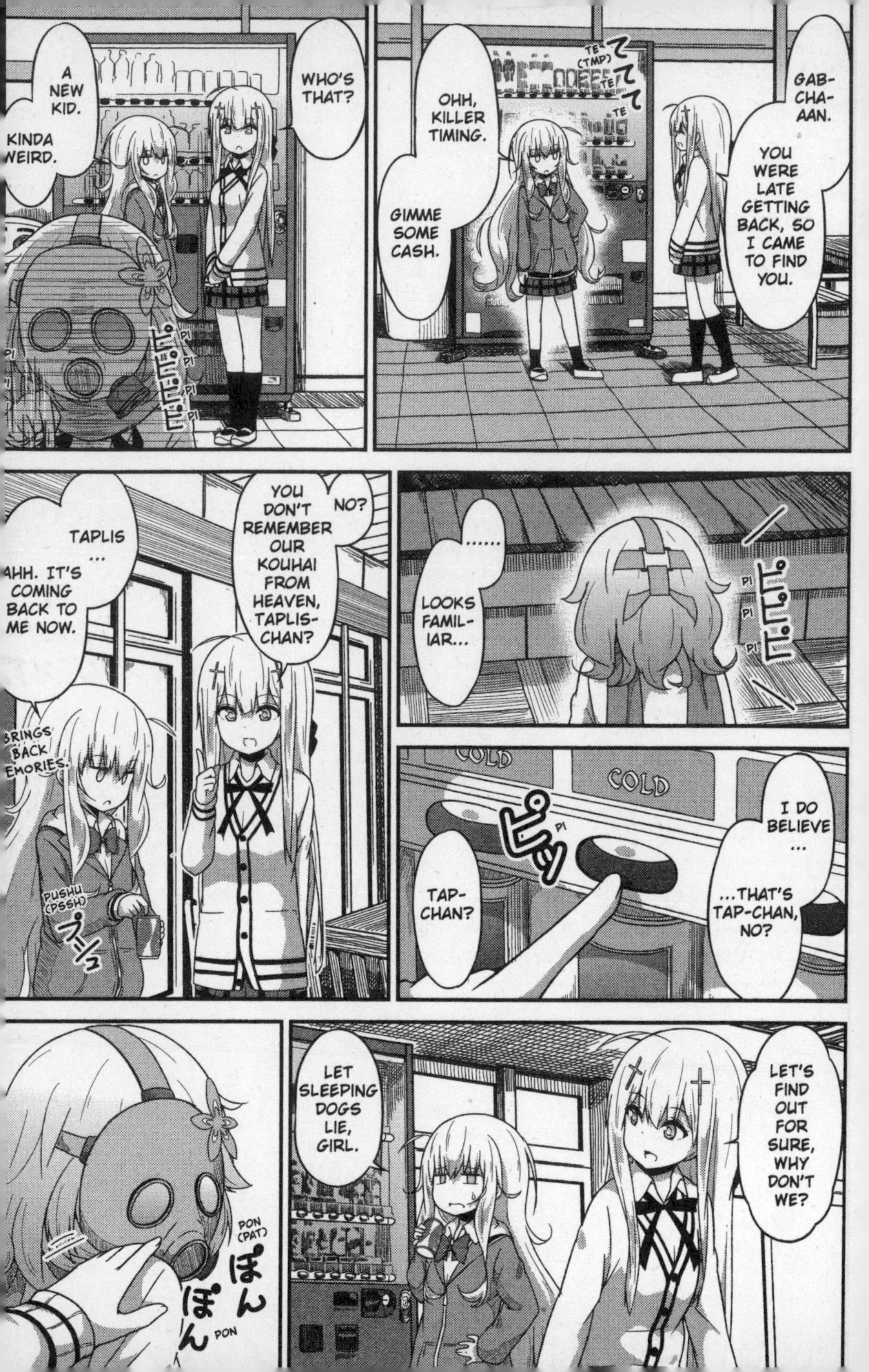
GAB-CHA-AAN.
YOU WERE LATE GETTING BACK, SO I CAME TO FIND YOU.
TE (TMP) TE TE
OHH, KILLER TIMING.
GIMME SOME CASH.
WHO'S THAT?
A NEW KID.
KINDA WEIRD.
PI PI PI PI
......
LOOKS FAMILIAR...
PI PI PI
I DO BELIEVE...
...THAT'S TAP-CHAN, NO?
TAP-CHAN?
PI
NO?
YOU DON'T REMEMBER OUR KOUHAI FROM HEAVEN, TAPLIS-CHAN?
TAPLIS...
AHH. IT'S COMING BACK TO ME NOW.
BRINGS BACK EMORIES.
PUSHU (PSSH)
LET'S FIND OUT FOR SURE, WHY DON'T WE?
LET SLEEPING DOGS LIE, GIRL.
PON (PAT) PON

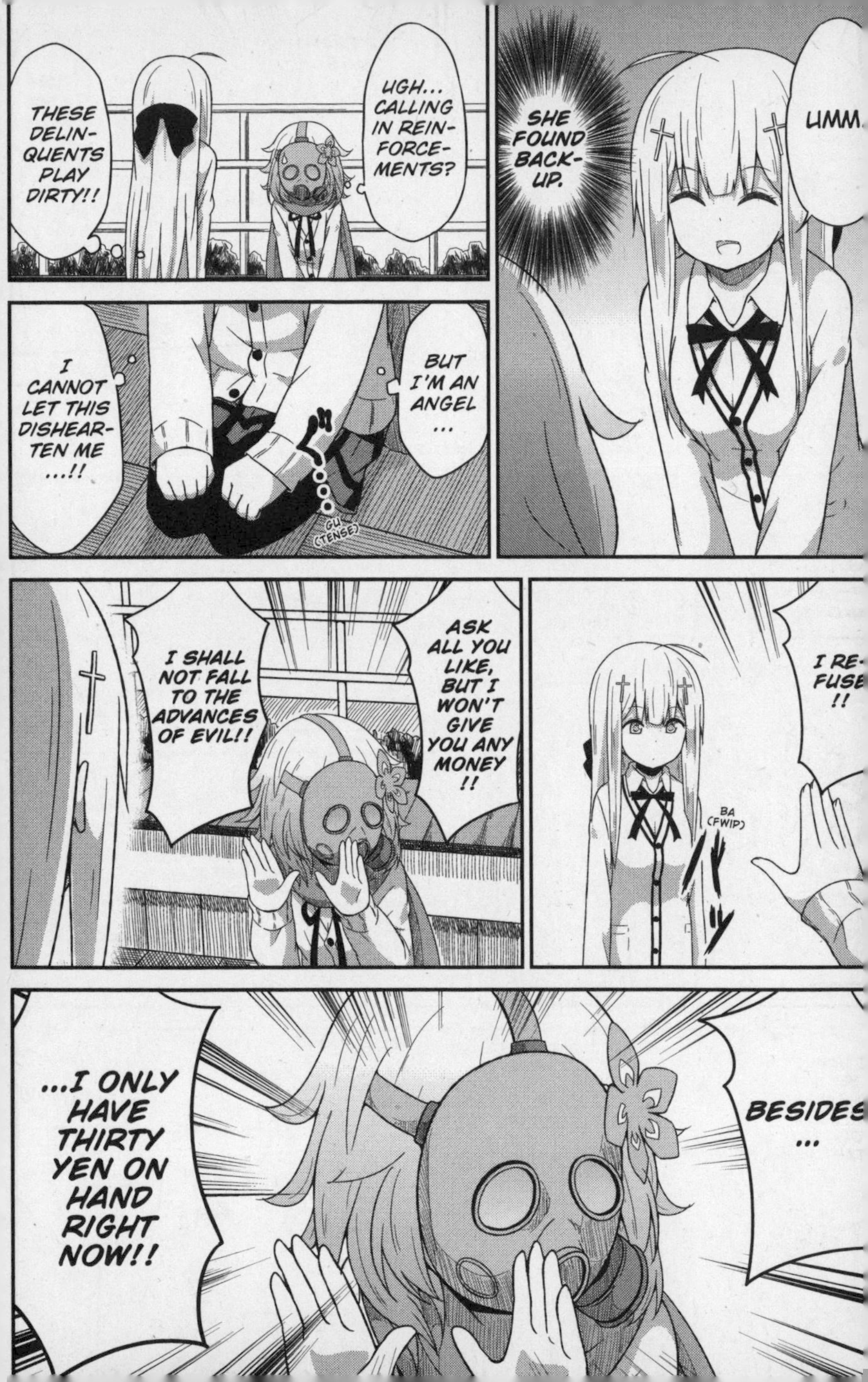
UMM.
SHE FOUND BACK-UP.
UGH... CALLING IN REINFORCEMENTS?
THESE DELINQUENTS PLAY DIRTY!!
BUT I'M AN ANGEL...
GU (TENSE)
I CANNOT LET THIS DISHEARTEN ME...!!
I REFUSE!!
BA (FWIP)
ASK ALL YOU LIKE, BUT I WON'T GIVE YOU ANY MONEY!!
I SHALL NOT FALL TO THE ADVANCES OF EVIL!!
BESIDES...
...I ONLY HAVE THIRTY YEN ON HAND RIGHT NOW!!

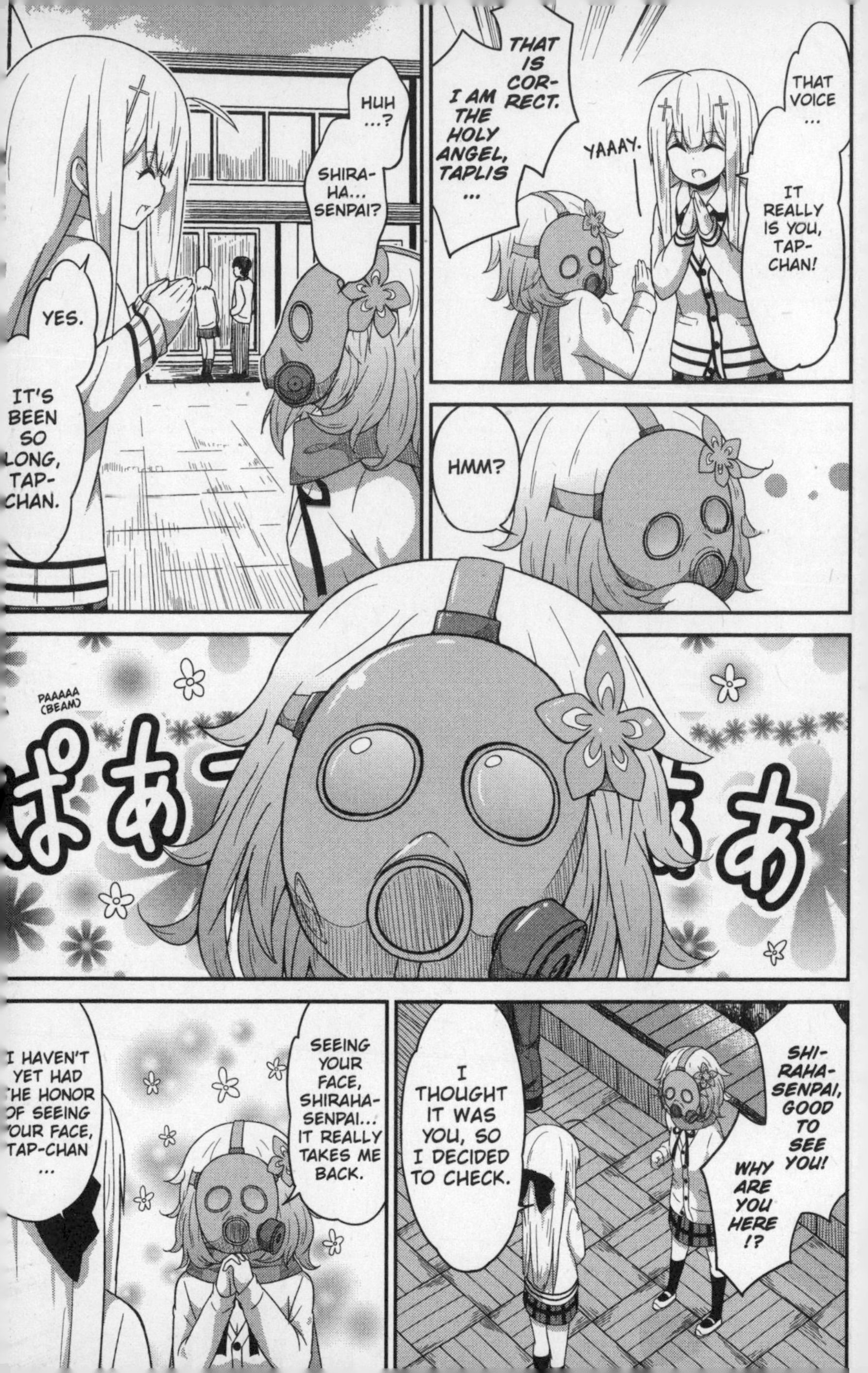
THAT VOICE...
IT REALLY IS YOU, TAP-CHAN!
YAAAY.
THAT IS CORRECT.
I AM THE HOLY ANGEL, TAPLIS...
HMM?
HUH...?
SHIRAHA... SENPAI?
YES.
IT'S BEEN SO LONG, TAP-CHAN.
PAAAAA (BEAM)
ぱあーーあ
SHIRAHA-SENPAI, GOOD TO SEE YOU!
WHY ARE YOU HERE!?
I THOUGHT IT WAS YOU, SO I DECIDED TO CHECK.
SEEING YOUR FACE, SHIRAHA-SENPAI... IT REALLY TAKES ME BACK.
I HAVEN'T YET HAD THE HONOR OF SEEING YOUR FACE, TAP-CHAN...

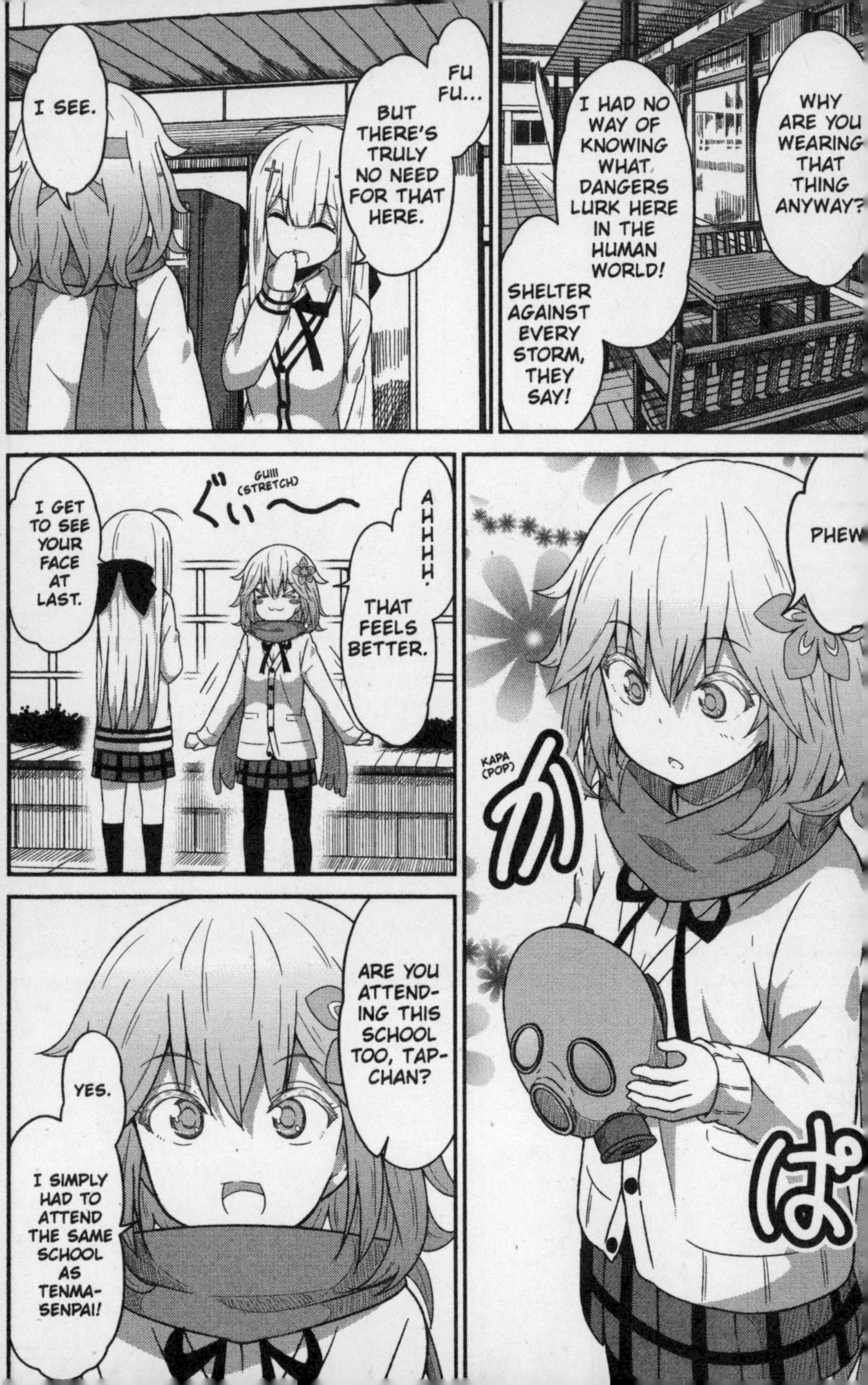
WHY ARE YOU WEARING THAT THING ANYWAY?
I HAD NO WAY OF KNOWING WHAT DANGERS LURK HERE IN THE HUMAN WORLD!
SHELTER AGAINST EVERY STORM, THEY SAY!
FU FU...
BUT THERE'S TRULY NO NEED FOR THAT HERE.
I SEE.
PHEW
かぱ
KAPA (POP)
AHHHH.
THAT FEELS BETTER.
ぐい〜〜
GUIII (STRETCH)
I GET TO SEE YOUR FACE AT LAST.
ARE YOU ATTENDING THIS SCHOOL TOO, TAP-CHAN?
YES.
I SIMPLY HAD TO ATTEND THE SAME SCHOOL AS TENMA-SENPAI!

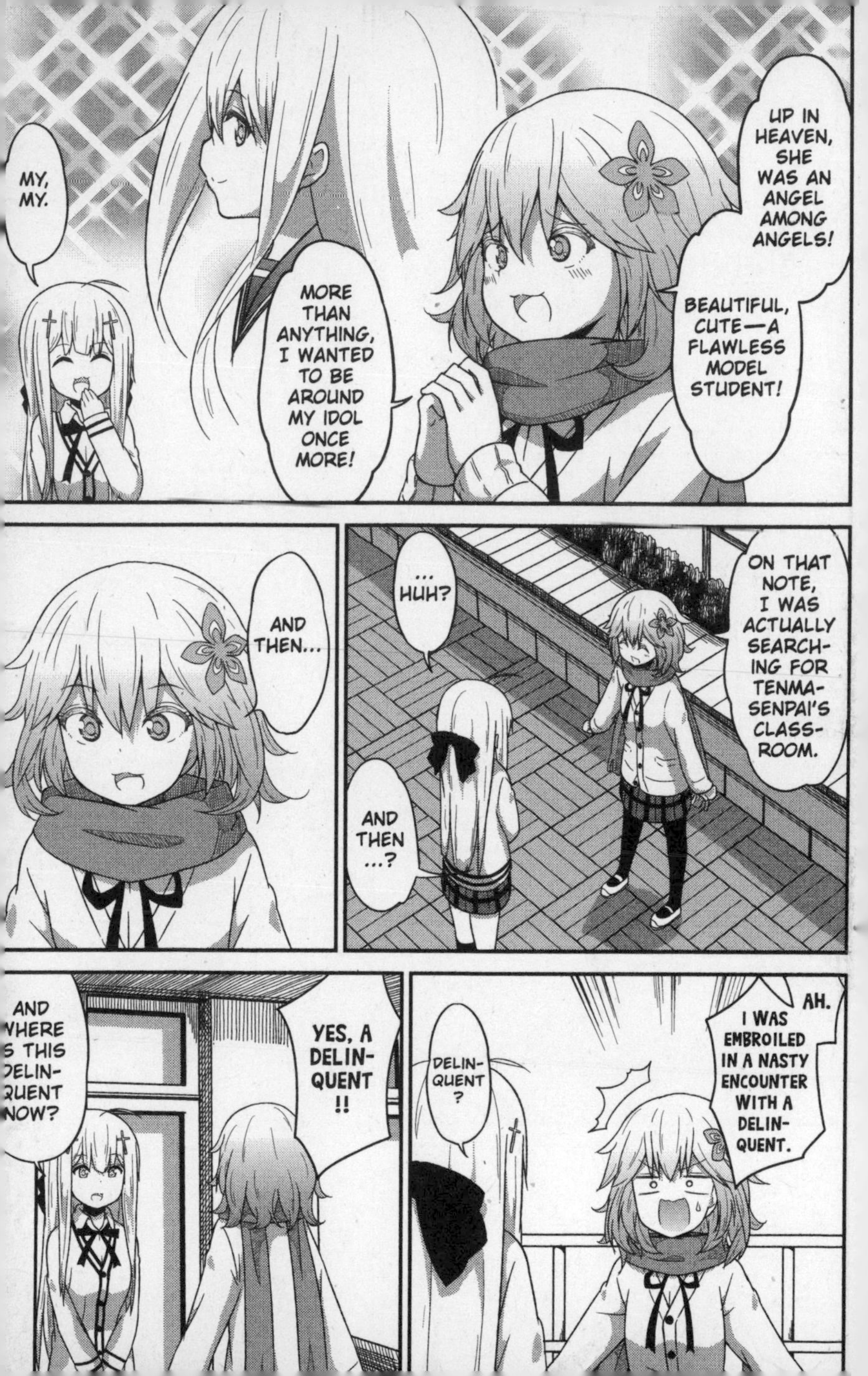
UP IN HEAVEN, SHE WAS AN ANGEL AMONG ANGELS!
BEAUTIFUL, CUTE—A FLAWLESS MODEL STUDENT!
MORE THAN ANYTHING, I WANTED TO BE AROUND MY IDOL ONCE MORE!
MY, MY.
ON THAT NOTE, I WAS ACTUALLY SEARCHING FOR TENMA-SENPAI'S CLASSROOM.
... HUH?
AND THEN ...?
AND THEN...
AH.
I WAS EMBROILED IN A NASTY ENCOUNTER WITH A DELINQUENT.
DELINQUENT ?
YES, A DELINQUENT !!
AND WHERE S THIS DELINQUENT NOW?

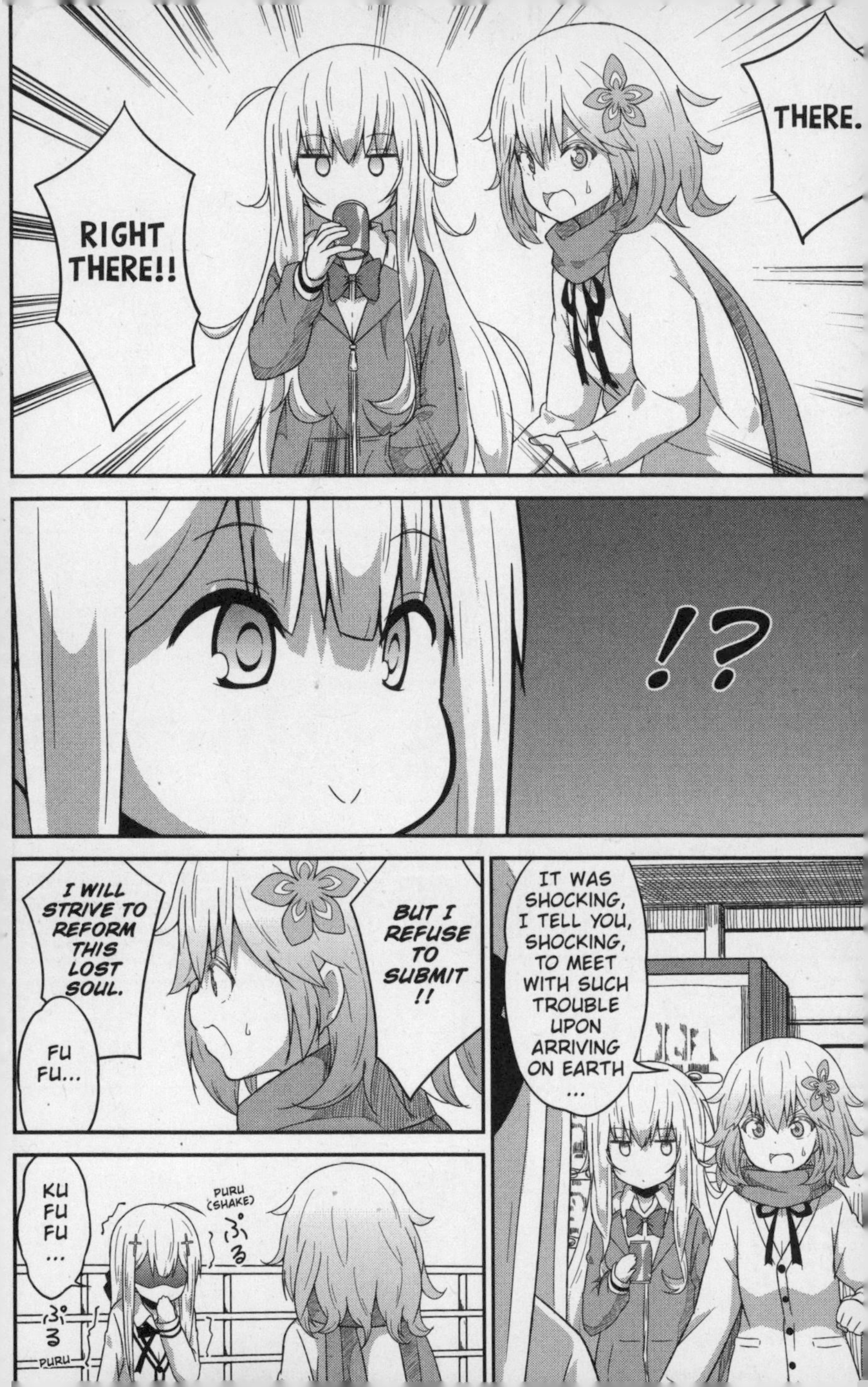
THERE.
RIGHT THERE!!
!?
IT WAS SHOCKING, I TELL YOU, SHOCKING, TO MEET WITH SUCH TROUBLE UPON ARRIVING ON EARTH ...
BUT I REFUSE TO SUBMIT !!
I WILL STRIVE TO REFORM THIS LOST SOUL.
FU FU...
PURU (SHAKE) ぷる
KU FU FU ...
ぷる PURU

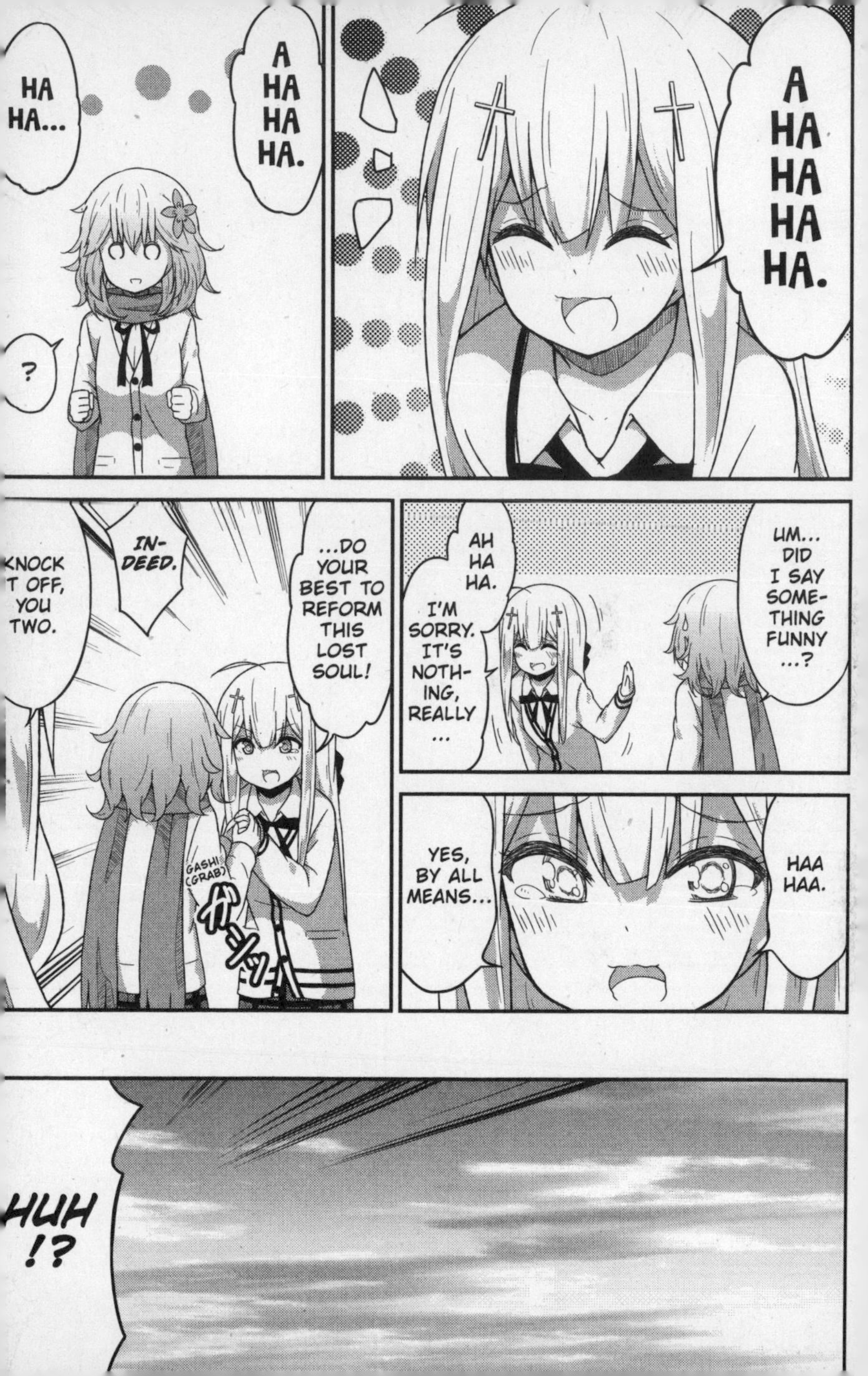
A HA HA HA HA HA.
A HA HA HA.
HA HA...
?
UM... DID I SAY SOME-THING FUNNY...?
AH HA HA.
I'M SORRY. IT'S NOTH-ING, REALLY...
HAA HAA.
YES, BY ALL MEANS...
...DO YOUR BEST TO REFORM THIS LOST SOUL!
IN-DEED.
GASHI (GRAB)
KNOCK T OFF, YOU TWO.
HUH !?

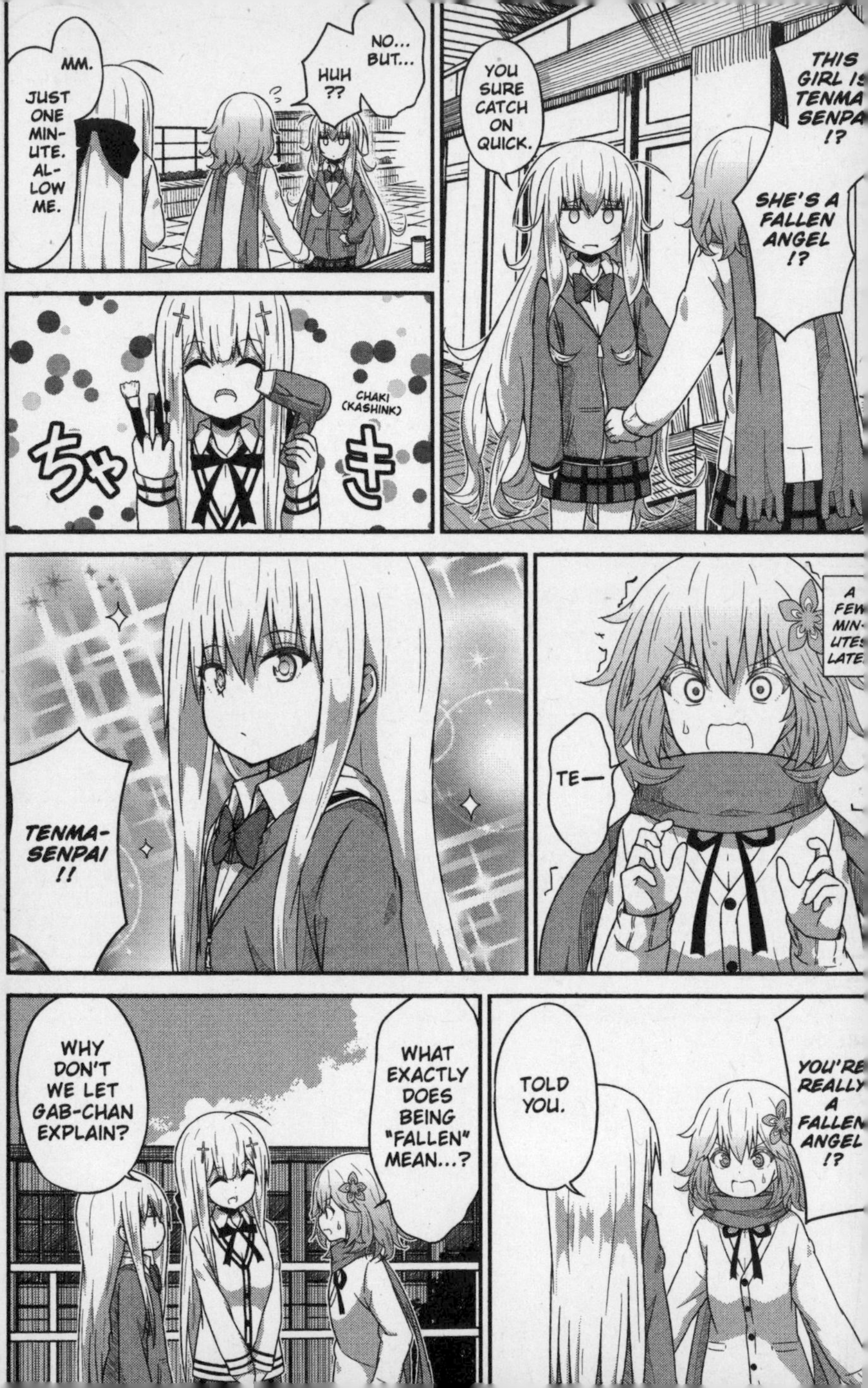
THIS GIRL IS TENMA SENPAI !?
SHE'S A FALLEN ANGEL !?
YOU SURE CATCH ON QUICK.
NO... BUT...
HUH ??
MM.
JUST ONE MIN-UTE. AL-LOW ME.
CHAKI (KASHINK)
ちゃき
A FEW MIN-UTES LATER
TE—
TENMA-SENPAI !!
YOU'RE REALLY A FALLEN ANGEL !?
TOLD YOU.
WHAT EXACTLY DOES BEING "FALLEN" MEAN...?
WHY DON'T WE LET GAB-CHAN EXPLAIN?

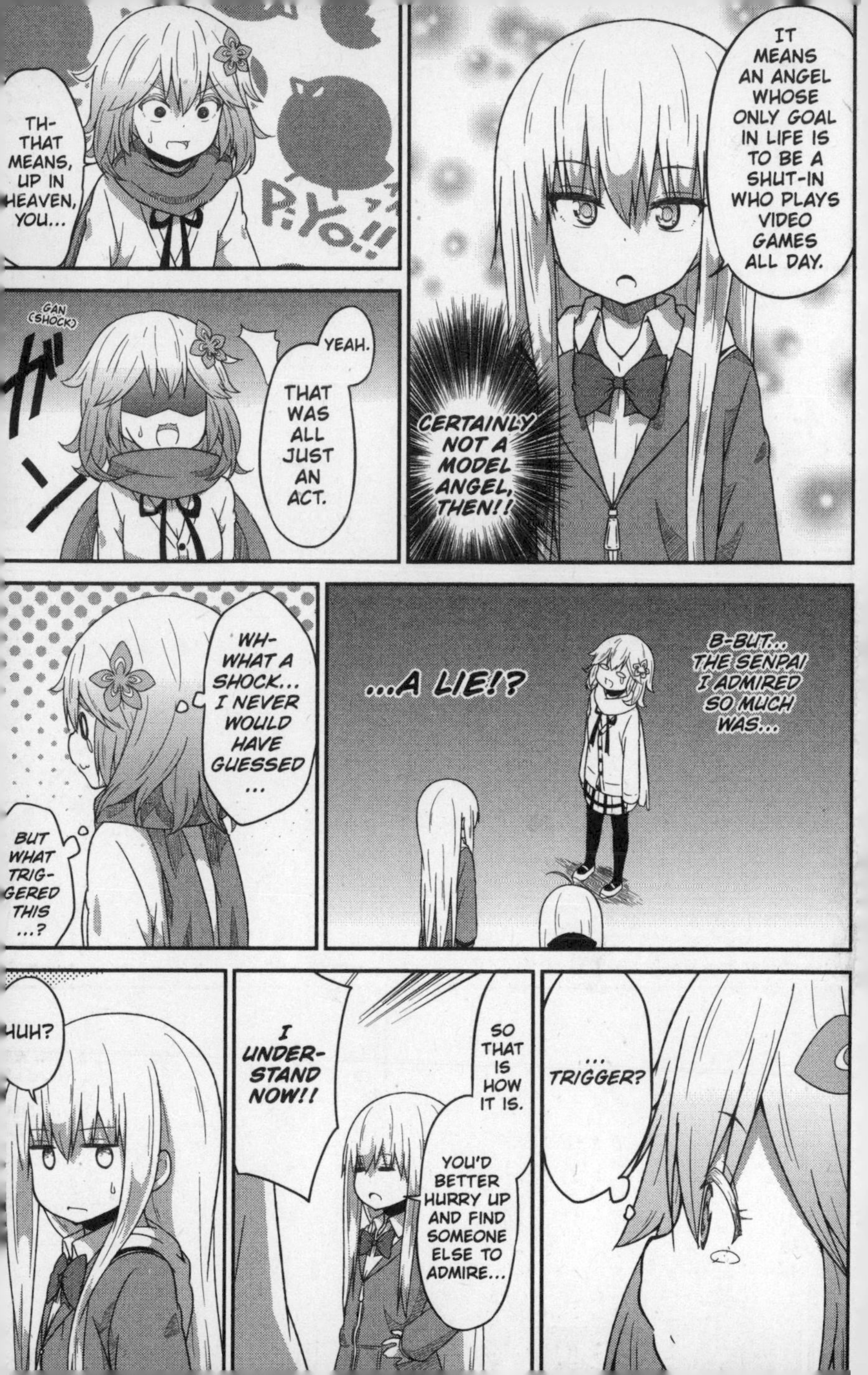
IT MEANS AN ANGEL WHOSE ONLY GOAL IN LIFE IS TO BE A SHUT-IN WHO PLAYS VIDEO GAMES ALL DAY.
CERTAINLY NOT A MODEL ANGEL, THEN!!
TH-THAT MEANS, UP IN HEAVEN, YOU...
P:YO!!
GAN (SHOCK)
YEAH.
THAT WAS ALL JUST AN ACT.
B-BUT... THE SENPAI I ADMIRED SO MUCH WAS...
...A LIE!?
WH-WHAT A SHOCK... I NEVER WOULD HAVE GUESSED...
BUT WHAT TRIG-GERED THIS...?
...TRIGGER?
SO THAT IS HOW IT IS.
I UNDER-STAND NOW!!
YOU'D BETTER HURRY UP AND FIND SOMEONE ELSE TO ADMIRE...
HUH?

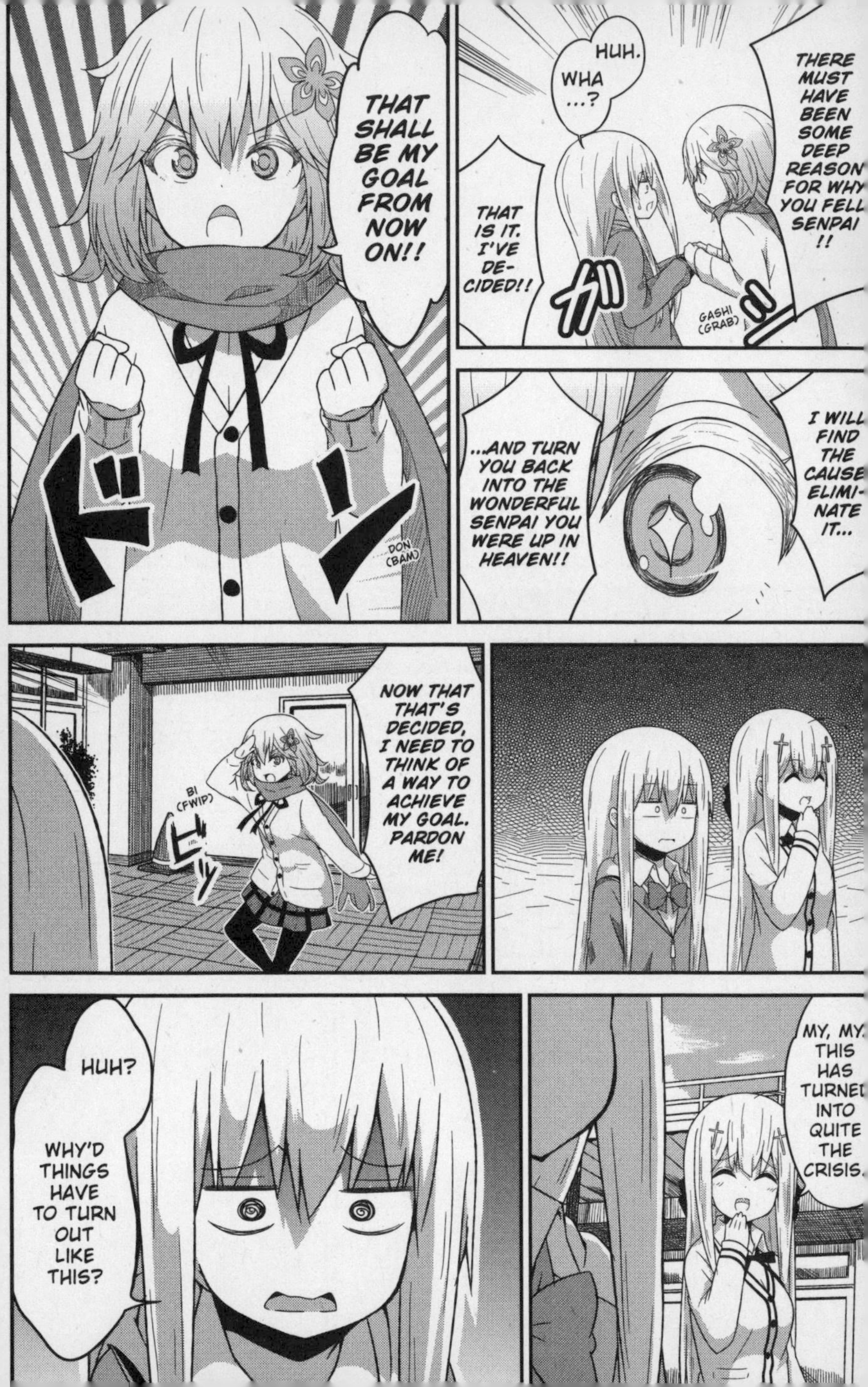
THERE MUST HAVE BEEN SOME DEEP REASON FOR WHY YOU FELL SENPAI!!
HUH.
WHA ...?
THAT IS IT. I'VE DE-CIDED!!
GASHI (GRAB)
I WILL FIND THE CAUSE ELIMI-NATE IT...
...AND TURN YOU BACK INTO THE WONDERFUL SENPAI YOU WERE UP IN HEAVEN!!
THAT SHALL BE MY GOAL FROM NOW ON!!
DON (BAM)
NOW THAT THAT'S DECIDED, I NEED TO THINK OF A WAY TO ACHIEVE MY GOAL. PARDON ME!
BI (FWIP)
MY, MY. THIS HAS TURNED INTO QUITE THE CRISIS.
HUH?
WHY'D THINGS HAVE TO TURN OUT LIKE THIS?

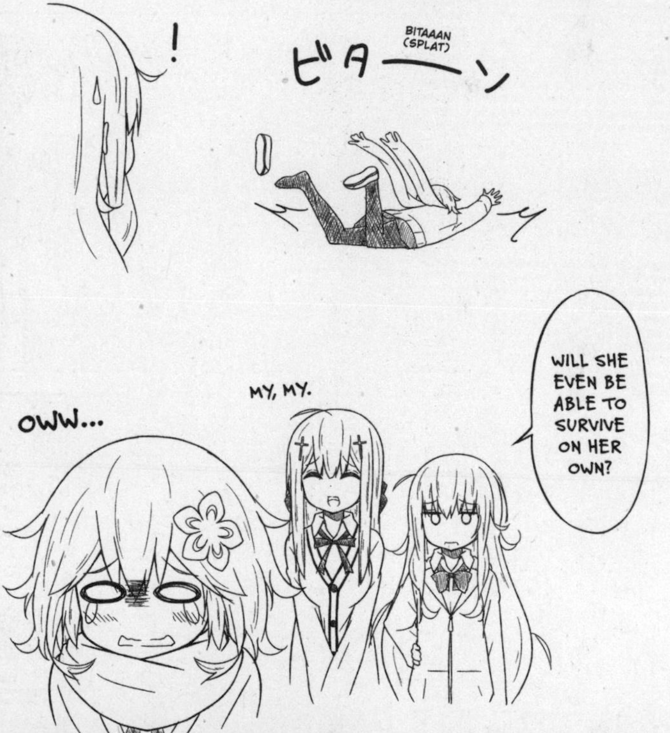

ビターーン
BITAAAN (SPLAT)
!
WILL SHE EVEN BE ABLE TO SURVIVE ON HER OWN?
MY, MY.
OWW...

Gabriel Dropout

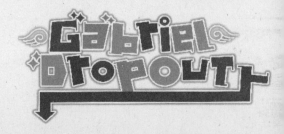

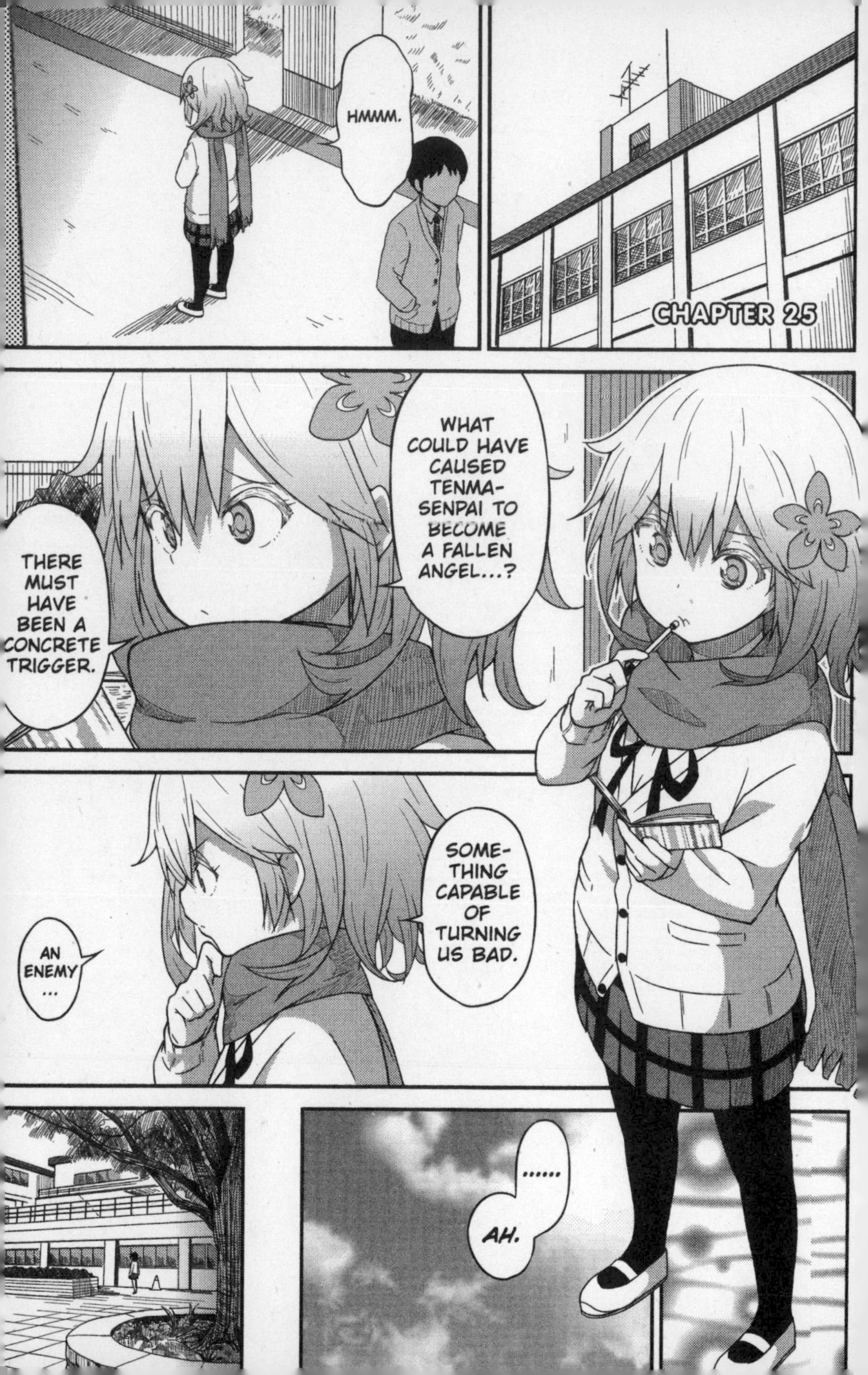

HMMM.
WHAT COULD HAVE CAUSED TENMA-SENPAI TO BECOME A FALLEN ANGEL...?
THERE MUST HAVE BEEN A CONCRETE TRIGGER.
SOME-THING CAPABLE OF TURNING US BAD.
AN ENEMY ...
......
AH.

CHAPTER 25

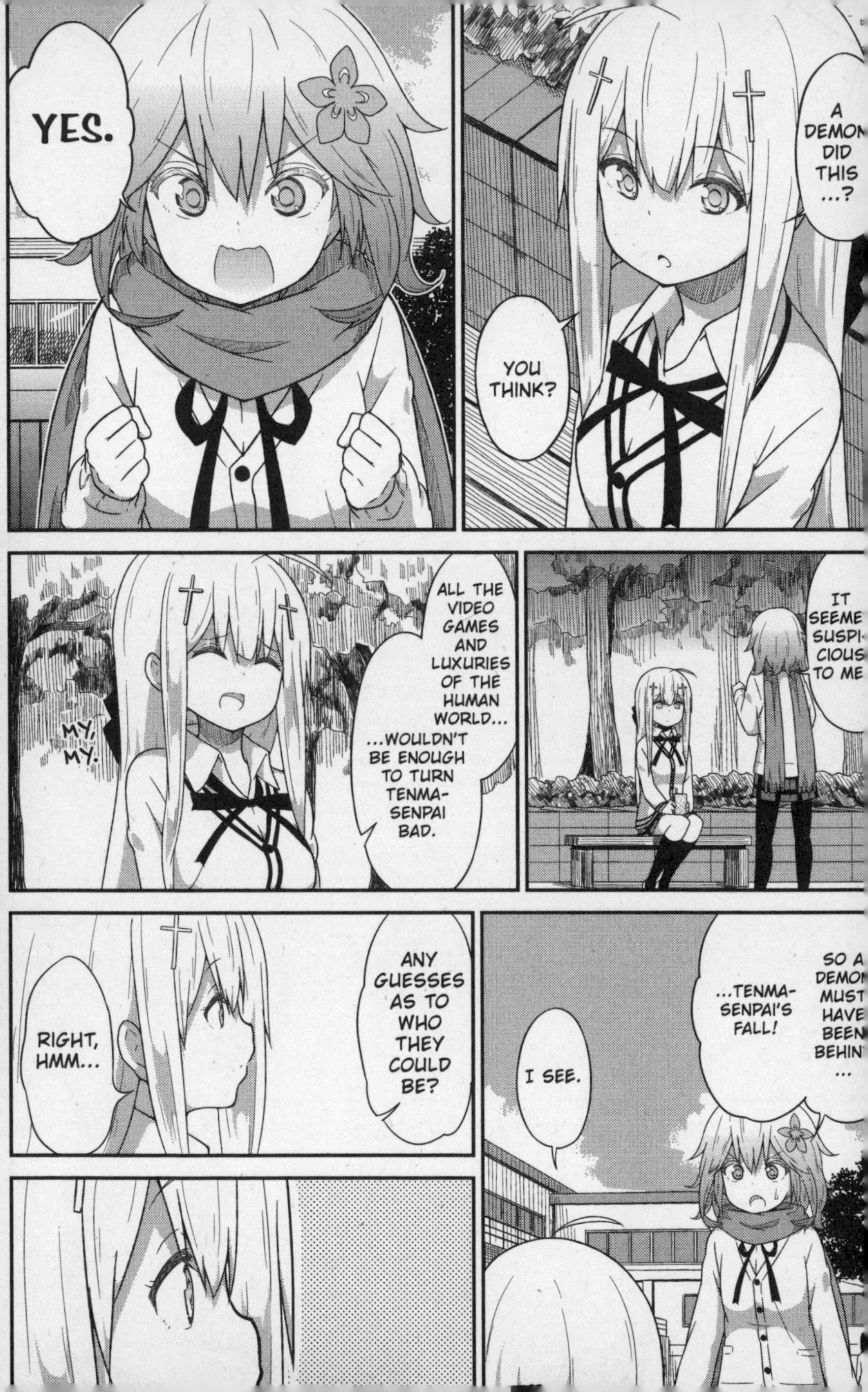
A DEMON DID THIS ...?
YOU THINK?
YES.
IT SEEME SUSPI-CIOUS TO ME
ALL THE VIDEO GAMES AND LUXURIES OF THE HUMAN WORLD...
...WOULDN'T BE ENOUGH TO TURN TENMA-SENPAI BAD.
MY, MY.
SO A DEMO MUST HAVE BEEN BEHIN ...
...TENMA-SENPAI'S FALL!
I SEE.
ANY GUESSES AS TO WHO THEY COULD BE?
RIGHT, HMM...

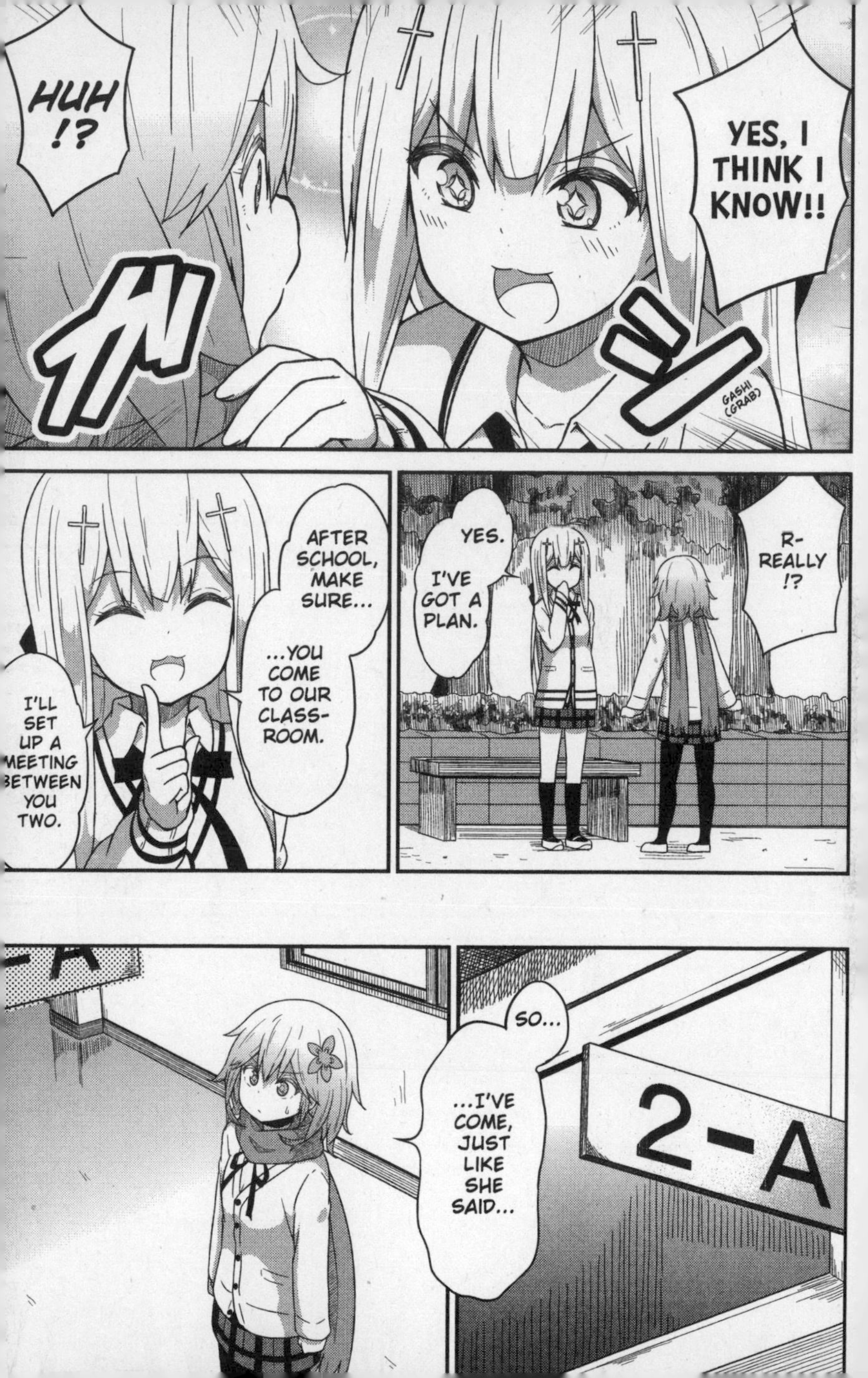
YES, I THINK I KNOW!!
GASHI (GRAB)
HUH!?
R-REALLY!?
YES. I'VE GOT A PLAN.
AFTER SCHOOL, MAKE SURE...
...YOU COME TO OUR CLASS-ROOM.
I'LL SET UP A MEETING BETWEEN YOU TWO.
SO...
...I'VE COME, JUST LIKE SHE SAID...
2-A

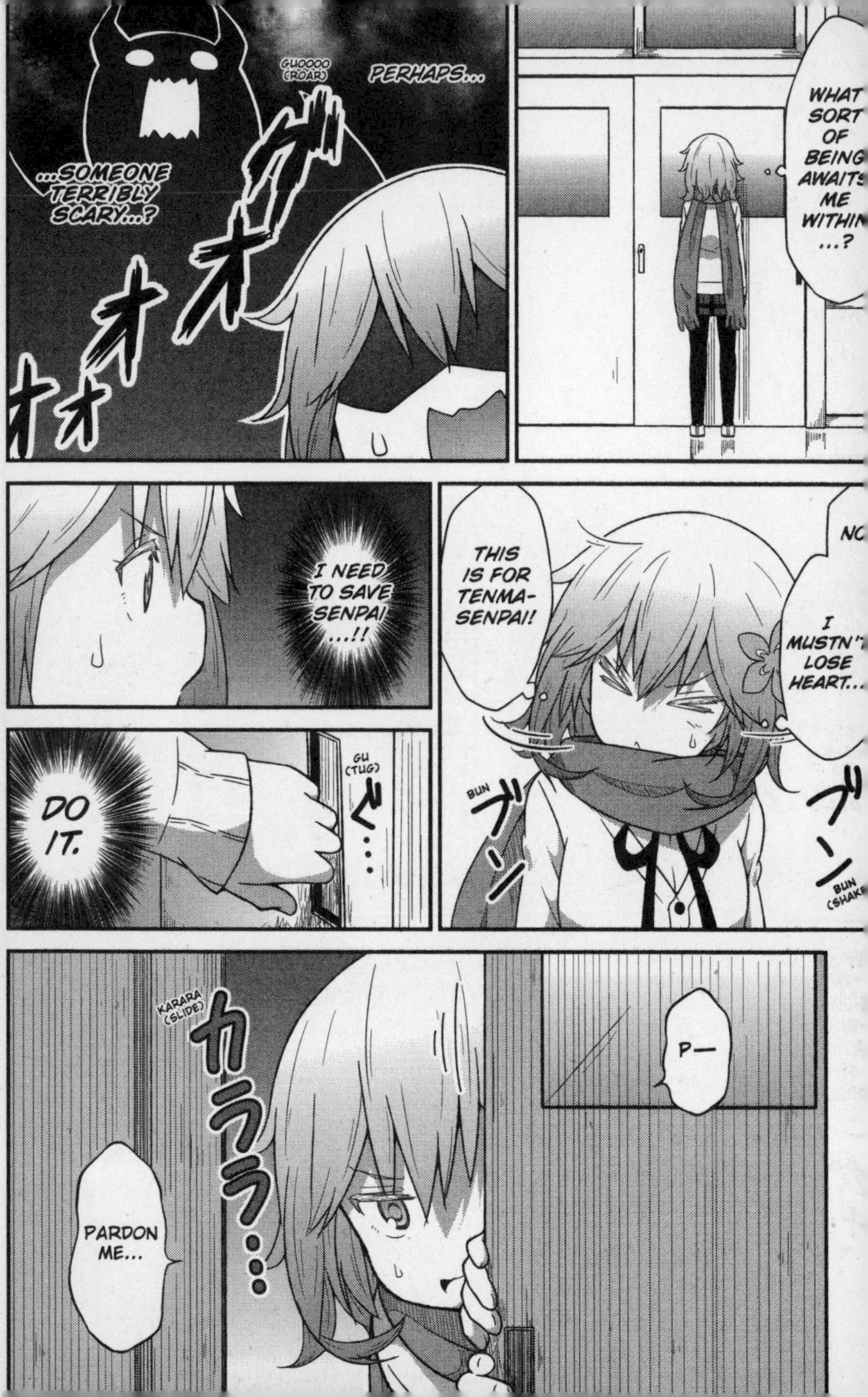
WHAT SORT OF BEING AWAITS ME WITHIN ...?
PERHAPS...
GUOOOO (ROAR)
...SOMEONE TERRIBLY SCARY...?
NO
I MUSTN'T LOSE HEART...
THIS IS FOR TENMA-SENPAI!
BUN (SHAKE)
BUN
I NEED TO SAVE SENPAI ...!!
GU (TUG)
DO IT.
P—
KARARA (SLIDE)
PARDON ME...

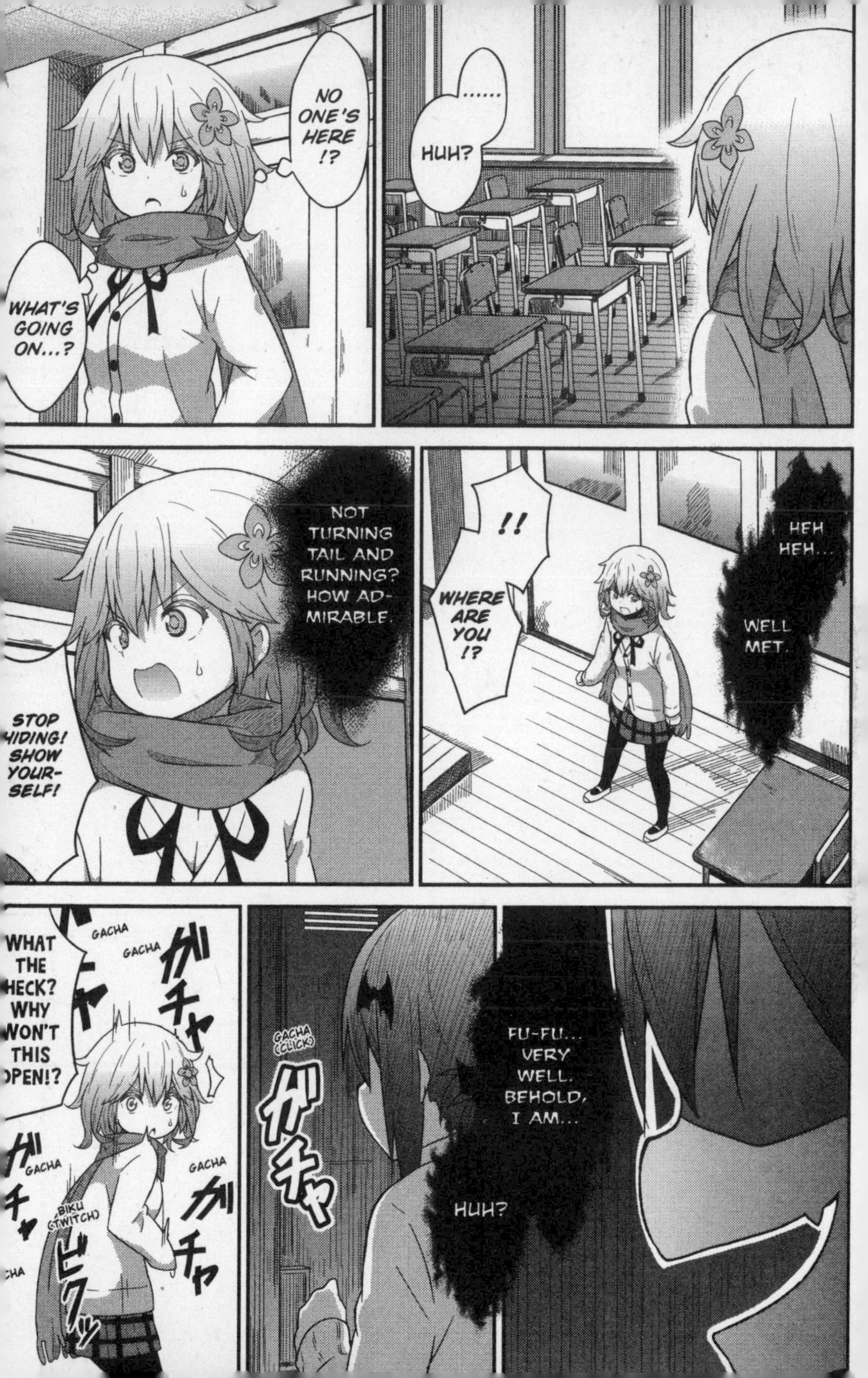
......
HUH?
NO ONE'S HERE !?
WHAT'S GOING ON...?
!!
HEH HEH...
WELL MET.
WHERE ARE YOU !?
NOT TURNING TAIL AND RUNNING? HOW AD-MIRABLE.
STOP HIDING! SHOW YOUR-SELF!
FU-FU... VERY WELL. BEHOLD, I AM...
GACHA (CLICK)
HUH?
GACHA
GACHA
WHAT THE HECK? WHY WON'T THIS OPEN!?
GACHA
GACHA
BIKU (TWITCH)

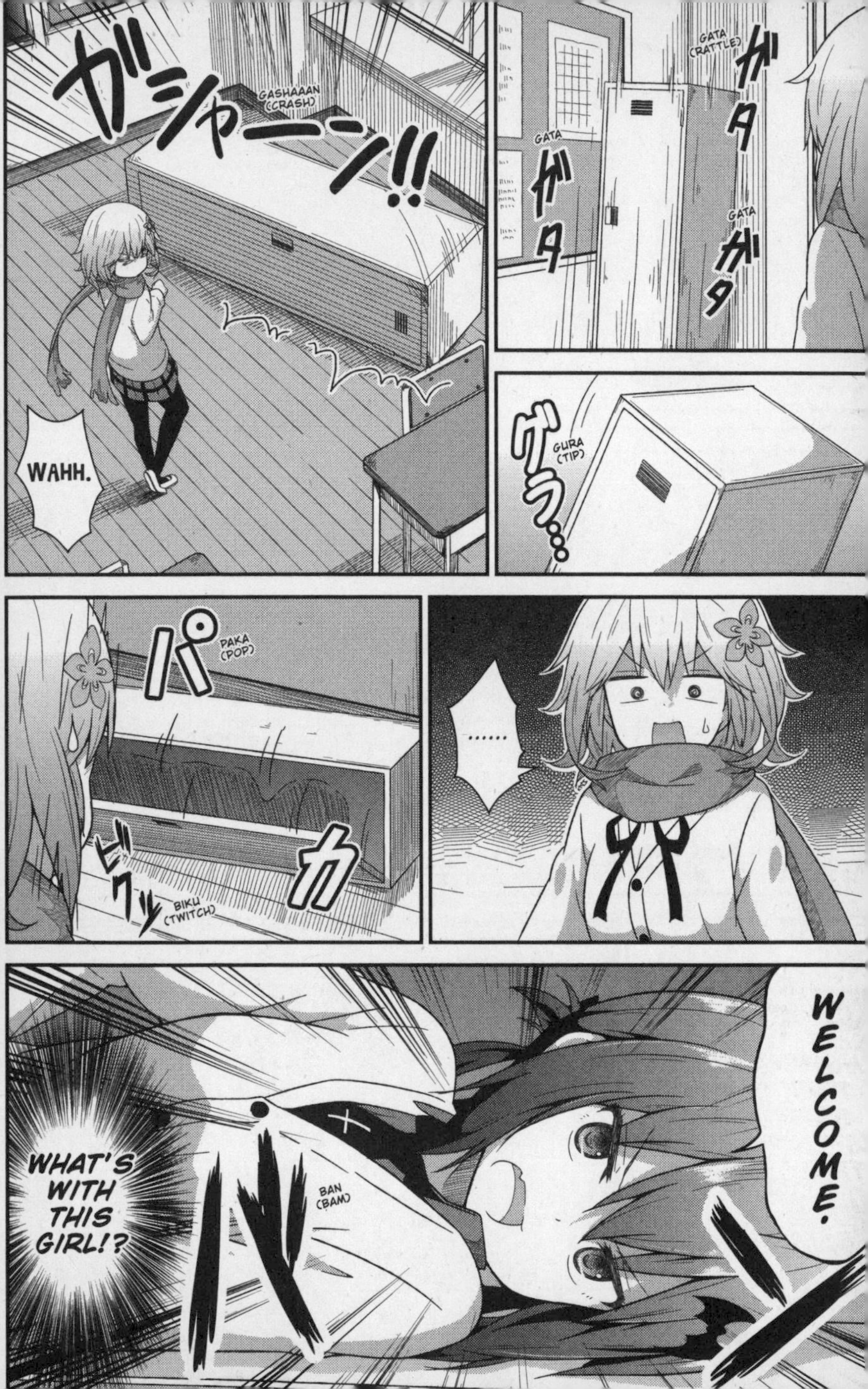
ガタ
GATA (RATTLE)
ガタ
GATA
ガタ
GATA
グラ…
GURA (TIP)
ガシャーーン!!
GASHAAAN (CRASH)
WAHH.
......
パカ
PAKA (POP)
ビクッ
BIKU (TWITCH)
WELCOME.
バン
BAN (BAM)
WHAT'S WITH THIS GIRL!?

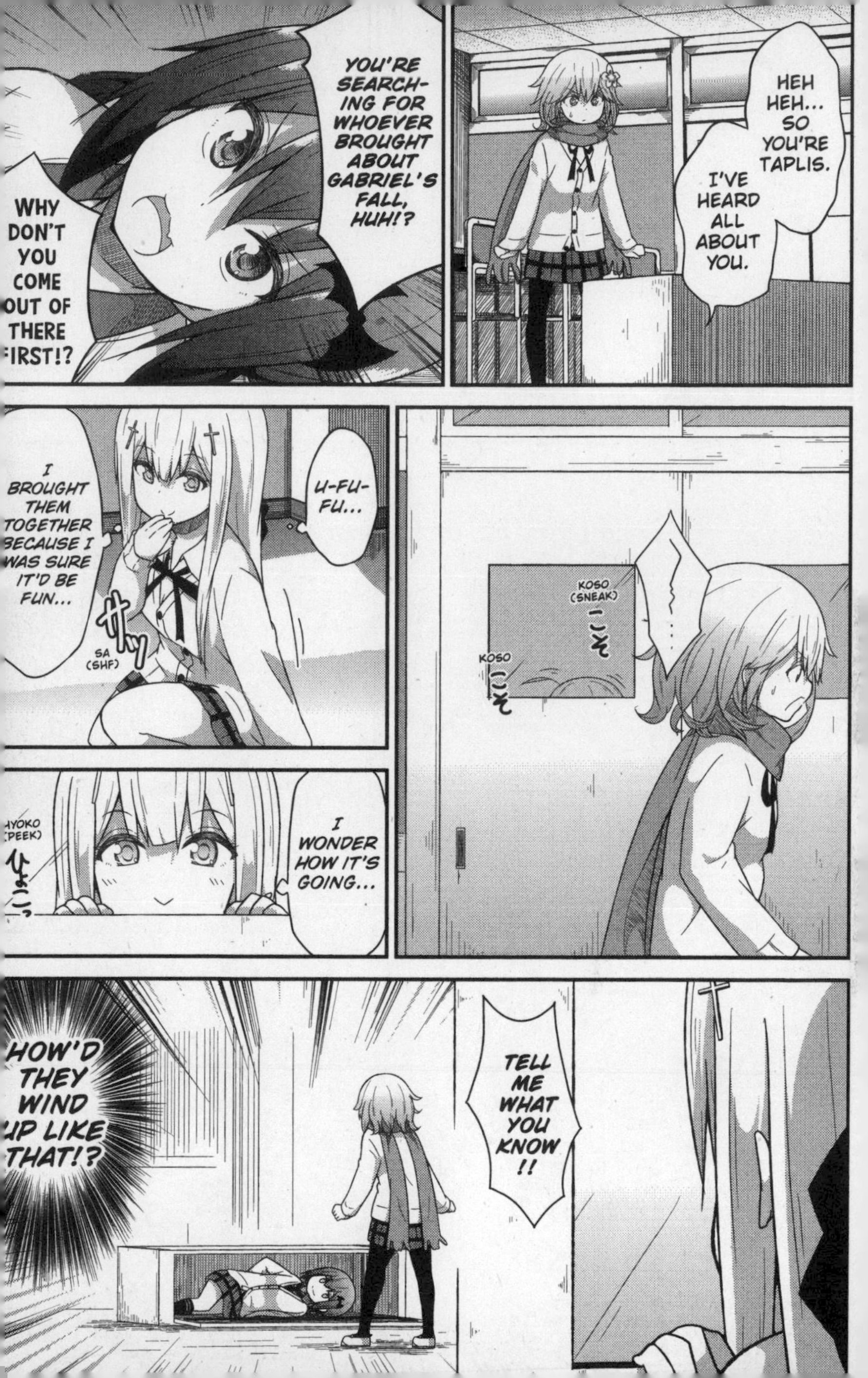
HEH HEH... SO YOU'RE TAPLIS.
I'VE HEARD ALL ABOUT YOU.
YOU'RE SEARCHING FOR WHOEVER BROUGHT ABOUT GABRIEL'S FALL, HUH!?
WHY DON'T YOU COME OUT OF THERE FIRST!?
KOSO (SNEAK)
こそ
KOSO
こそ
U-FU-FU...
I BROUGHT THEM TOGETHER BECAUSE I WAS SURE IT'D BE FUN...
SA (SHF)
サッ
I WONDER HOW IT'S GOING...
HYOKO (PEEK)
TELL ME WHAT YOU KNOW!!
HOW'D THEY WIND UP LIKE THAT!?

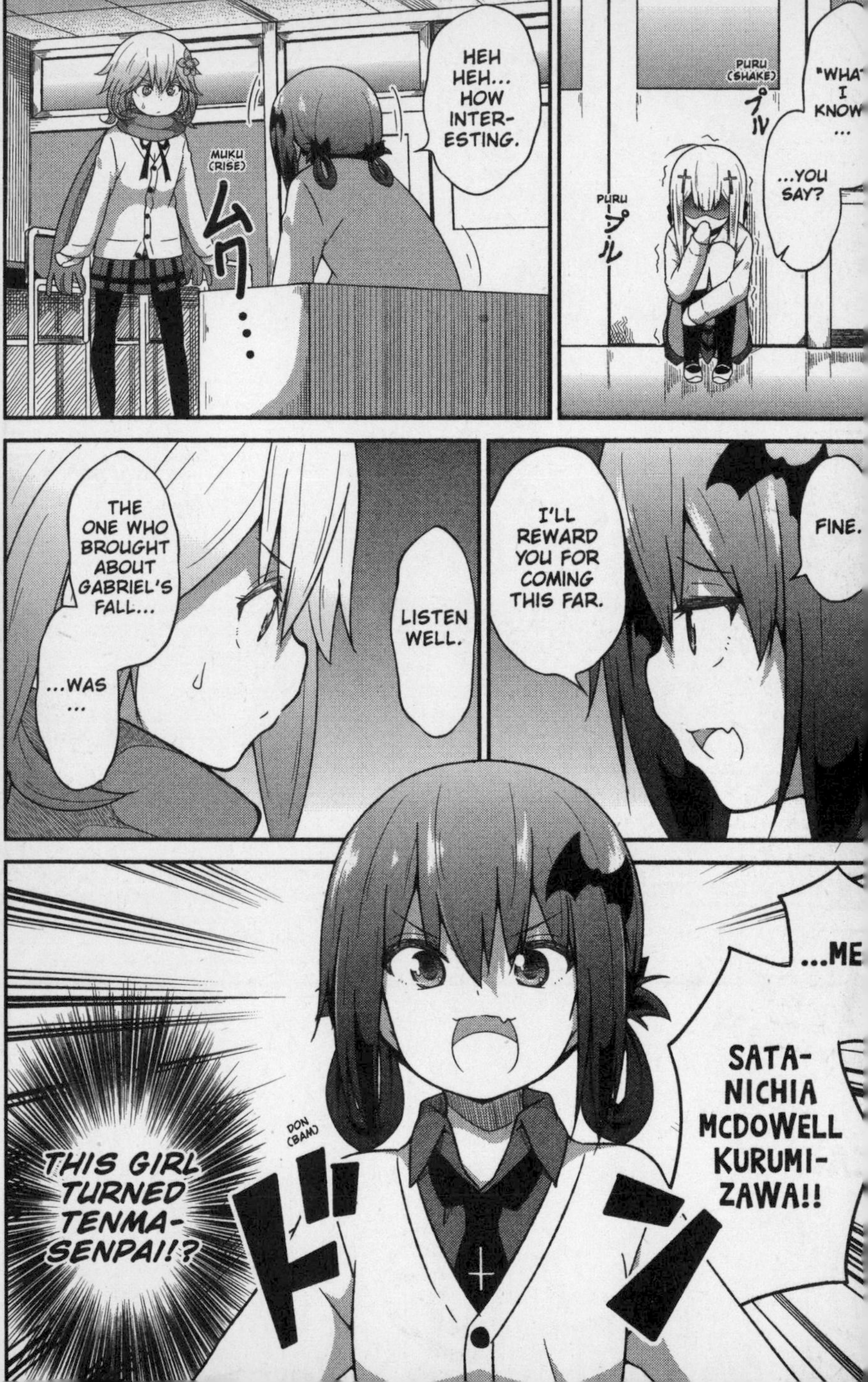
"WHA I KNOW ...
...YOU SAY?
PURU (SHAKE)
プル
PURU
プル
HEH HEH... HOW INTER-ESTING.
MUKU (RISE)
ムク...
FINE.
I'LL REWARD YOU FOR COMING THIS FAR.
LISTEN WELL.
THE ONE WHO BROUGHT ABOUT GABRIEL'S FALL...
...WAS ...
...ME
SATA-NICHIA MCDOWELL KURUMI-ZAWA!!
DON (BAM)
ドン
THIS GIRL TURNED TENMA-SENPAI!?

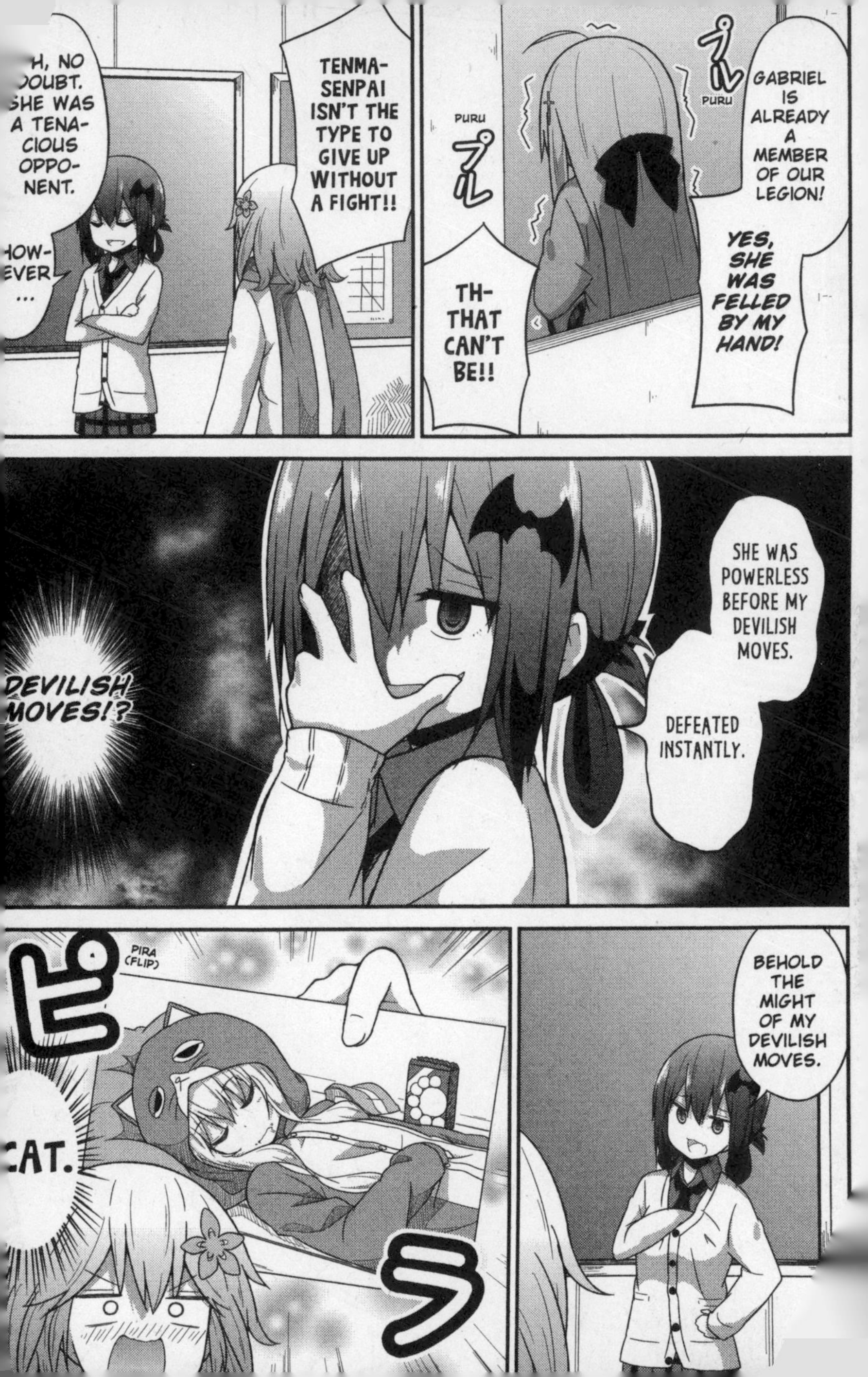

GABRIEL IS ALREADY A MEMBER OF OUR LEGION!
プル PURU
YES, SHE WAS FELLED BY MY HAND!
プル PURU
TH-THAT CAN'T BE!!
TENMA-SENPAI ISN'T THE TYPE TO GIVE UP WITHOUT A FIGHT!!
H, NO DOUBT. SHE WAS A TENACIOUS OPPONENT.
HOWEVER ...
SHE WAS POWERLESS BEFORE MY DEVILISH MOVES.
DEFEATED INSTANTLY.
DEVILISH MOVES!?
BEHOLD THE MIGHT OF MY DEVILISH MOVES.
ピラ PIRA (FLIP)
CAT.

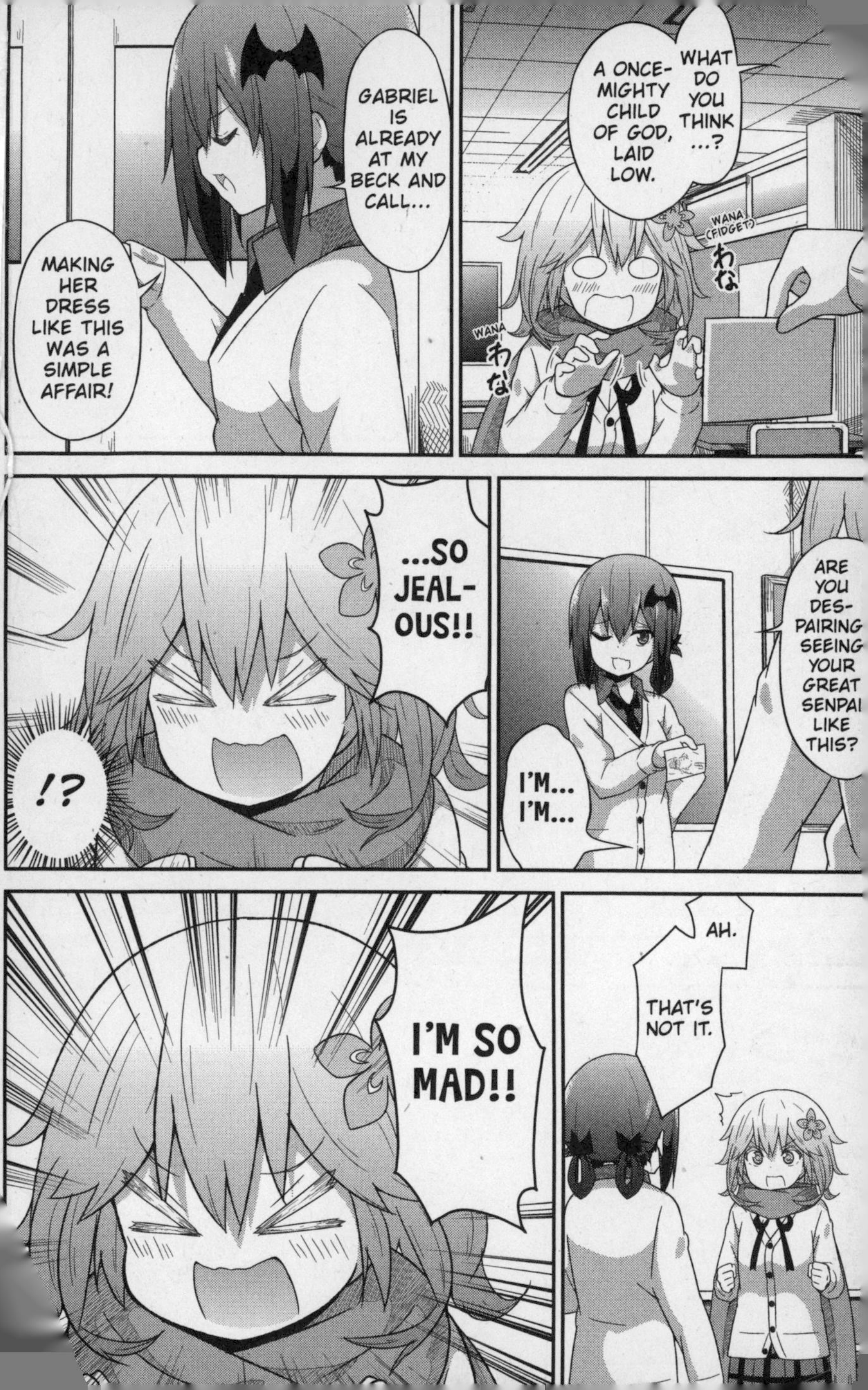
WHAT DO YOU THINK ...?
A ONCE-MIGHTY CHILD OF GOD, LAID LOW.
WANA (FIDGET:)
わな
WANA
わな
GABRIEL IS ALREADY AT MY BECK AND CALL...
MAKING HER DRESS LIKE THIS WAS A SIMPLE AFFAIR!
ARE YOU DES-PAIRING SEEING YOUR GREAT SENPAI LIKE THIS?
I'M... I'M...
...SO JEAL-OUS!!
!?
AH.
THAT'S NOT IT.
I'M SO MAD!!

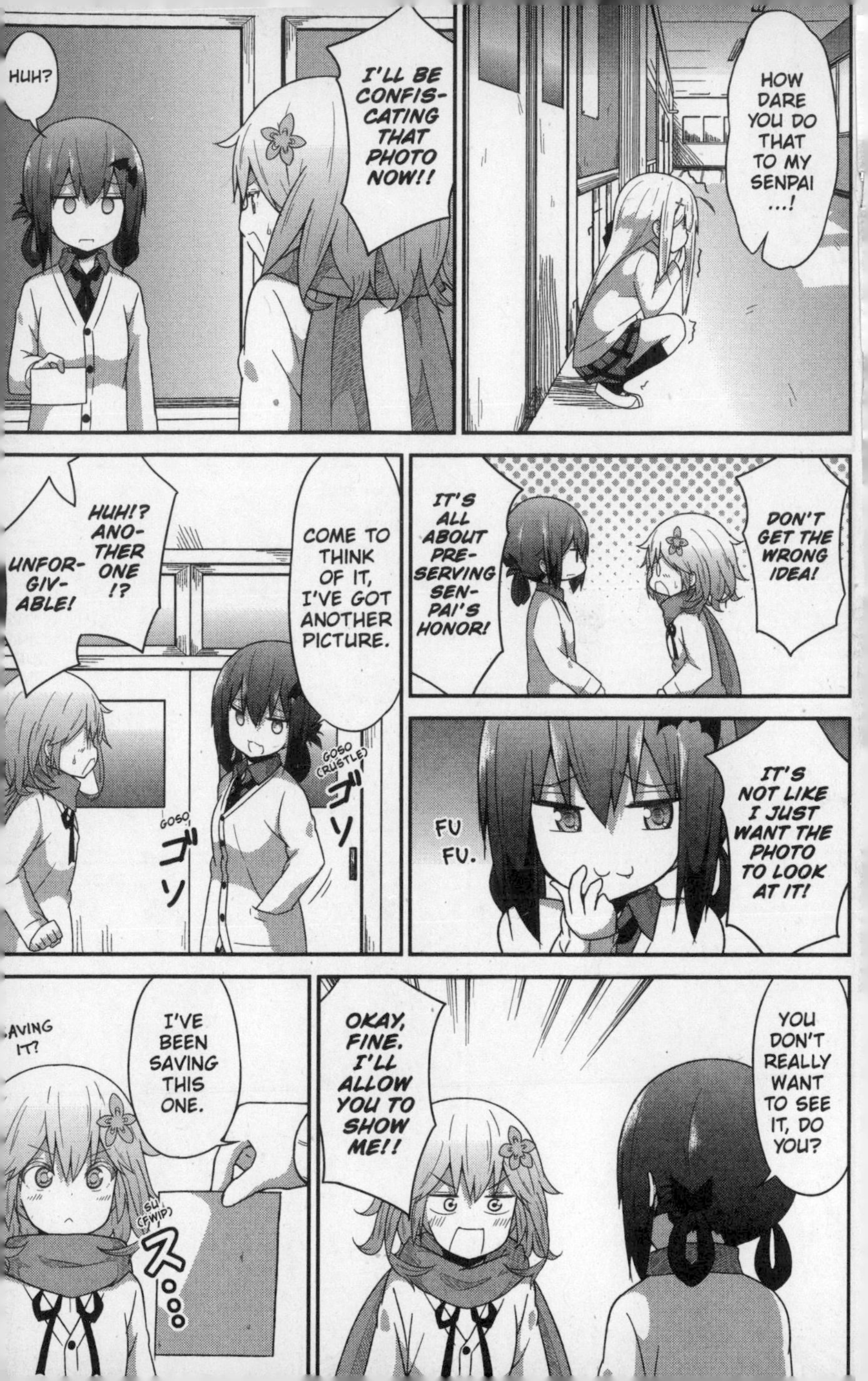
HOW DARE YOU DO THAT TO MY SENPAI ...!
I'LL BE CONFISCATING THAT PHOTO NOW!!
HUH?
DON'T GET THE WRONG IDEA!
IT'S ALL ABOUT PRESERVING SENPAI'S HONOR!
IT'S NOT LIKE I JUST WANT THE PHOTO TO LOOK AT IT!
FU FU.
COME TO THINK OF IT, I'VE GOT ANOTHER PICTURE.
HUH!? ANOTHER ONE !?
UNFORGIVABLE!
GOSO (RUSTLE)
ゴソ
GOSO
ゴソ
YOU DON'T REALLY WANT TO SEE IT, DO YOU?
OKAY, FINE. I'LL ALLOW YOU TO SHOW ME!!
I'VE BEEN SAVING THIS ONE.
AVING IT?
SU (FWIP)
ス

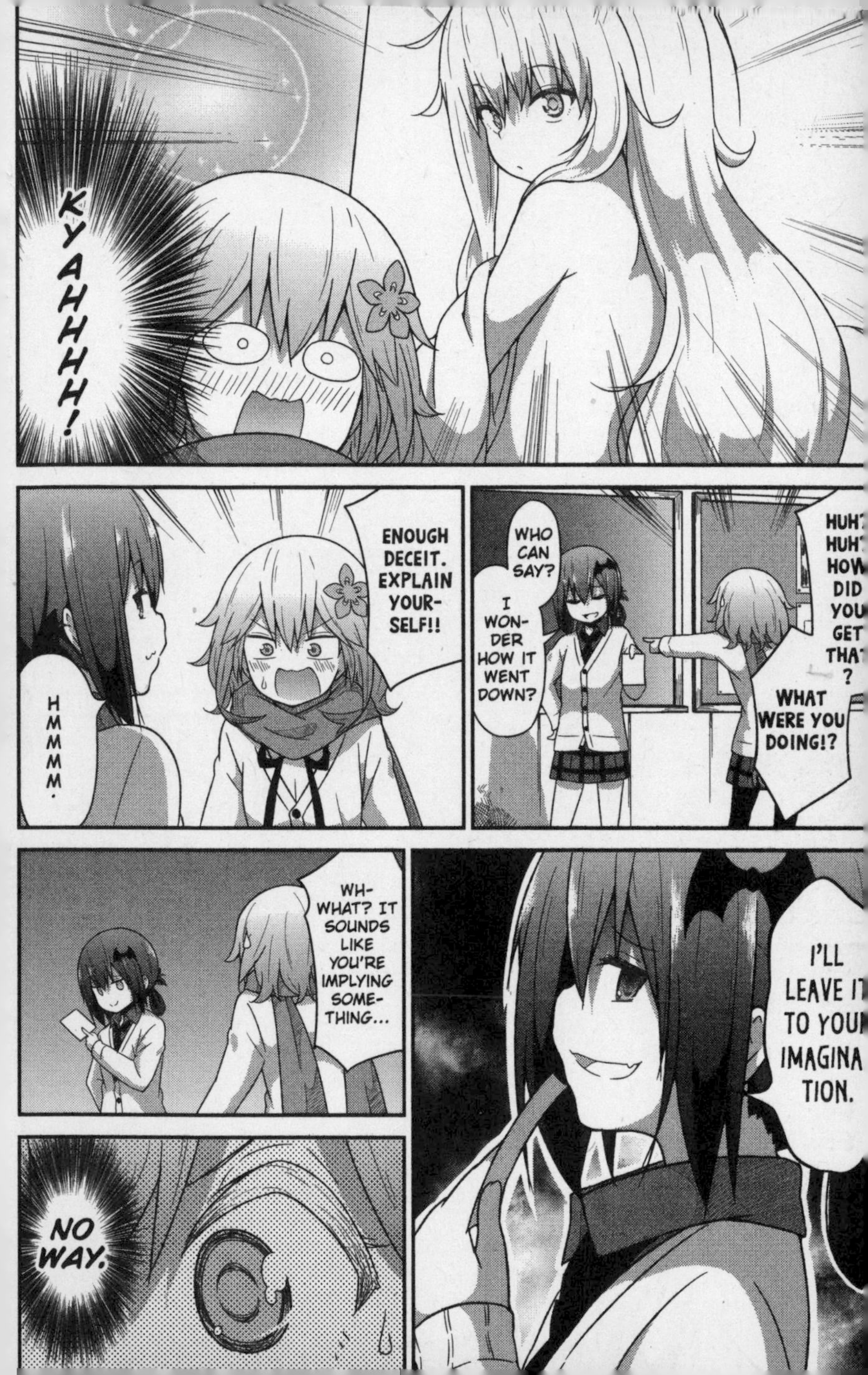
KYAHHHHH!
HUH? HUH? HOW DID YOU GET THAT?
WHAT WERE YOU DOING!?
WHO CAN SAY?
I WON-DER HOW IT WENT DOWN?
ENOUGH DECEIT. EXPLAIN YOUR-SELF!!
HMMMM.
I'LL LEAVE IT TO YOUR IMAGINA TION.
WH-WHAT? IT SOUNDS LIKE YOU'RE IMPLYING SOME-THING...
NO WAY.

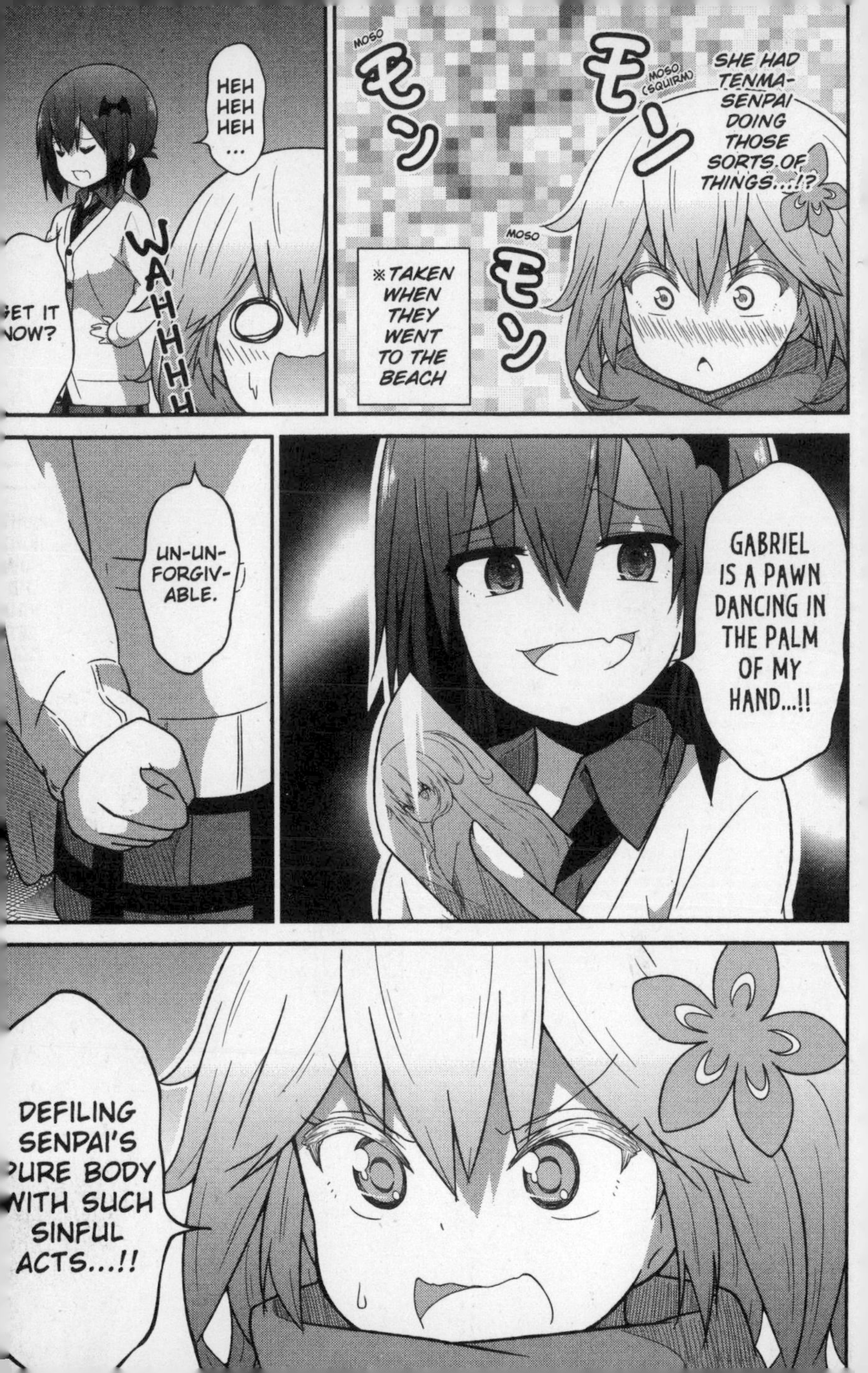
MOSO
MOSO (SQUIRM)
SHE HAD TENMA-SENPAI DOING THOSE SORTS OF THINGS...!?
MOSO
※TAKEN WHEN THEY WENT TO THE BEACH
HEH HEH HEH ...
WAHHHH
GET IT NOW?
GABRIEL IS A PAWN DANCING IN THE PALM OF MY HAND...!!
UN-UN-FORGIV-ABLE.
DEFILING SENPAI'S PURE BODY WITH SUCH SINFUL ACTS...!!

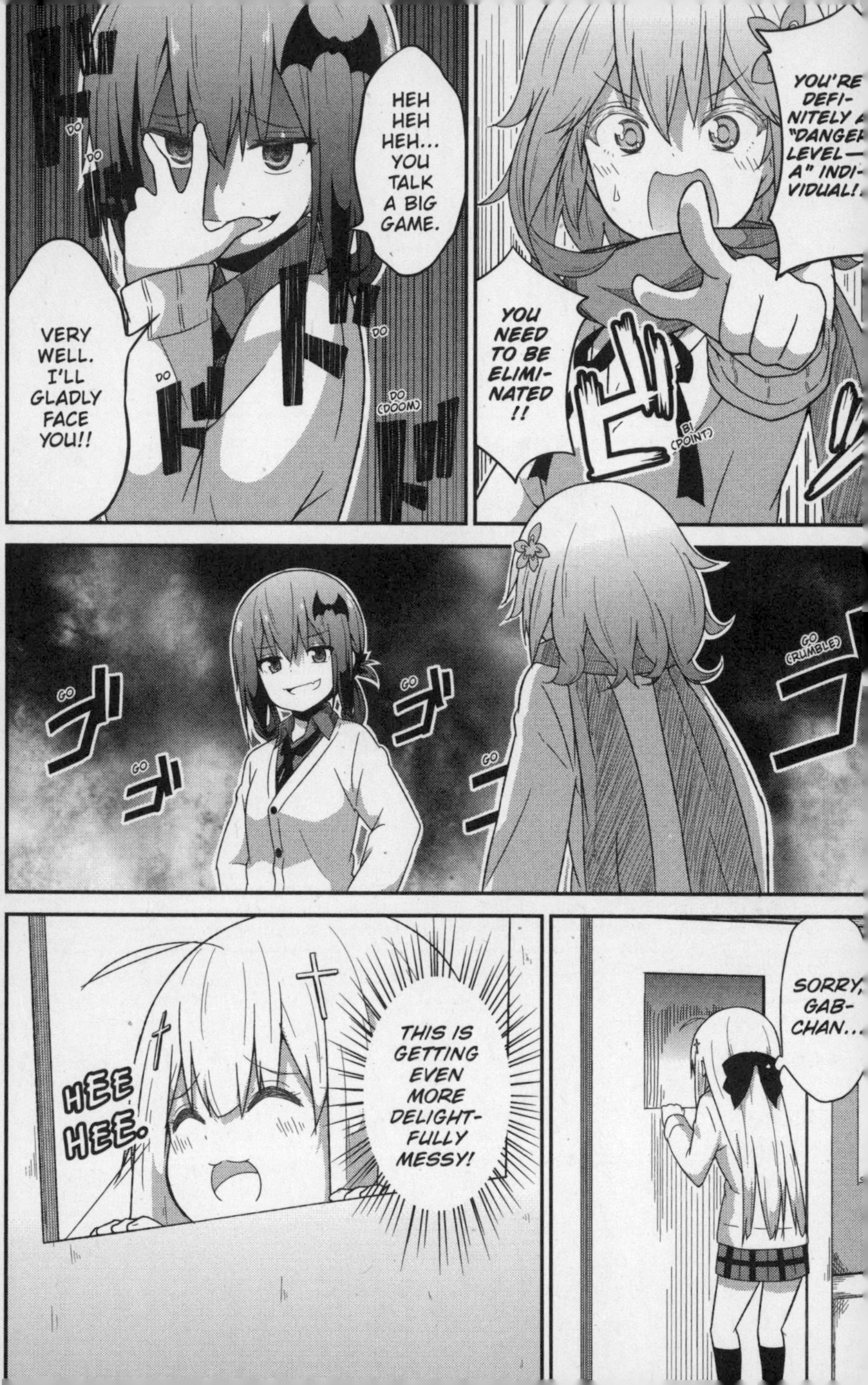
YOU'RE DEFINITELY A "DANGER LEVEL—A" INDIVIDUAL!!
YOU NEED TO BE ELIMINATED!!
BI (POINT)
HEH HEH HEH... YOU TALK A BIG GAME.
VERY WELL. I'LL GLADLY FACE YOU!!
DO
DO
DO
DO
DO (DOOM)
GO (RUMBLE)
GO
GO
GO
GO
SORRY, GAB-CHAN...
THIS IS GETTING EVEN MORE DELIGHTFULLY MESSY!
HEE HEE.

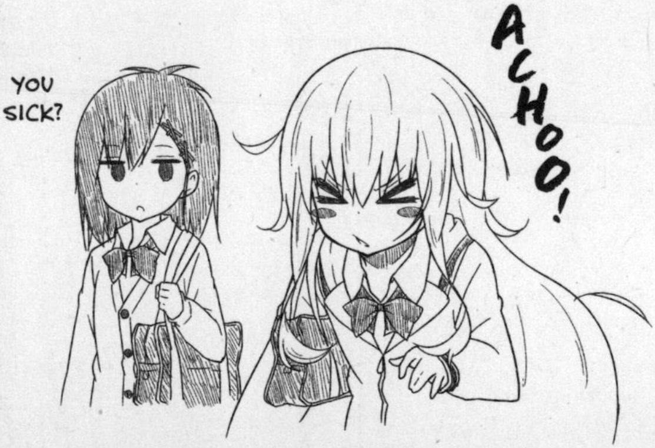
ACHOO!
YOU SICK?

✦✦TRANSLATION NOTES✦✦

COMMON HONORIFICS

no honorific: Indicates familiarity or closeness; if used without permission or reason, addressing someone in this manner would constitute an insult.

-san: The Japanese equivalent of Mr./Mrs./Miss. If a situation calls for politeness, this is the fail-safe honorific.

-sama: Conveys great respect; may also indicate that the social status of the speaker is lower than that of the addressee.

-kun: Used most often when referring to boys, this indicates affection or familiarity. Occasionally used by older men among their peers, but it may also be used by anyone referring to a person of lower standing.

-chan: An affectionate honorific indicating familiarity used mostly in reference to girls; also used in reference to cute persons or animals of either gender.

-senpai: A suffix used to address upperclassmen or more experienced coworkers.

-sensei: A respectful term for teachers, artists, or high-level professionals.

GENERAL

One hundred yen is roughly equivalent to one US dollar.

PAGE 19

In Japan, the first shrine visit of the new year is known as **hatsumoude**. As Vignette says, traditions like this are intended to help start the year off right, which is why millions of people flock to popular shrines all over the country during the New Year's holiday.

PAGE 28

In the original Japanese, Satanya's confusion regarding the "New Year's Bills" is due to her unfamiliarity with the practice of **otoshidama**. Otoshidama is a gift of money that children typically receive from parents and relatives during New Year's. Satanya's misinterpretation is understandable, though — the word can also be read as "ball drop".

PAGE 31

Gabriel and friends are ringing in the new year at **Yasukuni Shrine**, established in Tokyo in 1869 to honor the spirits of those who died in service to the Emperor of Japan. It attracts millions of visitors annually and hosts various celebrations throughout the year.

Takoyaki are fried octopus dumplings commonly sold at food stands in Japan. They're easy to eat with one hand, so they make for a great snack while walking around at a festival.

Amazake is a sweet traditional drink with very low- or no-alcohol content made from fermented rice.

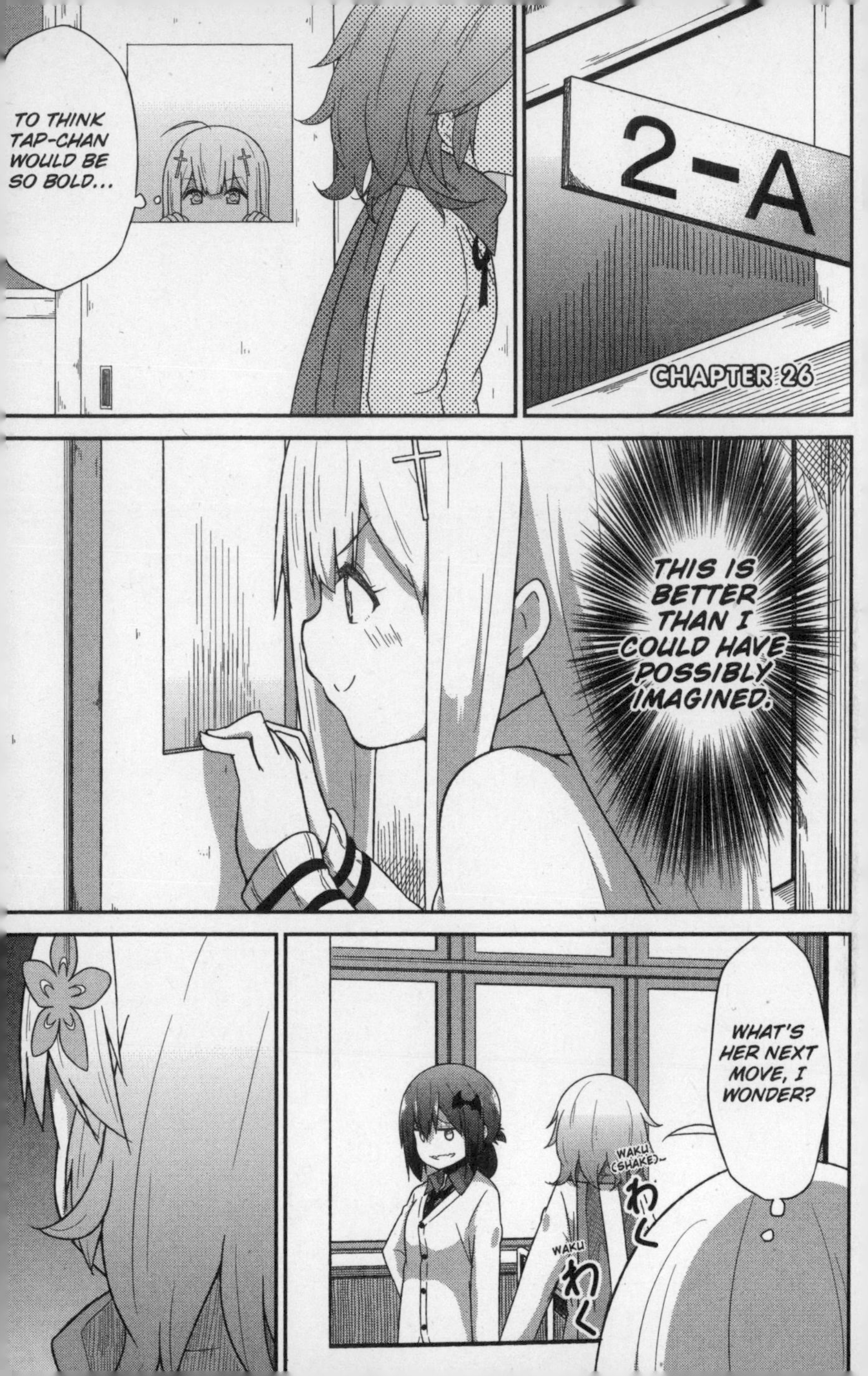
2-A
CHAPTER 26
TO THINK TAP-CHAN WOULD BE SO BOLD...
THIS IS BETTER THAN I COULD HAVE POSSIBLY IMAGINED.
WHAT'S HER NEXT MOVE, I WONDER?
WAKU (SHAKE)
わく
WAKU
わく

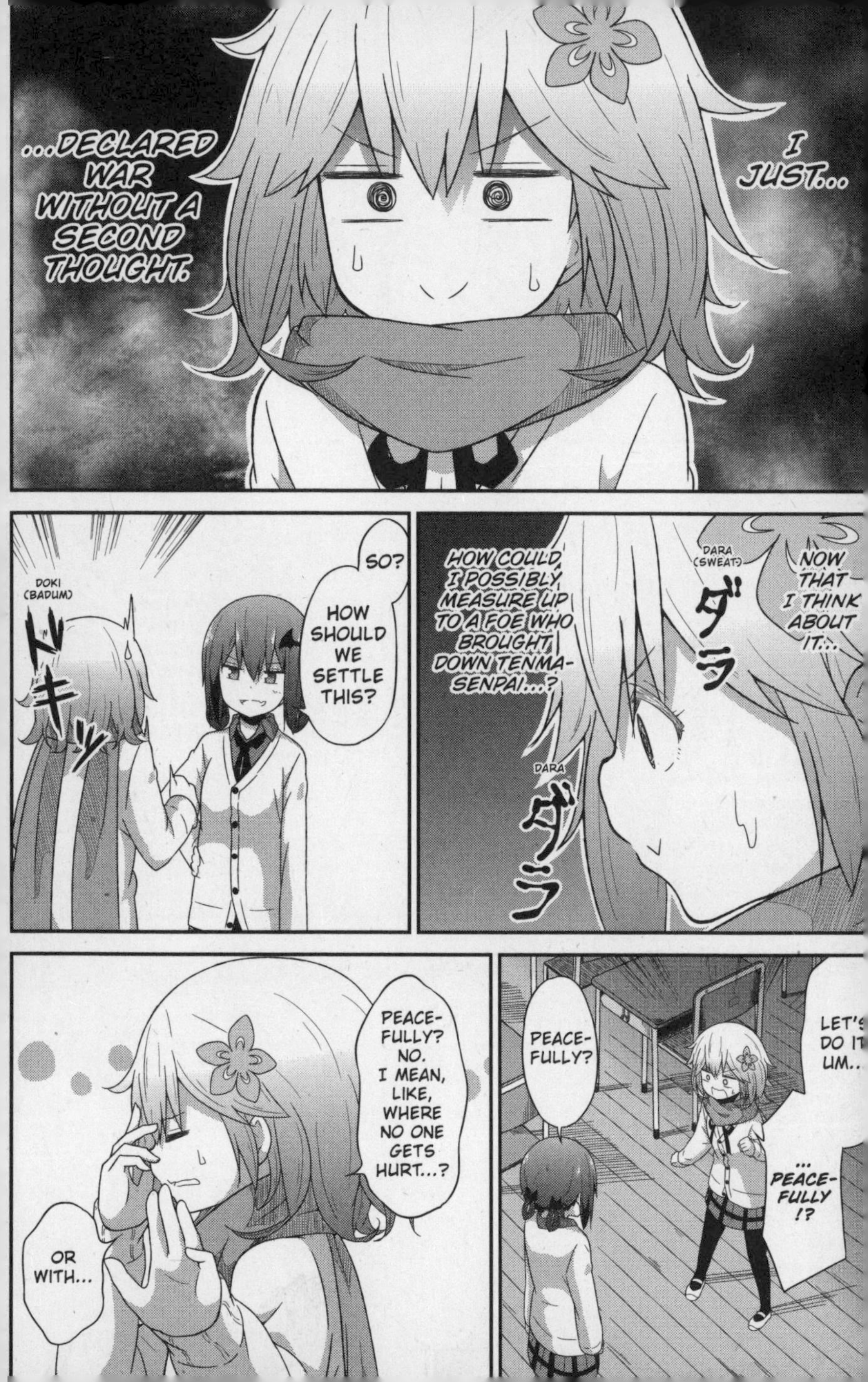
I JUST...
...DECLARED WAR WITHOUT A SECOND THOUGHT.
DARA (SWEAT)
NOW THAT I THINK ABOUT IT...
HOW COULD I POSSIBLY MEASURE UP TO A FOE WHO BROUGHT DOWN TENMA-SENPAI...?
DARA
SO?
HOW SHOULD WE SETTLE THIS?
DOKI (BADUM)
LET'S DO IT UM...
...PEACEFULLY!?
PEACEFULLY?
PEACEFULLY? NO. I MEAN, LIKE, WHERE NO ONE GETS HURT...?
OR WITH...

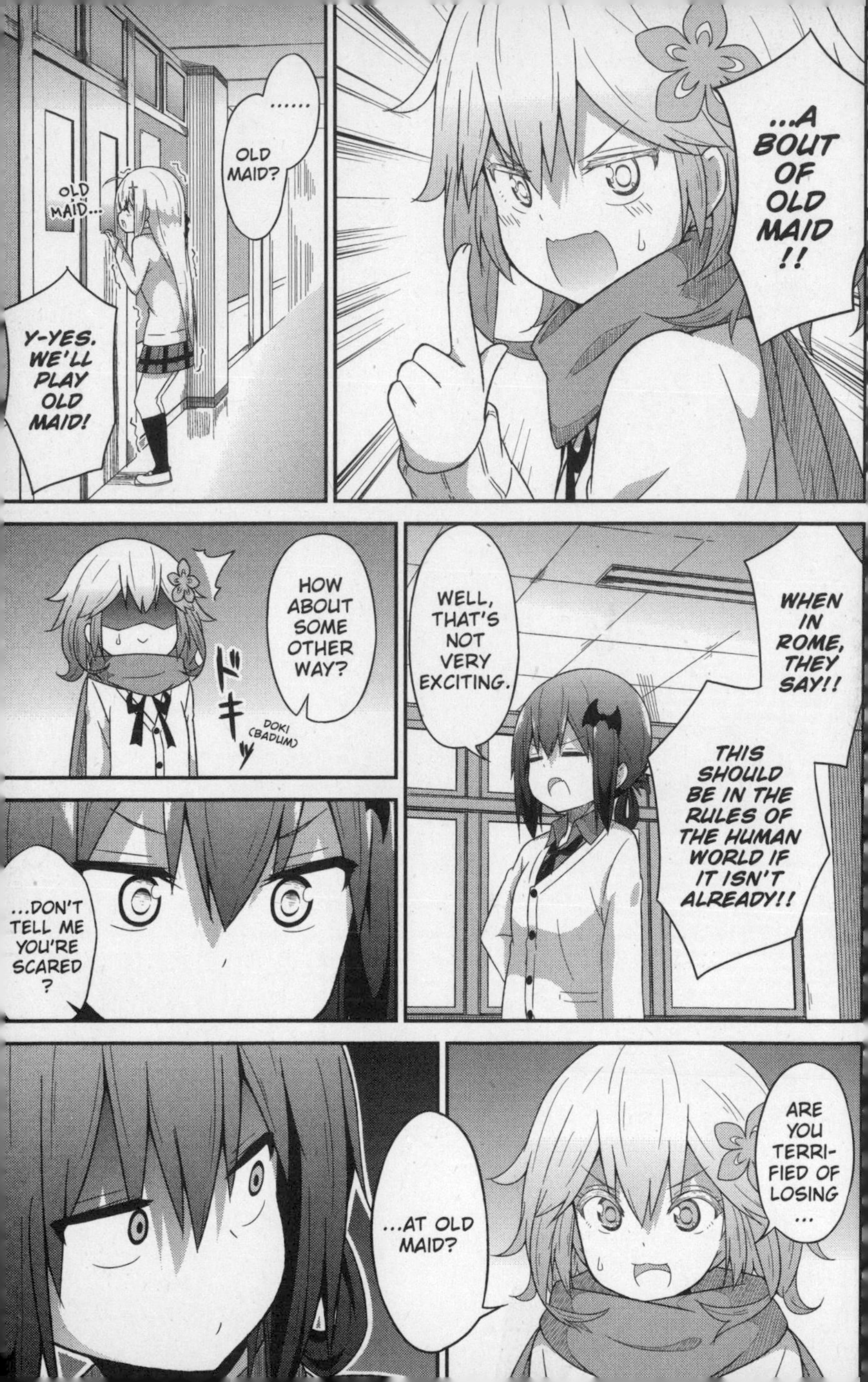
...A BOUT OF OLD MAID!!
......
OLD MAID?
OLD MAID...
Y-YES. WE'LL PLAY OLD MAID!
WHEN IN ROME, THEY SAY!!
WELL, THAT'S NOT VERY EXCITING.
THIS SHOULD BE IN THE RULES OF THE HUMAN WORLD IF IT ISN'T ALREADY!!
HOW ABOUT SOME OTHER WAY?
ドキッ
DOKI (BADUM)
...DON'T TELL ME YOU'RE SCARED?
ARE YOU TERRI-FIED OF LOSING...
...AT OLD MAID?

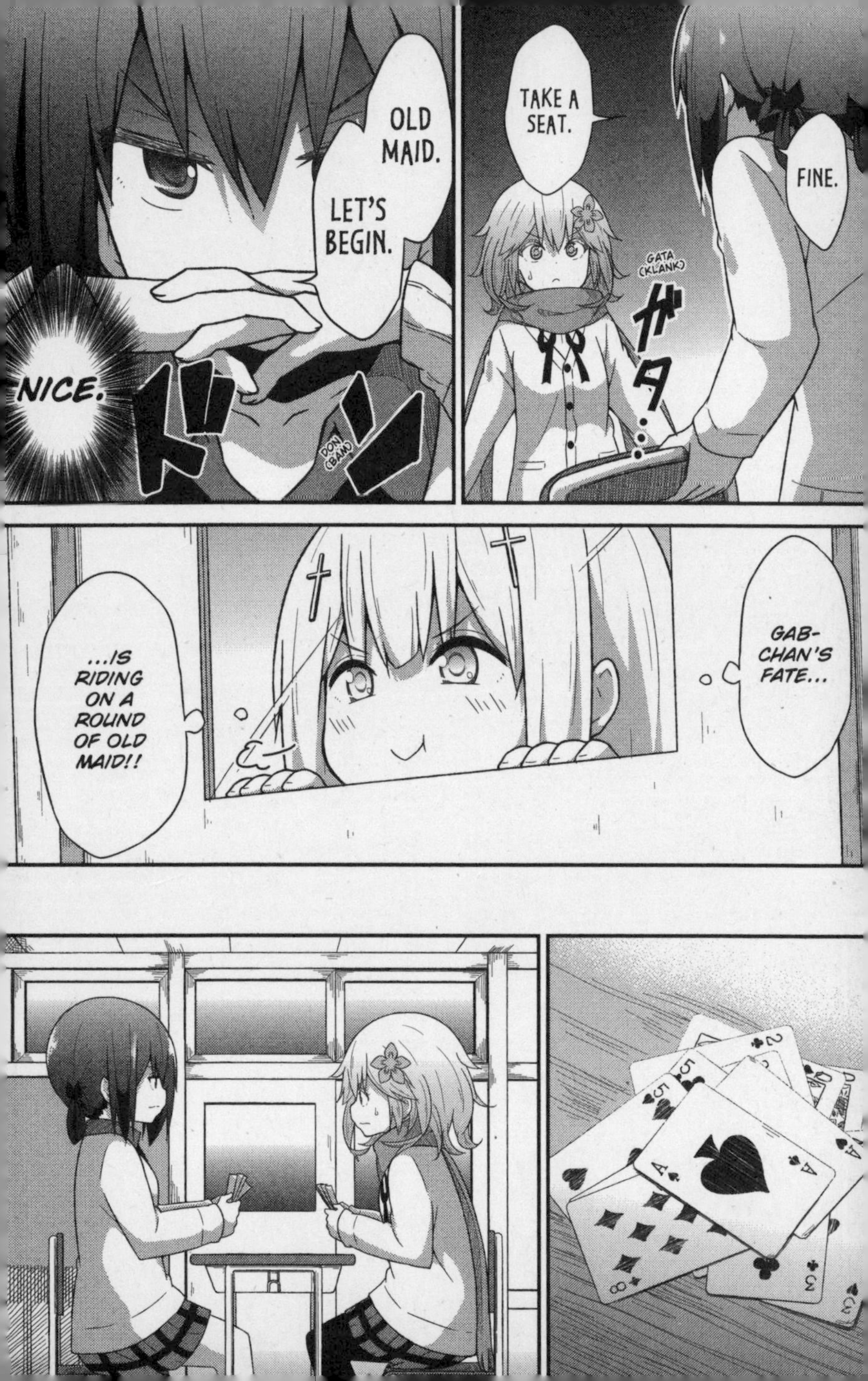
TAKE A SEAT.
FINE.
GATA (KLANK)
ガタ
OLD MAID.
LET'S BEGIN.
NICE.
DON (BAN)
ドン
GAB-CHAN'S FATE...
...IS RIDING ON A ROUND OF OLD MAID!!

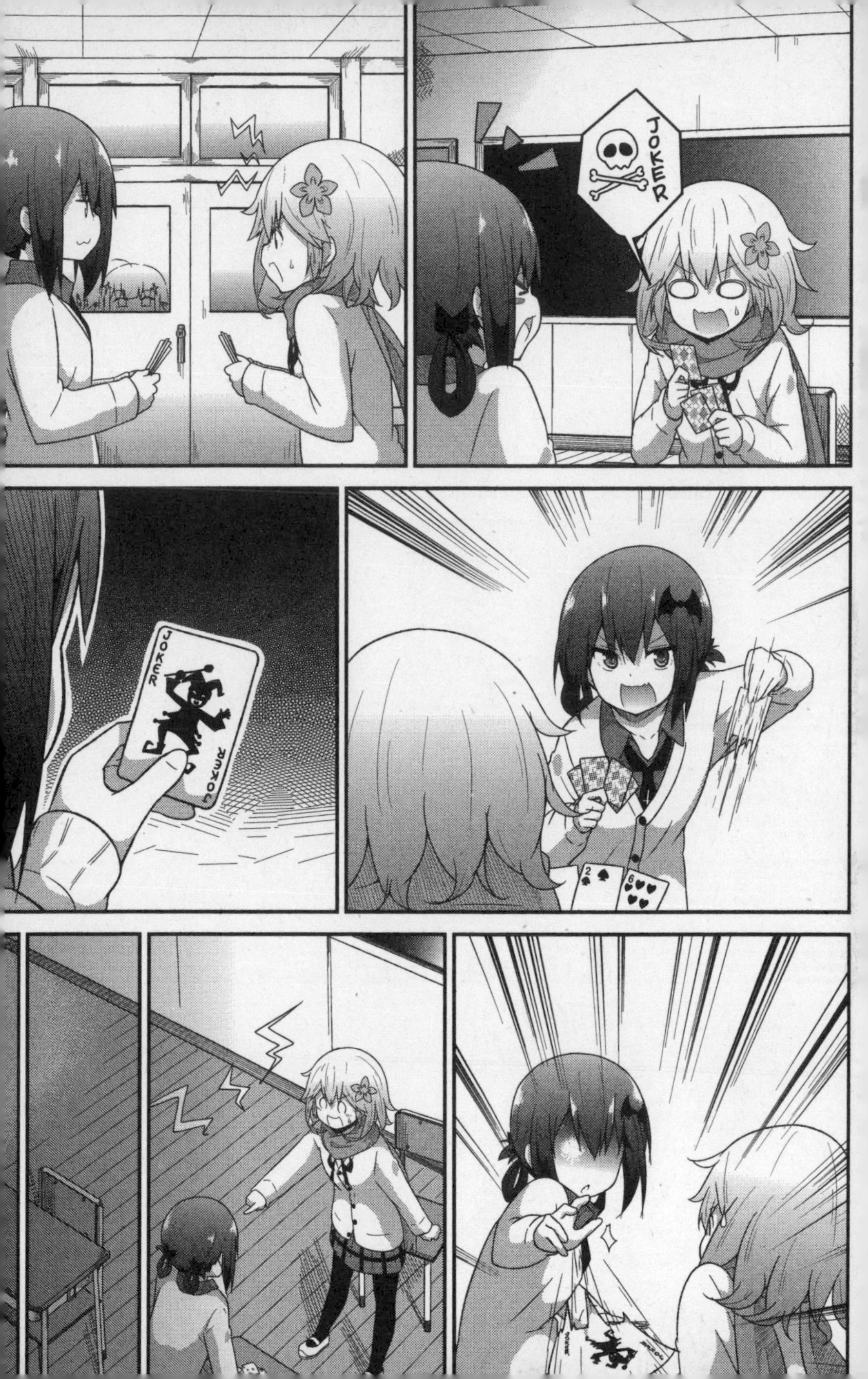
JOKER
JOKER

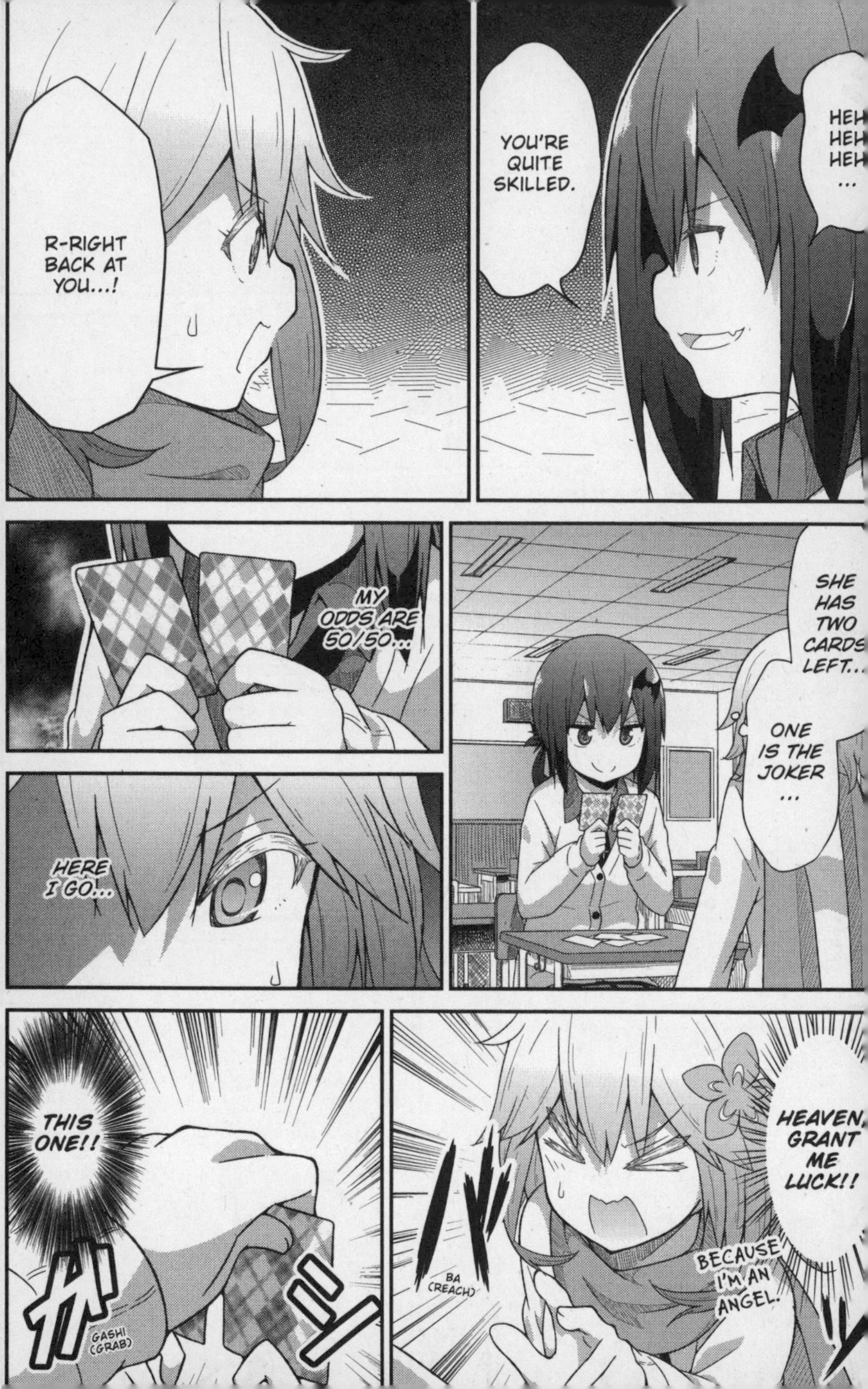
HEH HEH HEH ...
YOU'RE QUITE SKILLED.
R-RIGHT BACK AT YOU...!
SHE HAS TWO CARDS LEFT...
ONE IS THE JOKER ...
MY ODDS ARE 50/50...
HERE I GO...
HEAVEN, GRANT ME LUCK!!
BECAUSE I'M AN ANGEL.
BA (REACH)
THIS ONE!!
GASHI (GRAB)

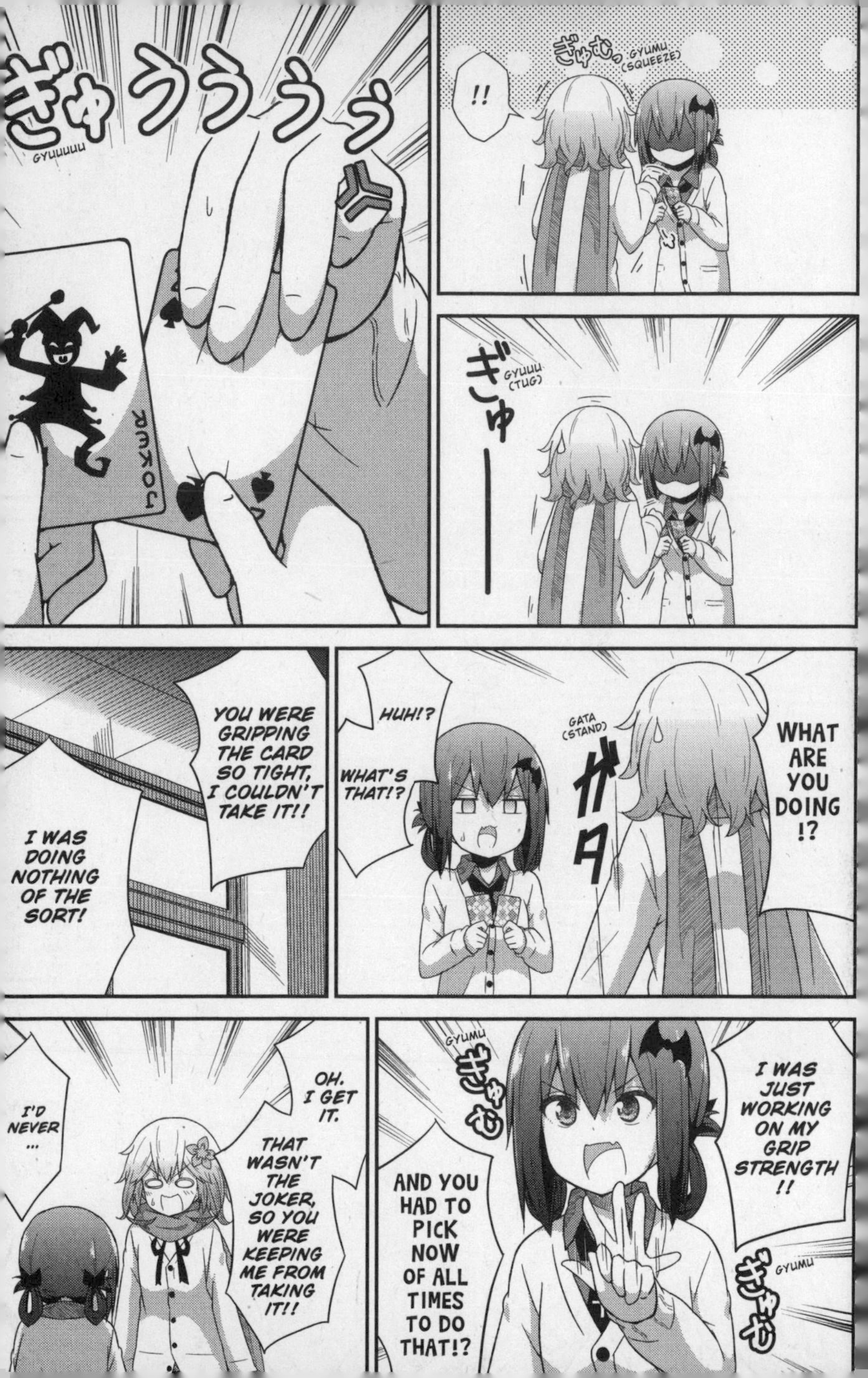
ぎゅむっ
GYUMU (SQUEEZE)
!!
ぎゅー
GYUUU (TUG)
ぎゅううううっ
GYUUUUU
WHAT ARE YOU DOING!?
ガタ
GATA (STAND)
HUH!?
WHAT'S THAT!?
YOU WERE GRIPPING THE CARD SO TIGHT, I COULDN'T TAKE IT!!
I WAS DOING NOTHING OF THE SORT!
I WAS JUST WORKING ON MY GRIP STRENGTH!!
ぎゅむ
GYUMU
ぎゅむ
GYUMU
AND YOU HAD TO PICK NOW OF ALL TIMES TO DO THAT!?
OH. I GET IT.
THAT WASN'T THE JOKER, SO YOU WERE KEEPING ME FROM TAKING IT!!
I'D NEVER...

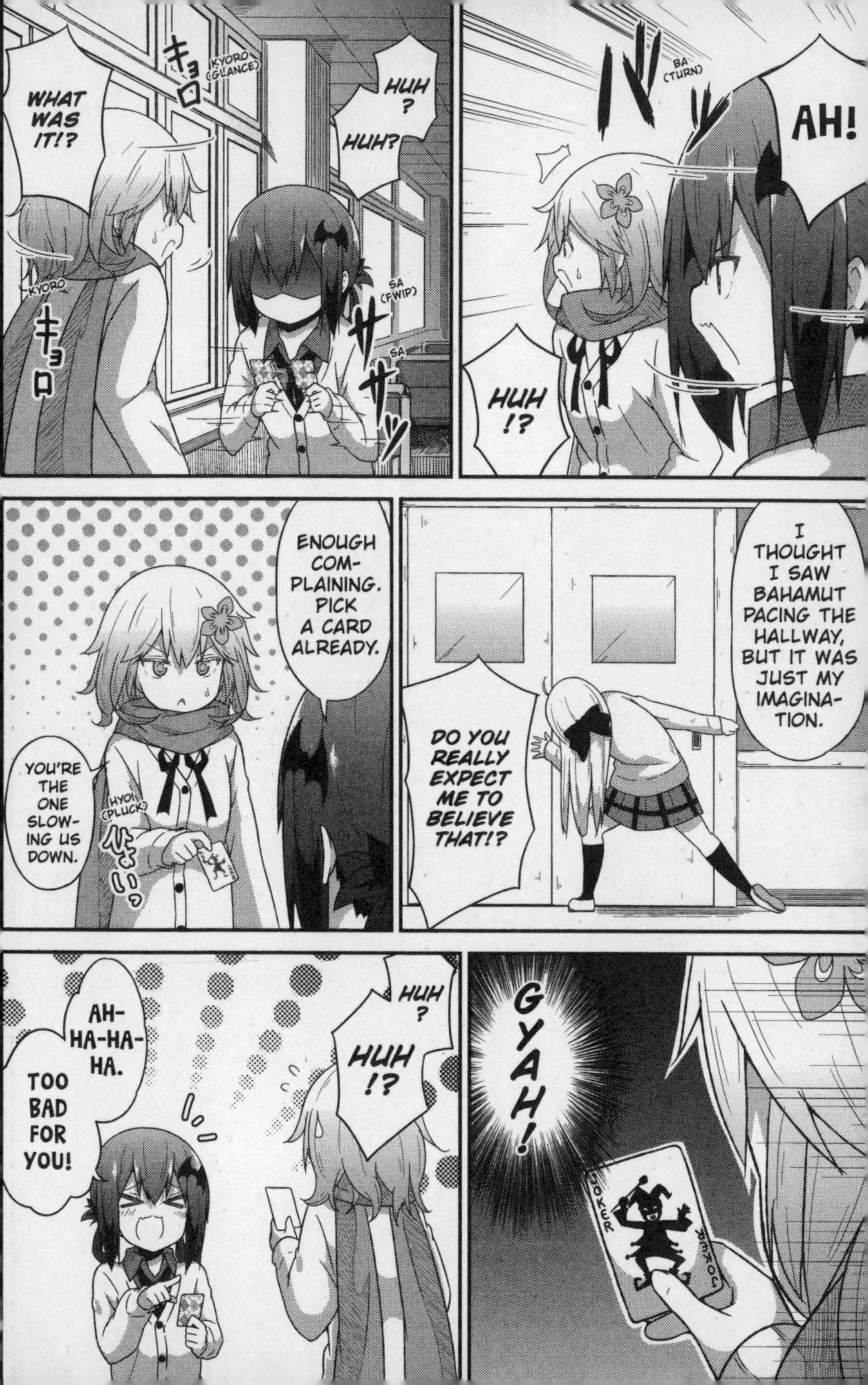
BA (TURN)
AH!
HUH!?
HUH?
HUH?
KYORO (GLANCE)
WHAT WAS IT!?
KYORO
SA (FWIP)
SA
I THOUGHT I SAW BAHAMUT PACING THE HALLWAY, BUT IT WAS JUST MY IMAGINATION.
DO YOU REALLY EXPECT ME TO BELIEVE THAT!?
ENOUGH COM-PLAINING. PICK A CARD ALREADY.
YOU'RE THE ONE SLOWING US DOWN.
HYOI (PLUCK)
GYAH!
JOKER
HUH?
HUH!?
AH-HA-HA-HA.
TOO BAD FOR YOU!

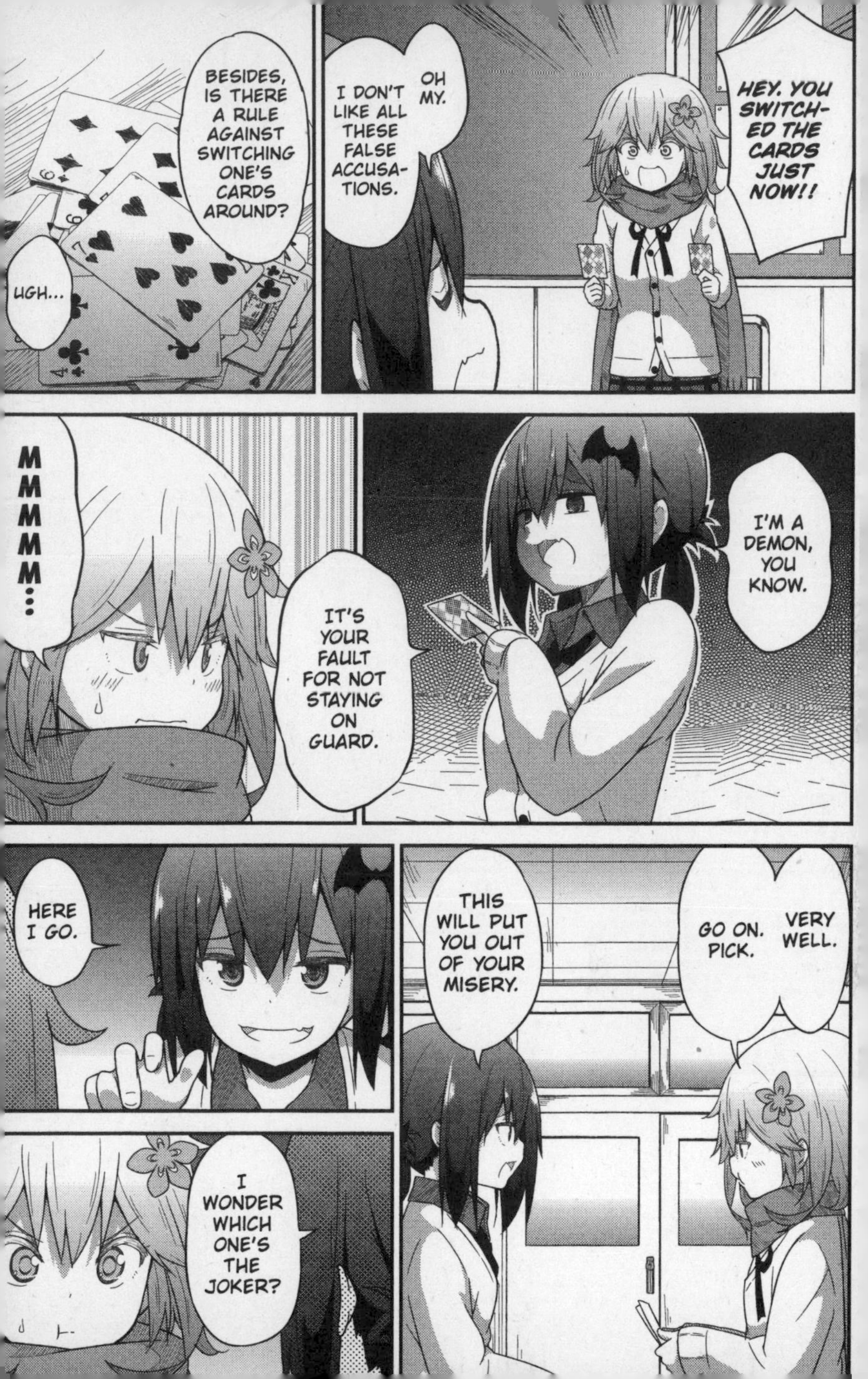
HEY. YOU SWITCHED THE CARDS JUST NOW!!
OH MY.
I DON'T LIKE ALL THESE FALSE ACCUSATIONS.
BESIDES, IS THERE A RULE AGAINST SWITCHING ONE'S CARDS AROUND?
UGH...
I'M A DEMON, YOU KNOW.
IT'S YOUR FAULT FOR NOT STAYING ON GUARD.
MMMMM...
VERY WELL.
GO ON. PICK.
THIS WILL PUT YOU OUT OF YOUR MISERY.
HERE I GO.
I WONDER WHICH ONE'S THE JOKER?

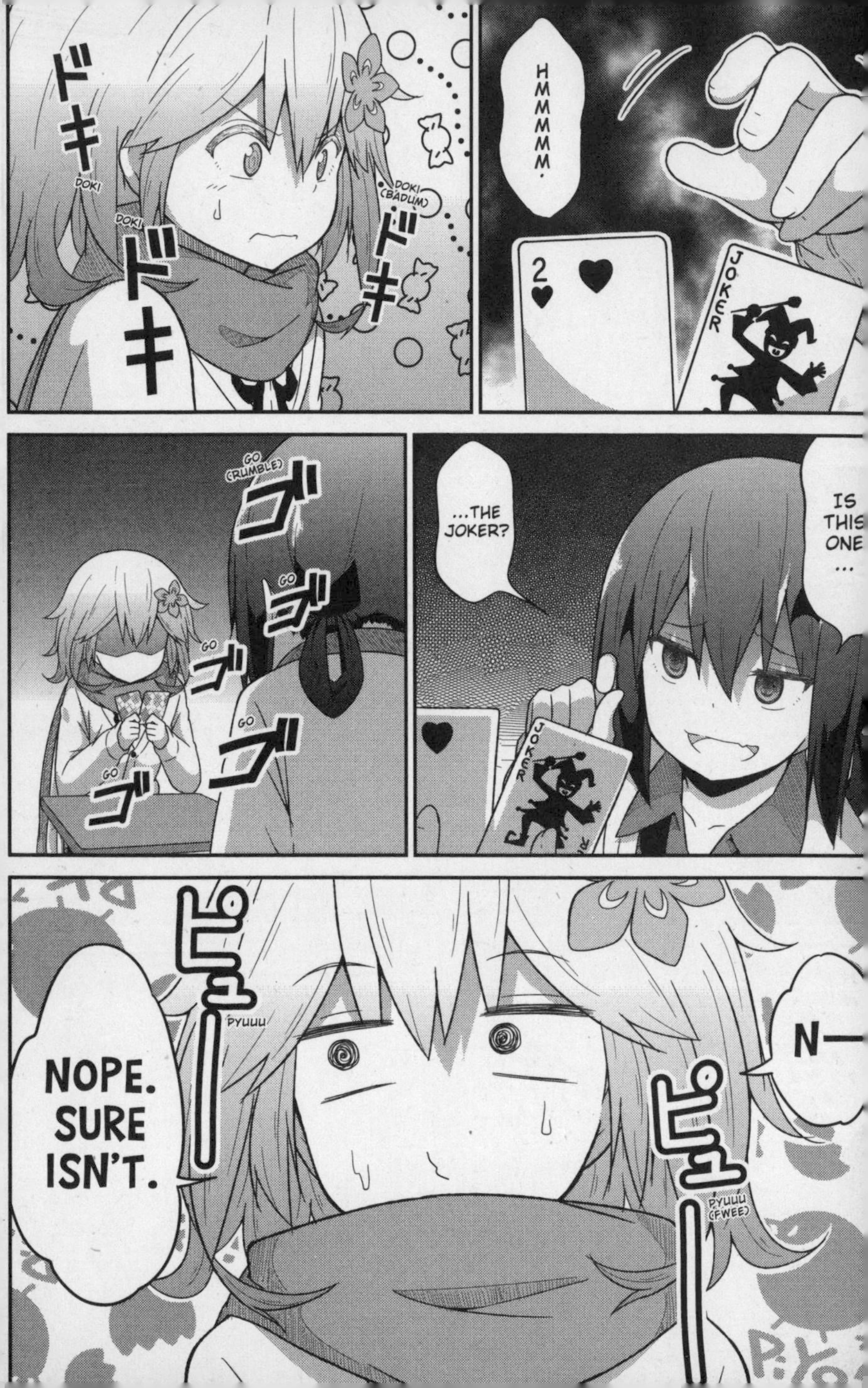

HMMMMM.
ドキ
DOKI
DOKI
ドキ
DOKI (BADUM)
ドキ
IS THIS ONE...
...THE JOKER?
GO (RUMBLE)
ゴ
GO
ゴ
GO
ゴ
GO
ゴ
GO
ゴ
N—
ピュー
PYUUU (FWEE)
NOPE. SURE ISN'T.
ピュー
PYUUU

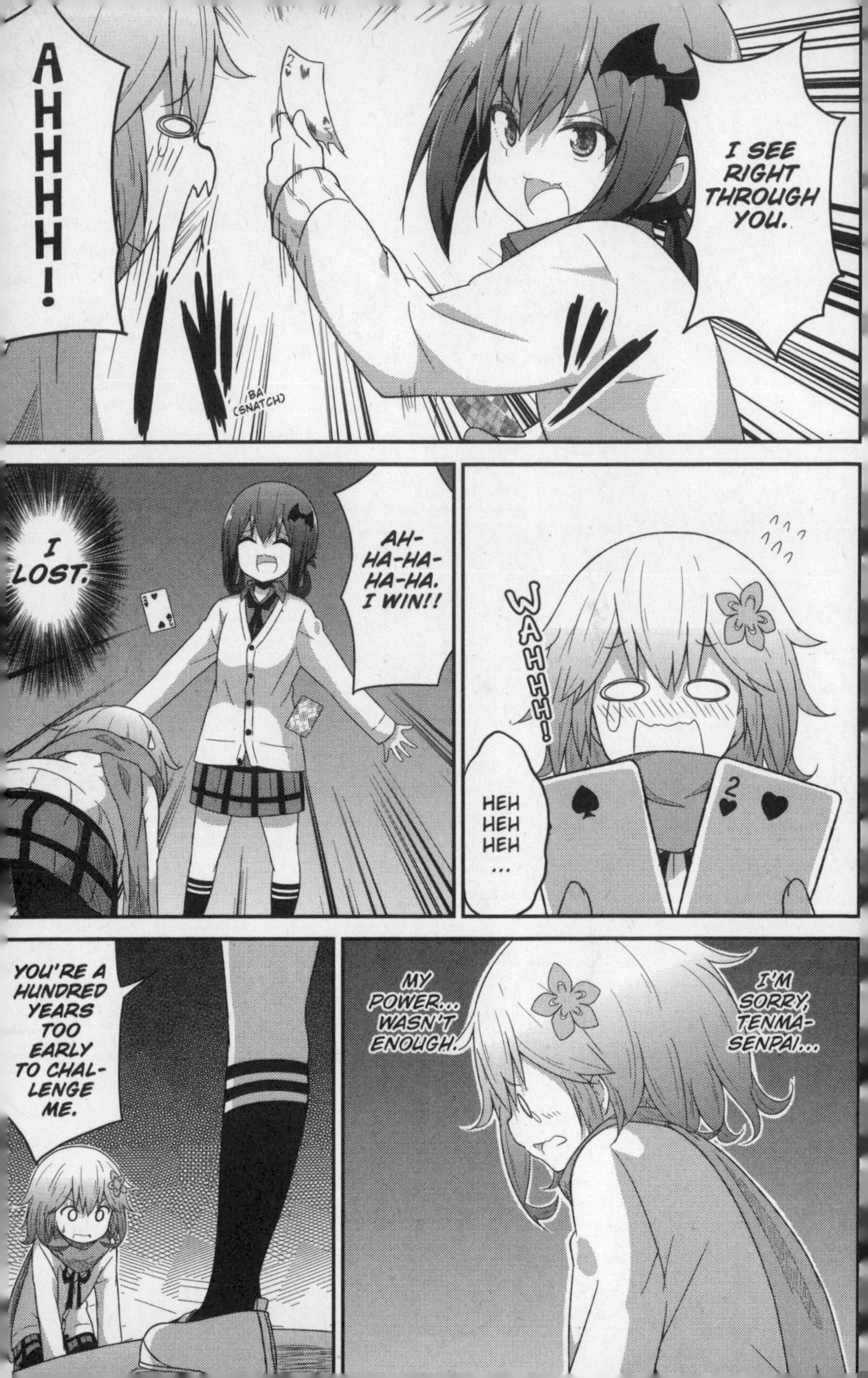
I SEE RIGHT THROUGH YOU.
AHHHHH!
BA (SNATCH)
WAHHHH!
HEH HEH HEH ...
AH-HA-HA-HA-HA. I WIN!!
I LOST.
I'M SORRY, TENMA-SENPAI...
MY POWER... WASN'T ENOUGH.
YOU'RE A HUNDRED YEARS TOO EARLY TO CHAL-LENGE ME.

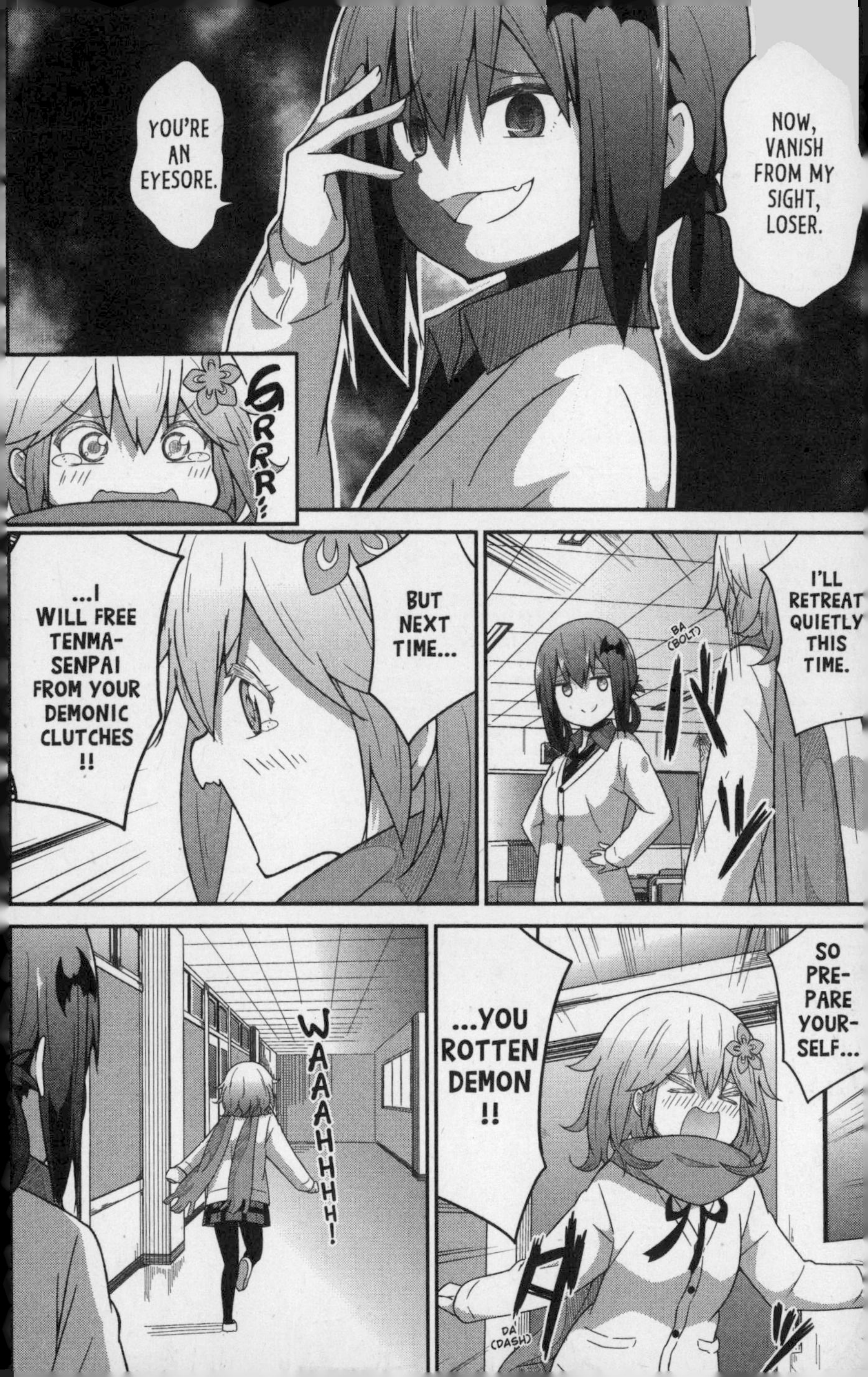
NOW, VANISH FROM MY SIGHT, LOSER.
YOU'RE AN EYESORE.
GRRR!!
I'LL RETREAT QUIETLY THIS TIME.
BA (BOLT)
BUT NEXT TIME...
...I WILL FREE TENMA-SENPAI FROM YOUR DEMONIC CLUTCHES!!
SO PRE-PARE YOUR-SELF...
...YOU ROTTEN DEMON!!
DA (DASH)
WAAAAHHHH!

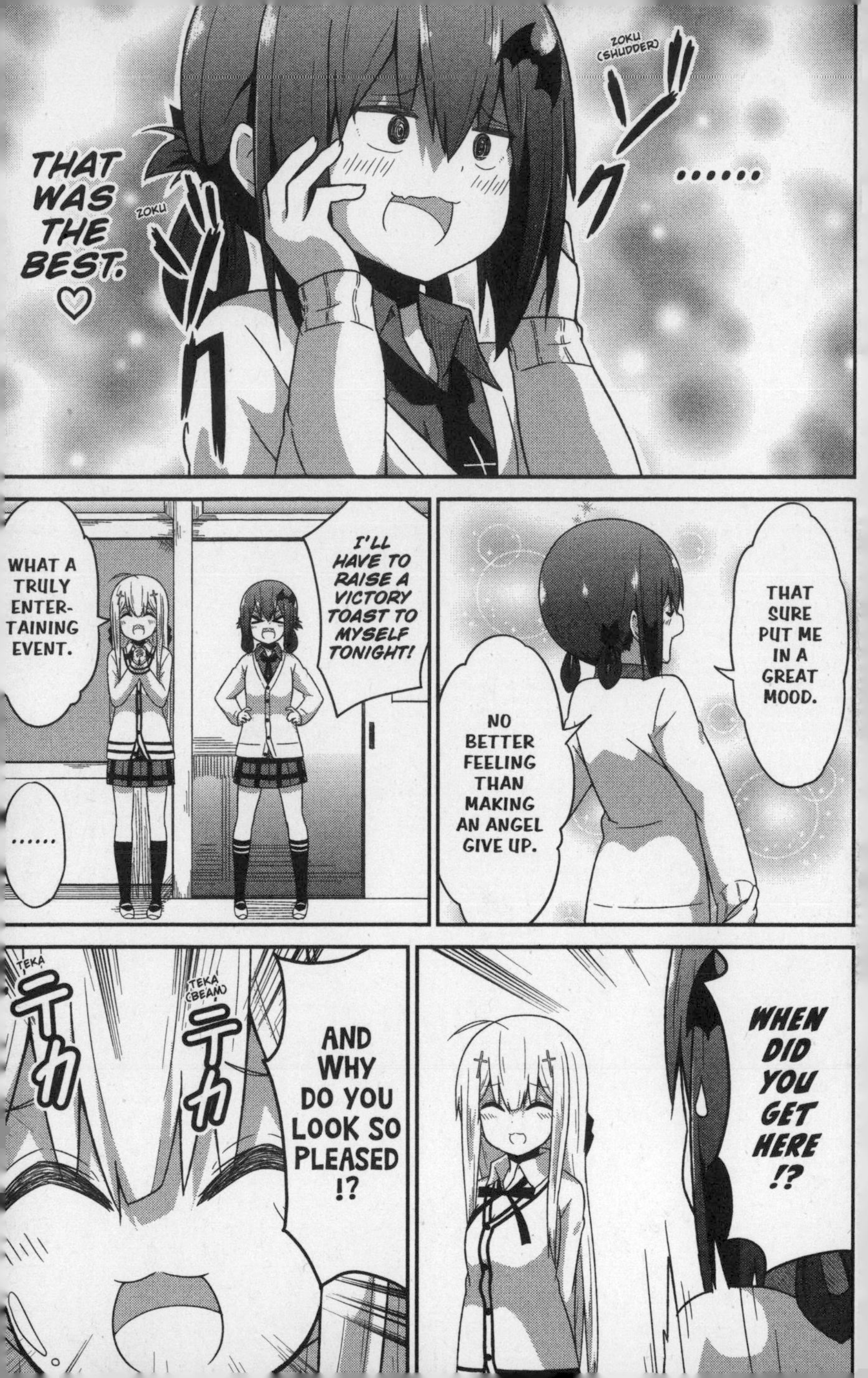
ZOKU (SHUDDER)
......
THAT WAS THE BEST. ♡
ZOKU
THAT SURE PUT ME IN A GREAT MOOD.
NO BETTER FEELING THAN MAKING AN ANGEL GIVE UP.
I'LL HAVE TO RAISE A VICTORY TOAST TO MYSELF TONIGHT!
WHAT A TRULY ENTER-TAINING EVENT.
......
WHEN DID YOU GET HERE!?
TEKA (BEAM)
TEKA
AND WHY DO YOU LOOK SO PLEASED!?

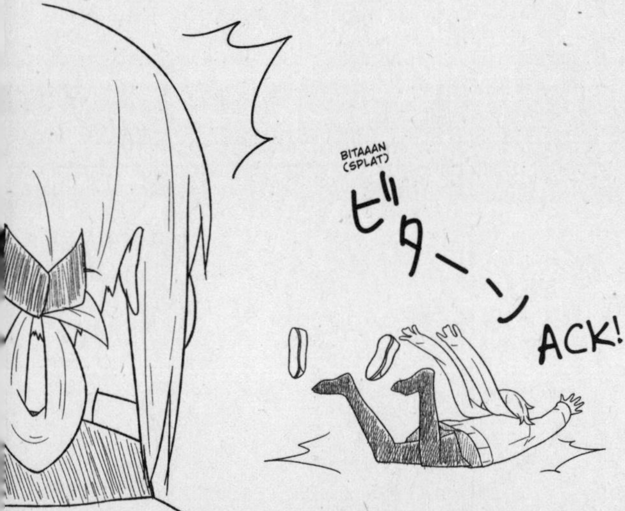
BITAAAN
(SPLAT)
ビターン
ACK!

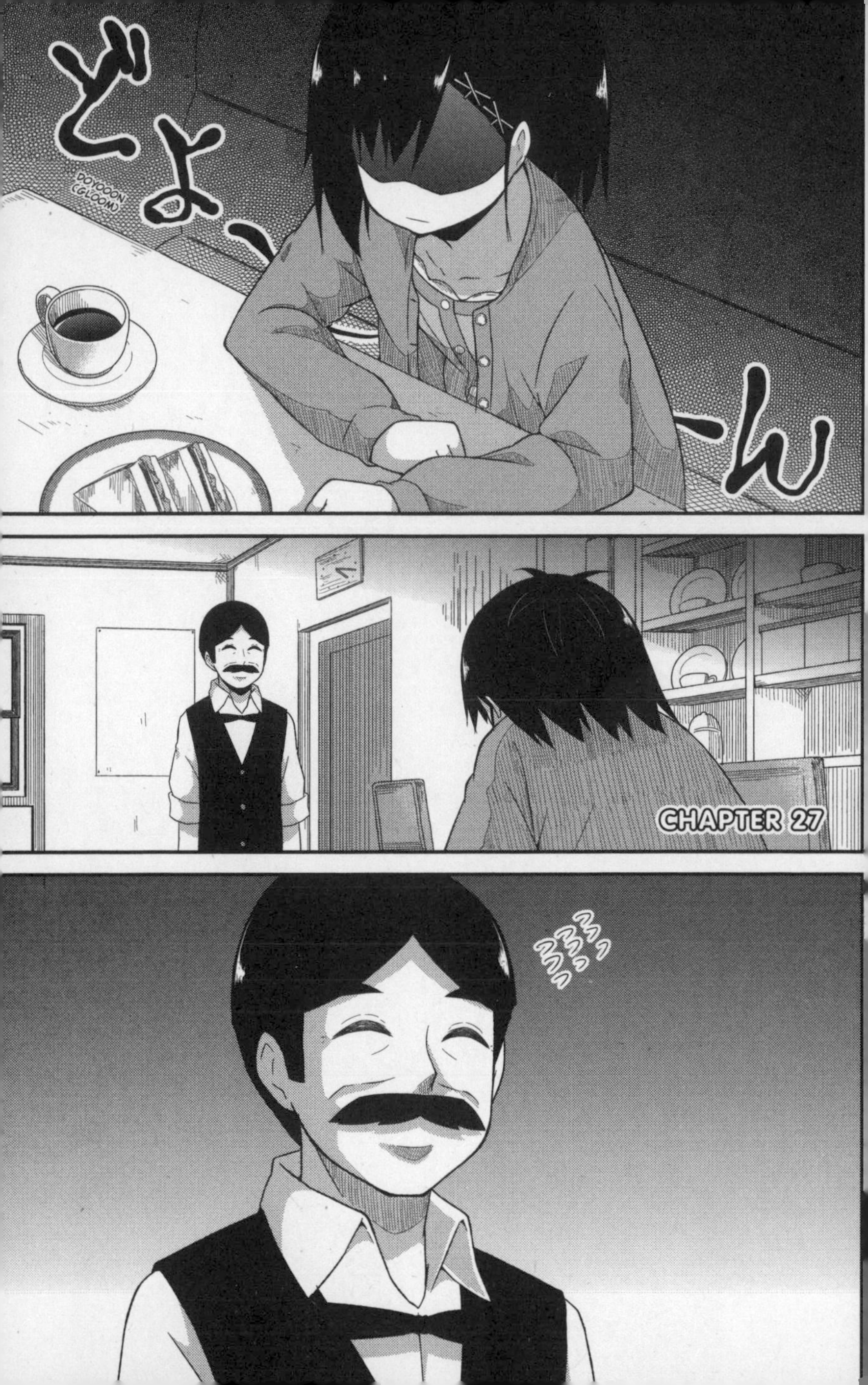
DOYOOON (GLOOM)
CHAPTER 27

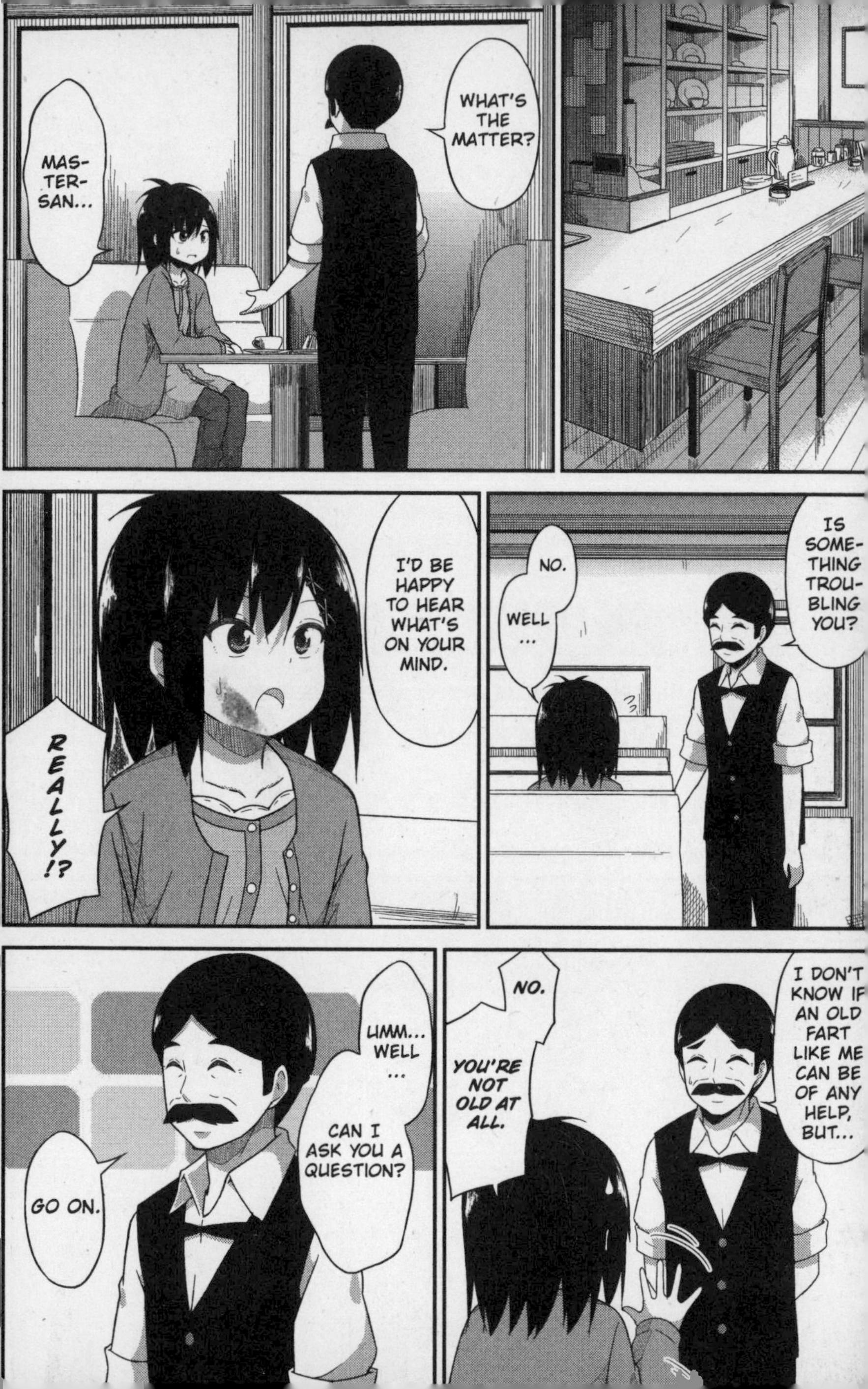
WHAT'S THE MATTER?
MAS-TER-SAN...
IS SOME-THING TROU-BLING YOU?
NO.
WELL ...
I'D BE HAPPY TO HEAR WHAT'S ON YOUR MIND.
REALLY!?
I DON'T KNOW IF AN OLD FART LIKE ME CAN BE OF ANY HELP, BUT...
NO.
YOU'RE NOT OLD AT ALL.
UMM... WELL ...
CAN I ASK YOU A QUESTION?
GO ON.

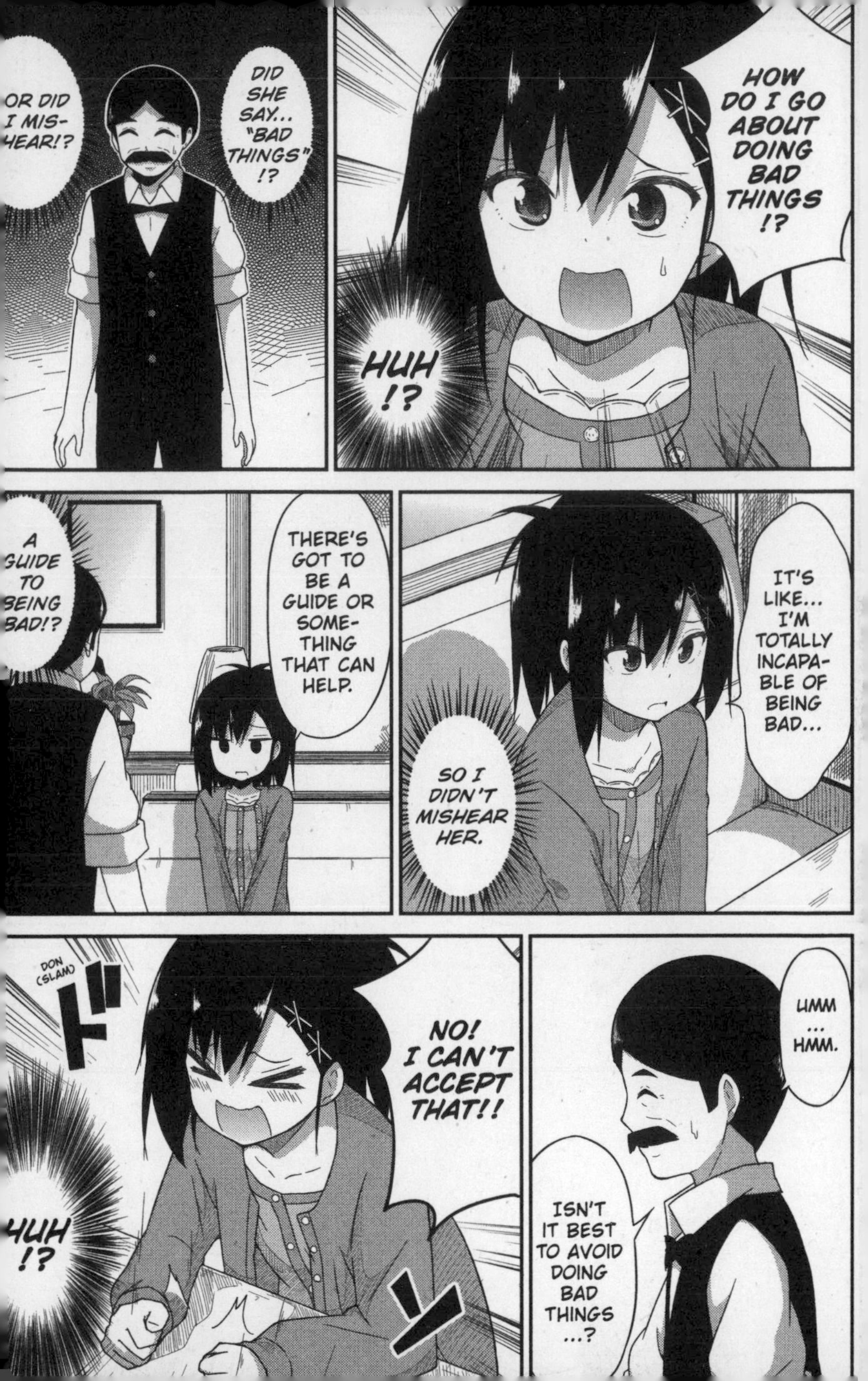
HOW DO I GO ABOUT DOING BAD THINGS!?
HUH!?
DID SHE SAY... "BAD THINGS"!?
OR DID I MIS-HEAR!?
IT'S LIKE... I'M TOTALLY INCAPA-BLE OF BEING BAD...
SO I DIDN'T MISHEAR HER.
THERE'S GOT TO BE A GUIDE OR SOME-THING THAT CAN HELP.
A GUIDE TO BEING BAD!?
UMM... HMM.
ISN'T IT BEST TO AVOID DOING BAD THINGS...?
NO! I CAN'T ACCEPT THAT!!
DON (SLAM)
HUH!?

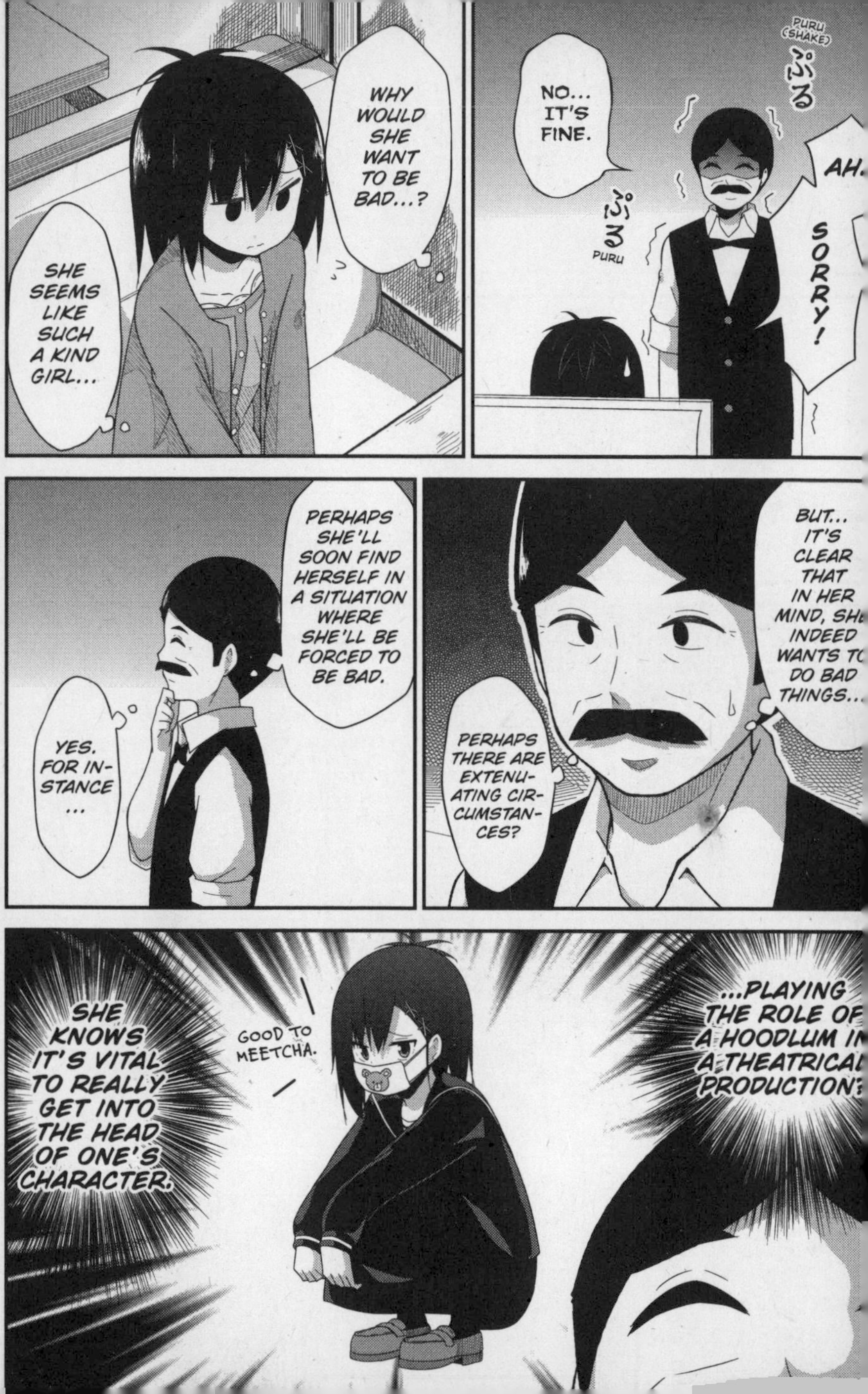
PURU (SHAKE)
ぷる
AH... SORRY!
NO... IT'S FINE.
ぷる
PURU
WHY WOULD SHE WANT TO BE BAD...?
SHE SEEMS LIKE SUCH A KIND GIRL...
BUT... IT'S CLEAR THAT IN HER MIND, SHE INDEED WANTS TO DO BAD THINGS...
PERHAPS THERE ARE EXTENUATING CIRCUMSTANCES?
PERHAPS SHE'LL SOON FIND HERSELF IN A SITUATION WHERE SHE'LL BE FORCED TO BE BAD.
YES. FOR INSTANCE...
...PLAYING THE ROLE OF A HOODLUM IN A THEATRICAL PRODUCTION?
GOOD TO MEETCHA.
SHE KNOWS IT'S VITAL TO REALLY GET INTO THE HEAD OF ONE'S CHARACTER.

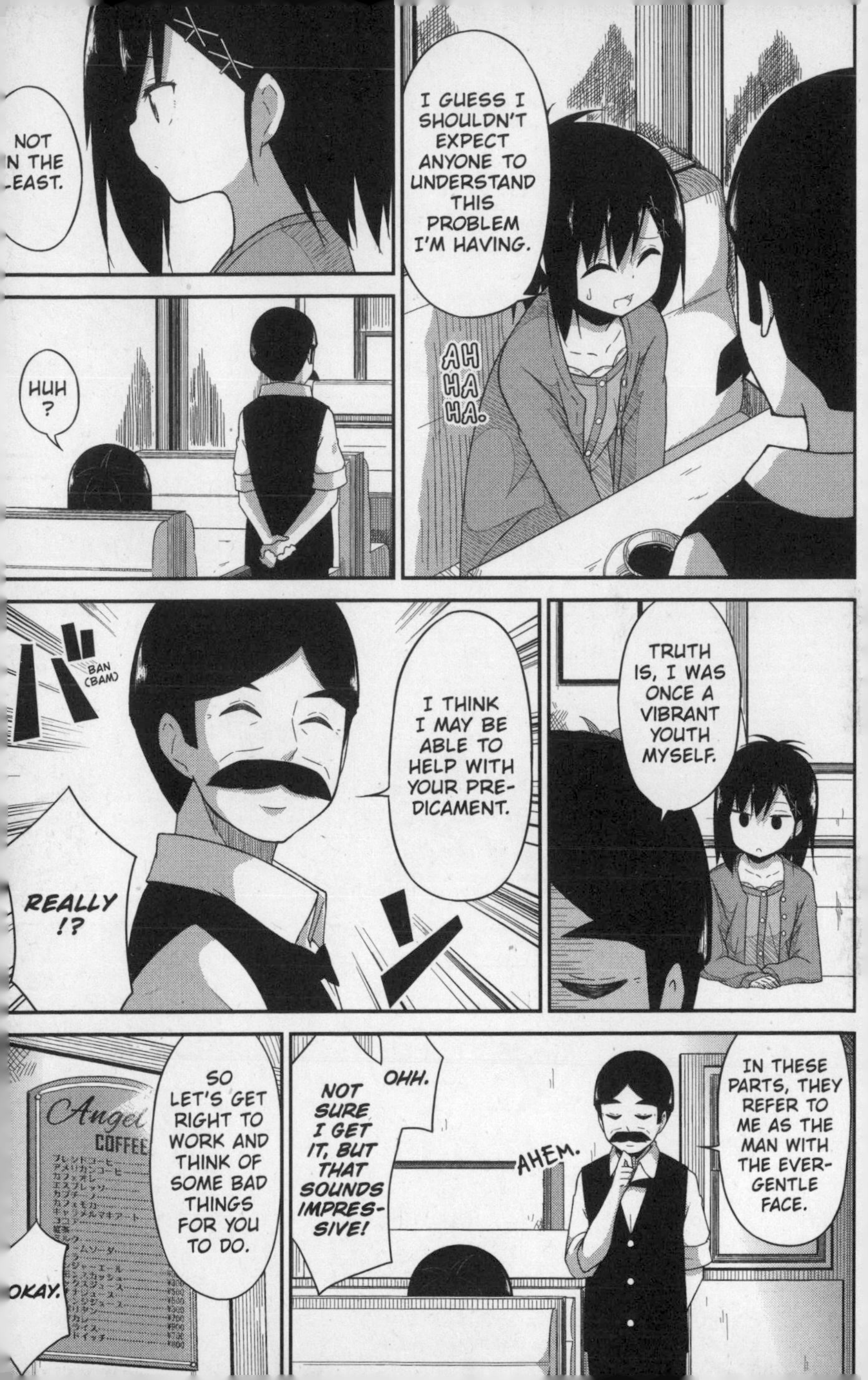
I GUESS I SHOULDN'T EXPECT ANYONE TO UNDERSTAND THIS PROBLEM I'M HAVING.
AH HA HA.
NOT N THE EAST.
HUH?
TRUTH IS, I WAS ONCE A VIBRANT YOUTH MYSELF.
I THINK I MAY BE ABLE TO HELP WITH YOUR PREDICAMENT.
BAN (BAM)
REALLY!?
IN THESE PARTS, THEY REFER TO ME AS THE MAN WITH THE EVER-GENTLE FACE.
AHEM.
OHH.
NOT SURE I GET IT, BUT THAT SOUNDS IMPRESSIVE!
SO LET'S GET RIGHT TO WORK AND THINK OF SOME BAD THINGS FOR YOU TO DO.
OKAY.
Angel
COFFEE

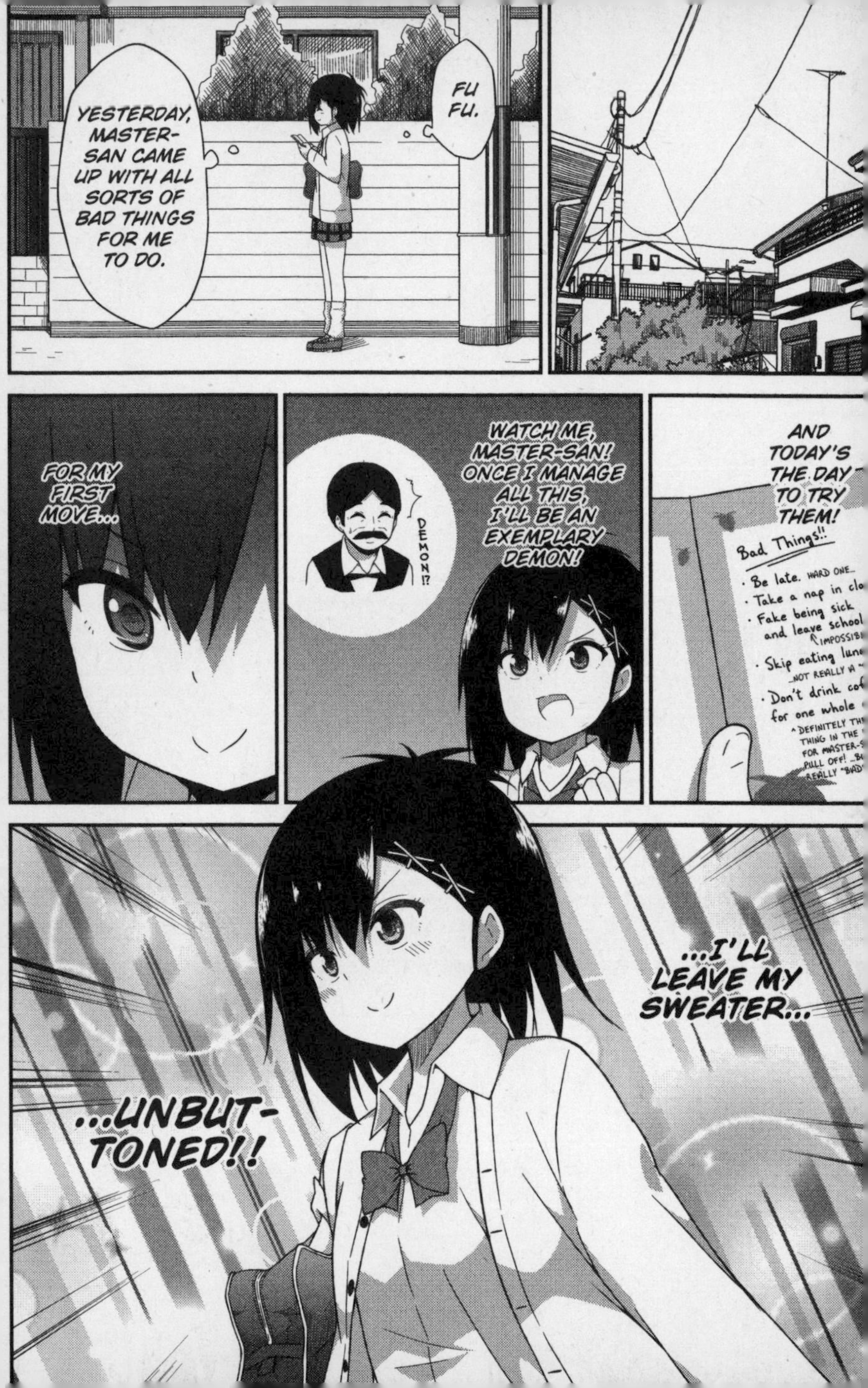
FU FU.
YESTERDAY, MASTER-SAN CAME UP WITH ALL SORTS OF BAD THINGS FOR ME TO DO.
AND TODAY'S THE DAY TO TRY THEM!
Bad Things!!
· Be late. HARD ONE...
· Take a nap in cl
· Fake being sick and leave school
IMPOSSIB
· Skip eating lun
...NOT REALLY A
· Don't drink co for one whole
DEFINITELY TH THING IN THE FOR MASTER-S PULL OFF! ...B REALLY "BAD"
WATCH ME, MASTER-SAN! ONCE I MANAGE ALL THIS, I'LL BE AN EXEMPLARY DEMON!
DEMON!?
FOR MY FIRST MOVE...
...I'LL LEAVE MY SWEATER...
...UNBUT-TONED!!

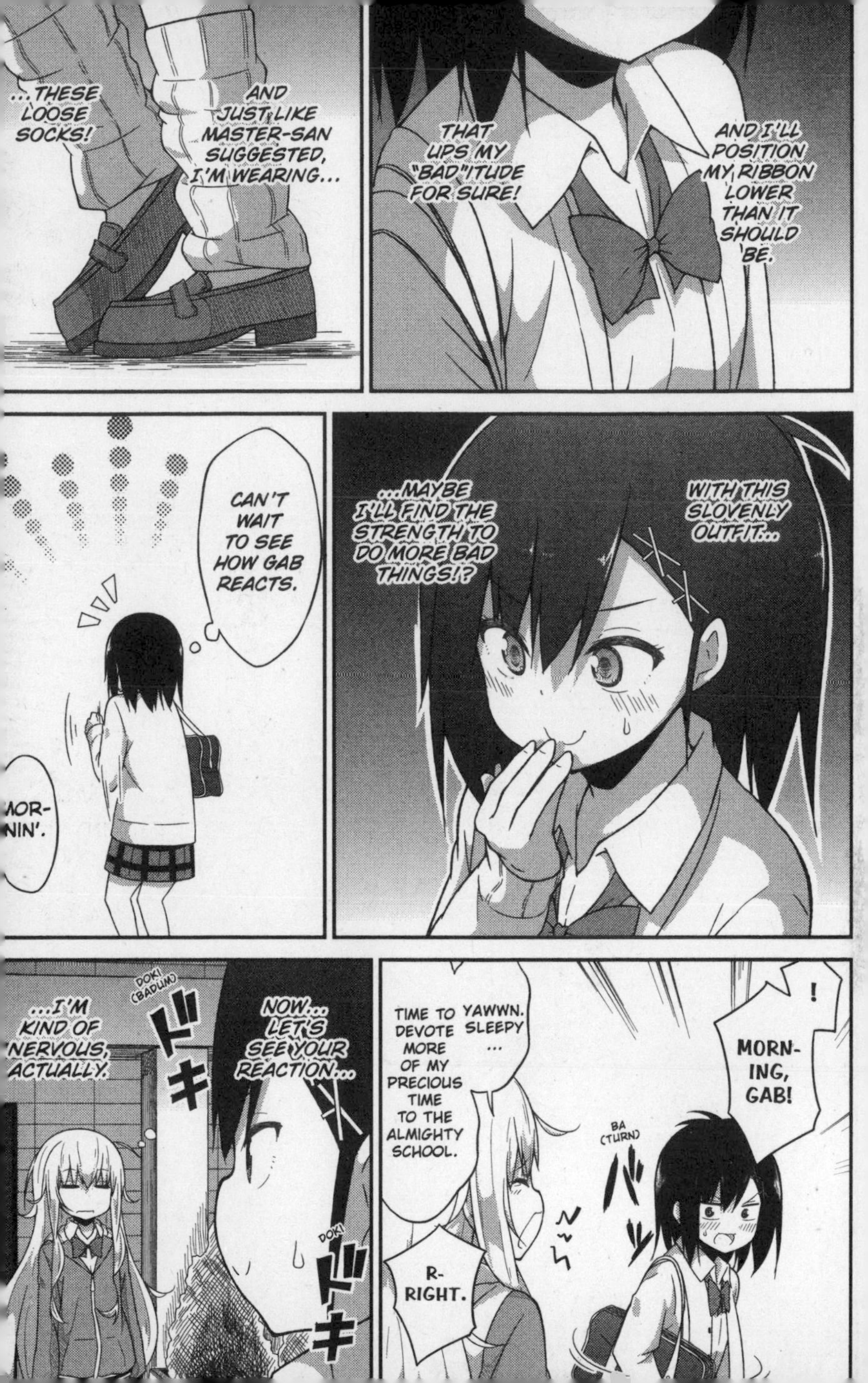
AND I'LL POSITION MY RIBBON LOWER THAN IT SHOULD BE.
THAT UPS MY "BAD"ITUDE FOR SURE!
AND JUST LIKE MASTER-SAN SUGGESTED, I'M WEARING...
...THESE LOOSE SOCKS!
WITH THIS SLOVENLY OUTFIT...
...MAYBE I'LL FIND THE STRENGTH TO DO MORE BAD THINGS!?
CAN'T WAIT TO SEE HOW GAB REACTS.
MOR-NIN'.
!
MORN-ING, GAB!
BA (TURN)
YAWWN. SLEEPY ...
TIME TO DEVOTE MORE OF MY PRECIOUS TIME TO THE ALMIGHTY SCHOOL.
R-RIGHT.
NOW... LET'S SEE YOUR REACTION...
DOKI (BADUM)
...I'M KIND OF NERVOUS, ACTUALLY.
DOKI

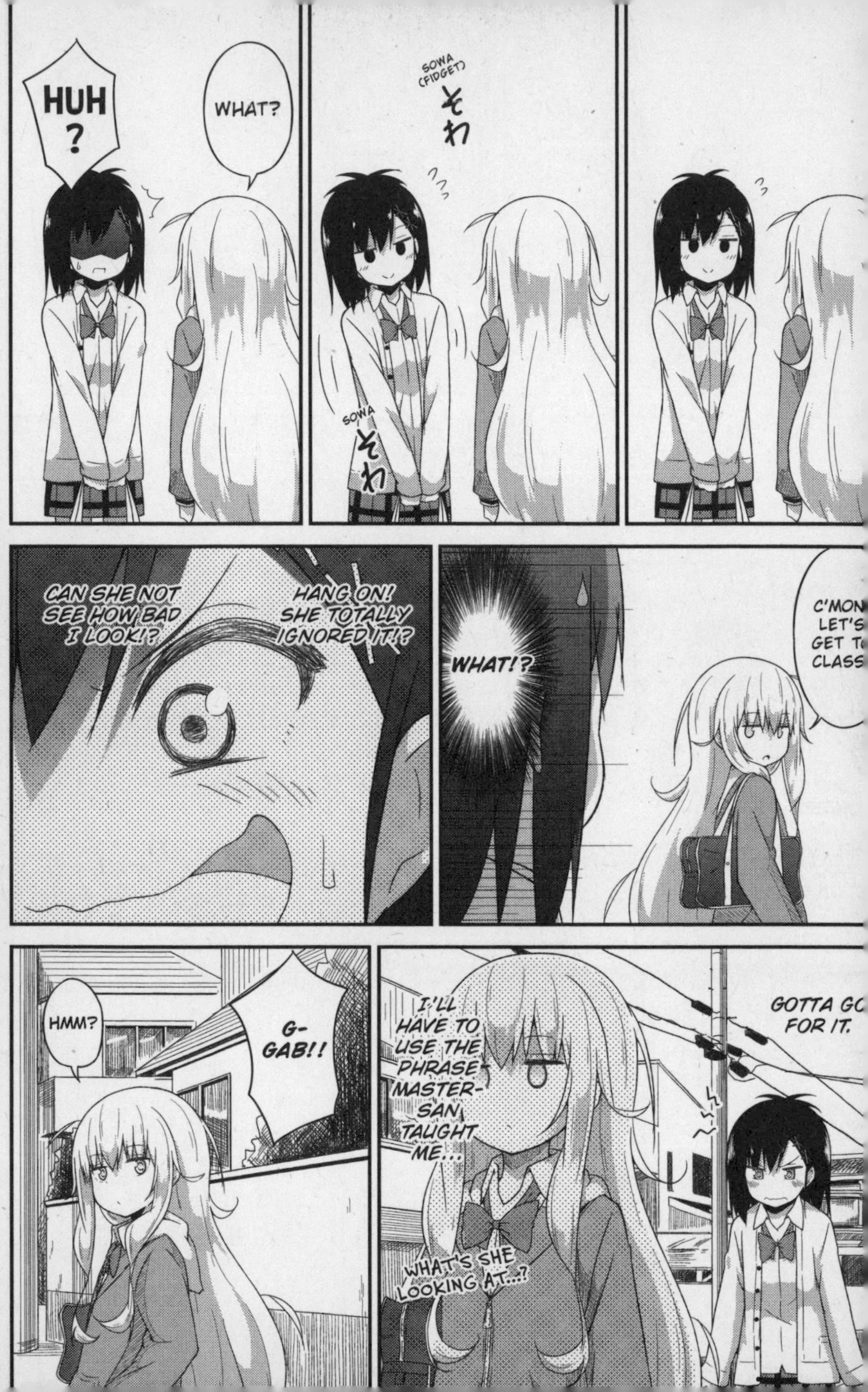
SOWA (FIDGET) そわ
SOWA そわ
WHAT?
HUH?
C'MON LET'S GET T CLASS
WHAT!?
HANG ON! SHE TOTALLY IGNORED IT!?
CAN SHE NOT SEE HOW BAD I LOOK!?
GOTTA GO FOR IT.
I'LL HAVE TO USE THE PHRASE-MASTER-SAN TAUGHT ME...
WHAT'S SHE LOOKING AT...?
G-GAB!!
HMM?

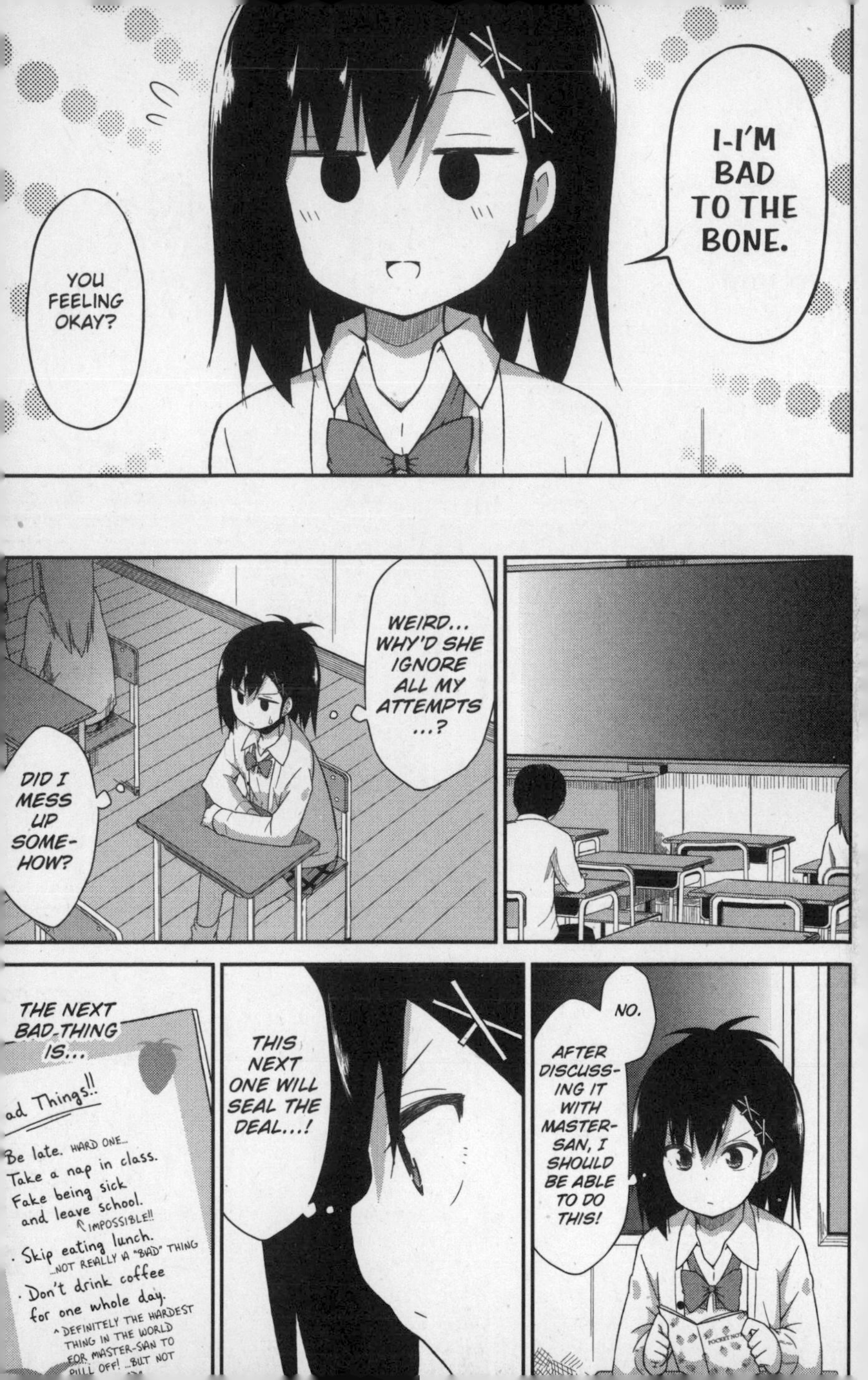
I-I'M BAD TO THE BONE.
YOU FEELING OKAY?
WEIRD... WHY'D SHE IGNORE ALL MY ATTEMPTS ...?
DID I MESS UP SOME-HOW?
NO.
AFTER DISCUSS-ING IT WITH MASTER-SAN, I SHOULD BE ABLE TO DO THIS!
THIS NEXT ONE WILL SEAL THE DEAL...!
THE NEXT BAD THING IS...
ad Things!!
Be late. HARD ONE...
Take a nap in class.
Fake being sick and leave school.
IMPOSSIBLE!!
· Skip eating lunch.
...NOT REALLY A "BAD" THING
· Don't drink coffee for one whole day.
DEFINITELY THE HARDEST THING IN THE WORLD FOR MASTER-SAN TO PULL OFF! ...BUT NOT

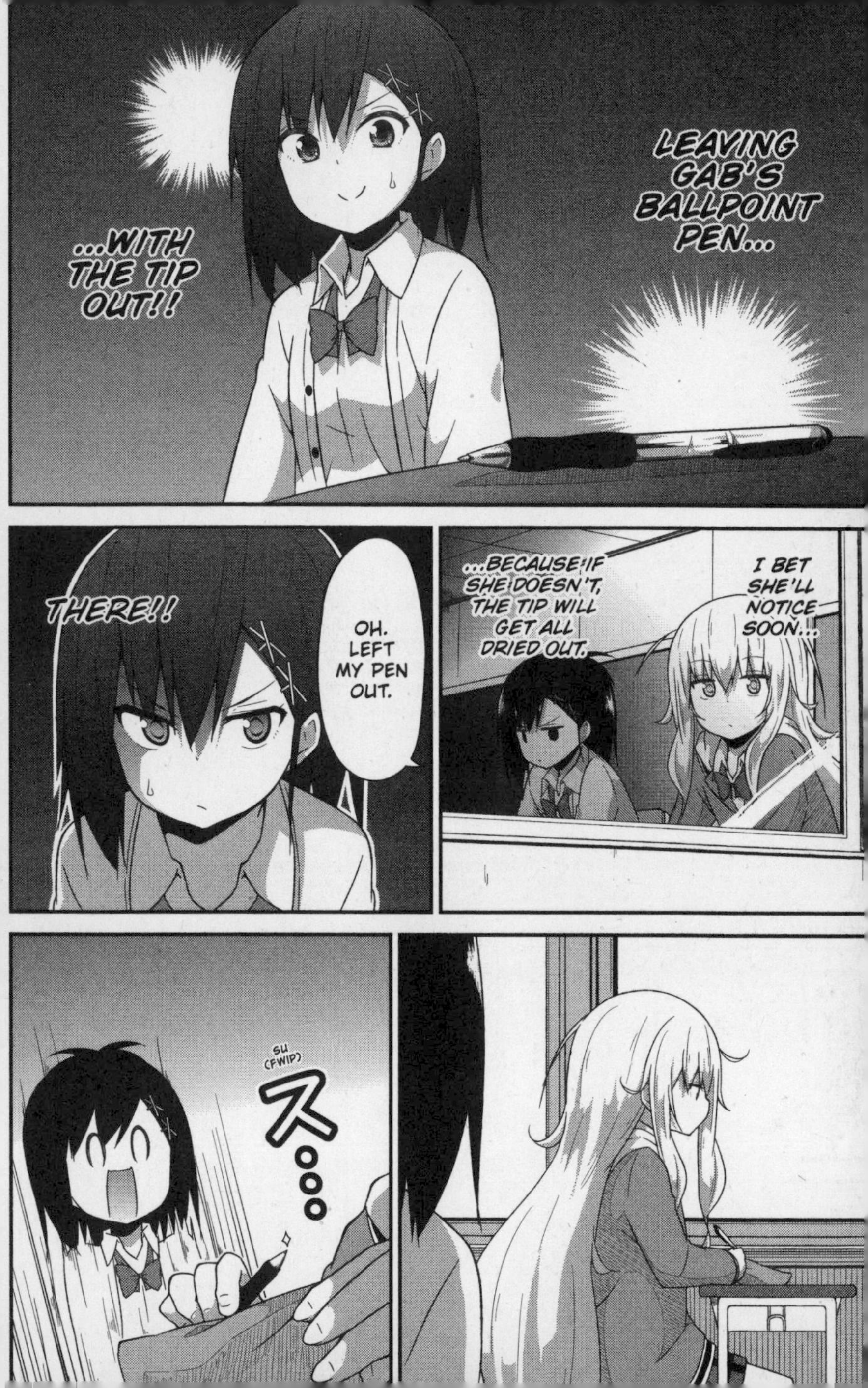
LEAVING GAB'S BALLPOINT PEN...
...WITH THE TIP OUT!!
I BET SHE'LL NOTICE SOON...
...BECAUSE IF SHE DOESN'T, THE TIP WILL GET ALL DRIED OUT.
OH. LEFT MY PEN OUT.
THERE!!
SU (FWIP)
スooo

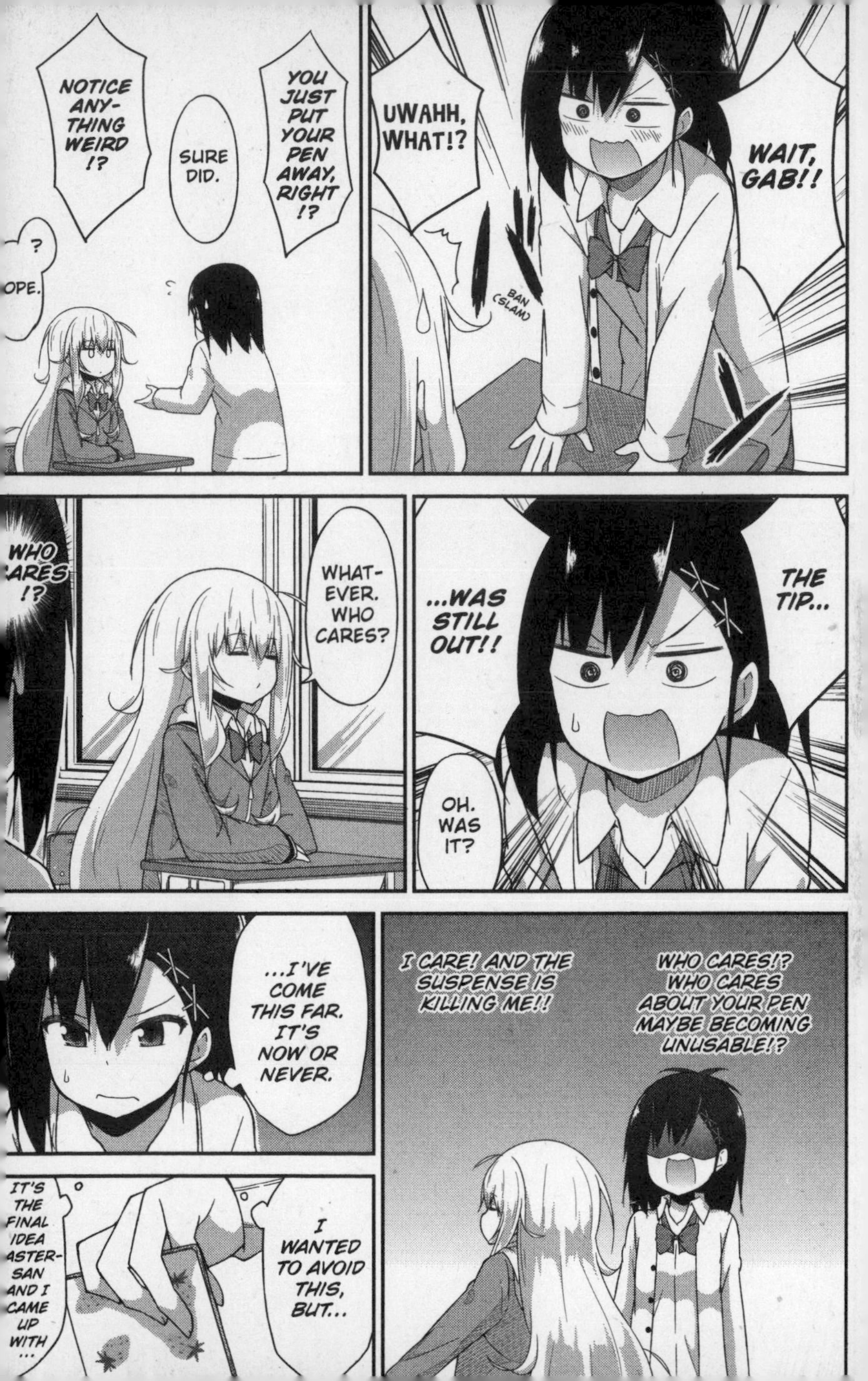
WAIT, GAB!!
UWAHH, WHAT!?
BAN (SLAM)
YOU JUST PUT YOUR PEN AWAY, RIGHT!?
SURE DID.
NOTICE ANY-THING WEIRD!?
?
OPE.
THE TIP...
...WAS STILL OUT!!
OH. WAS IT?
WHAT-EVER. WHO CARES?
WHO ARES!?
WHO CARES!? WHO CARES ABOUT YOUR PEN MAYBE BECOMING UNUSABLE!?
I CARE! AND THE SUSPENSE IS KILLING ME!!
...I'VE COME THIS FAR. IT'S NOW OR NEVER.
I WANTED TO AVOID THIS, BUT...
IT'S THE FINAL IDEA ASTER-SAN AND I CAME UP WITH...

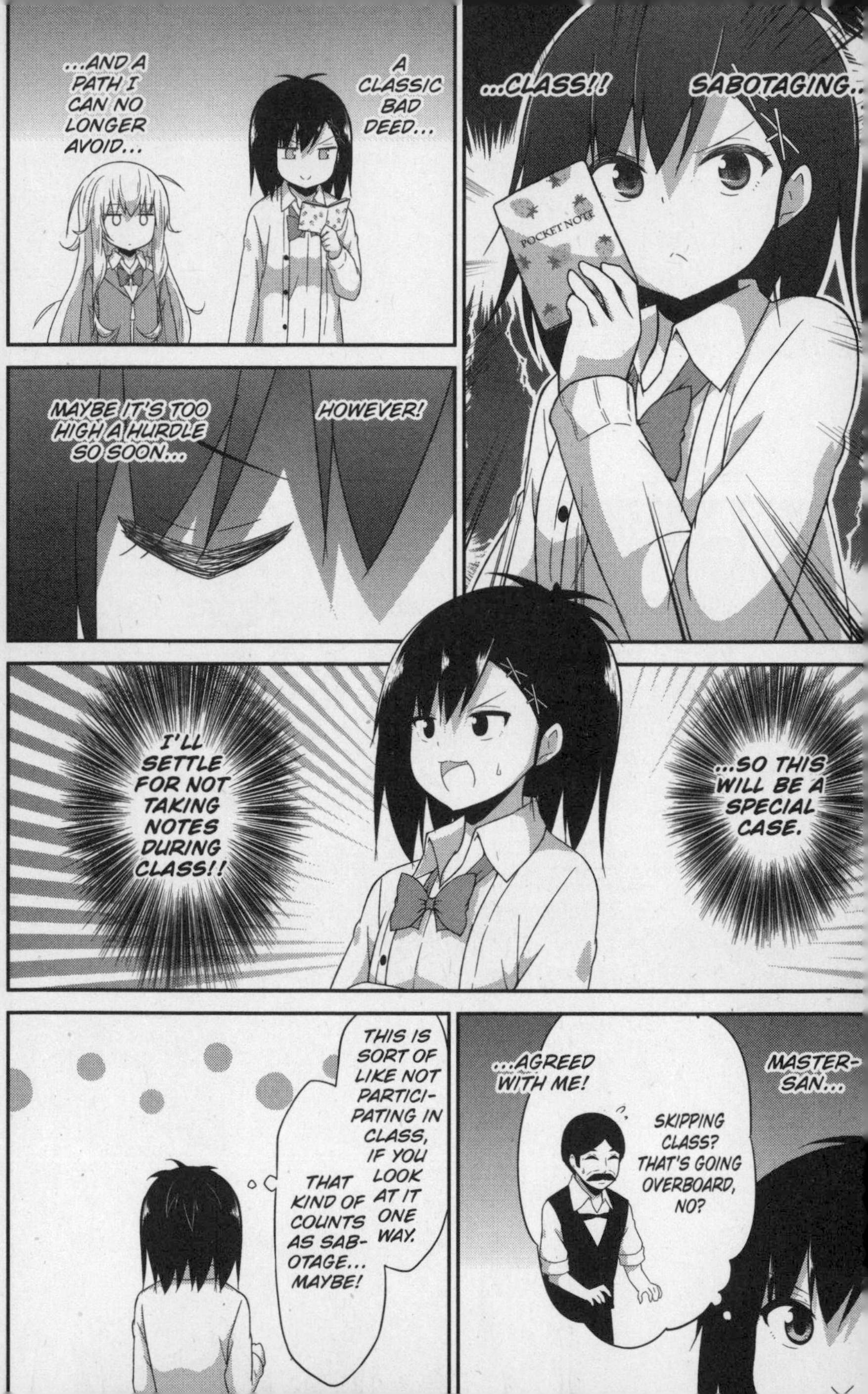
SABOTAGING...
...CLASS!!
POCKET NOTE
A CLASSIC BAD DEED...
...AND A PATH I CAN NO LONGER AVOID...
HOWEVER!
MAYBE IT'S TOO HIGH A HURDLE SO SOON...
...SO THIS WILL BE A SPECIAL CASE.
I'LL SETTLE FOR NOT TAKING NOTES DURING CLASS!!
MASTER-SAN...
SKIPPING CLASS? THAT'S GOING OVERBOARD, NO?
...AGREED WITH ME!
THIS IS SORT OF LIKE NOT PARTICI-PATING IN CLASS, IF YOU LOOK AT IT ONE WAY.
THAT KIND OF COUNTS AS SAB-OTAGE... MAYBE!

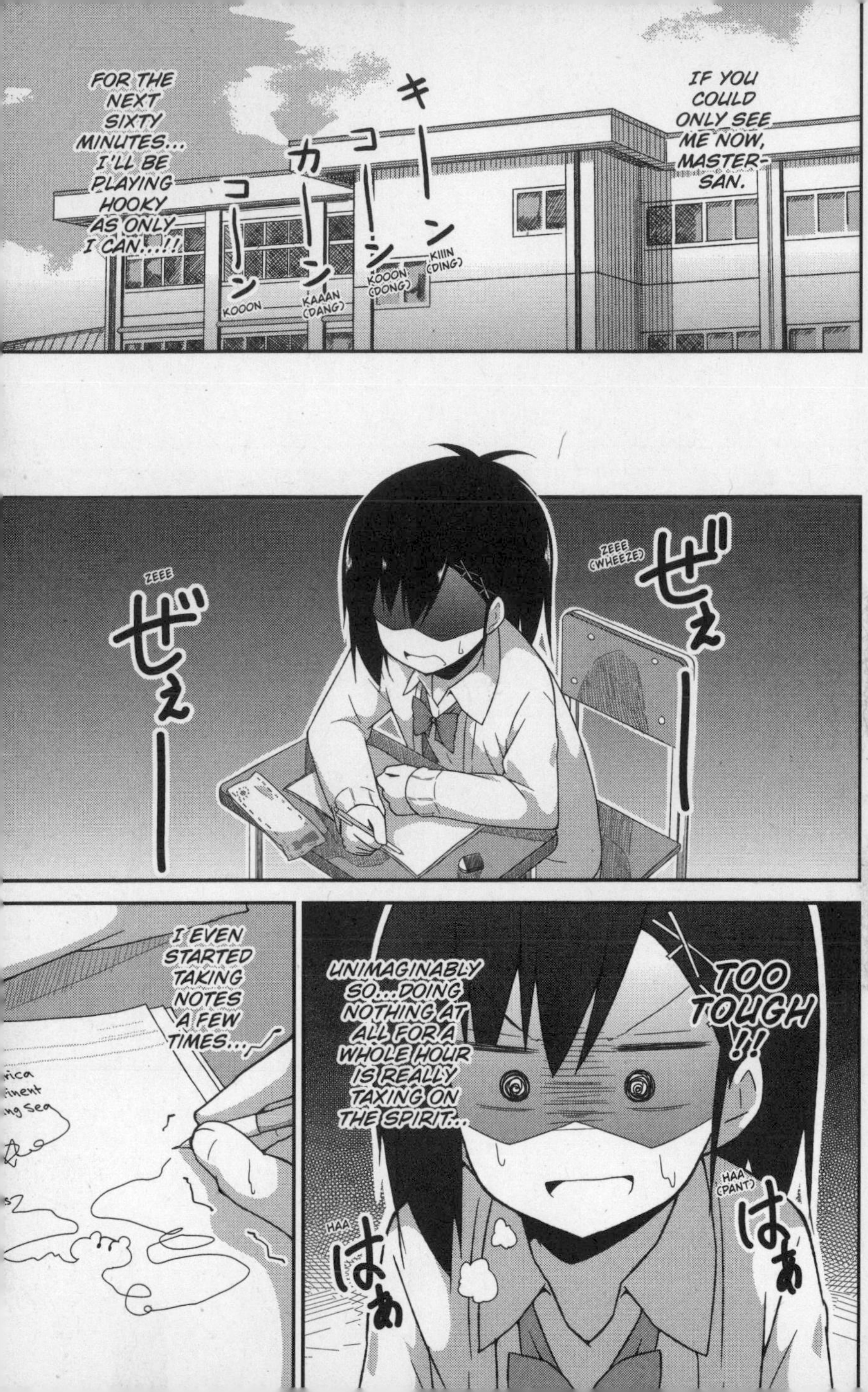
IF YOU COULD ONLY SEE ME NOW, MASTER-SAN.
キーン
KIIIN (DING)
コーン
KOOON (DONG)
カーン
KAAAN (DANG)
コーン
KOOON
FOR THE NEXT SIXTY MINUTES... I'LL BE PLAYING HOOKY AS ONLY I CAN...!!
ぜぇー
ZEEE (WHEEZE)
ぜぇー
ZEEE
TOO TOUGH!!
UNIMAGINABLY SO...DOING NOTHING AT ALL FOR A WHOLE HOUR IS REALLY TAXING ON THE SPIRIT...
はぁ
HAA (PANT)
はぁ
HAA
I EVEN STARTED TAKING NOTES A FEW TIMES...

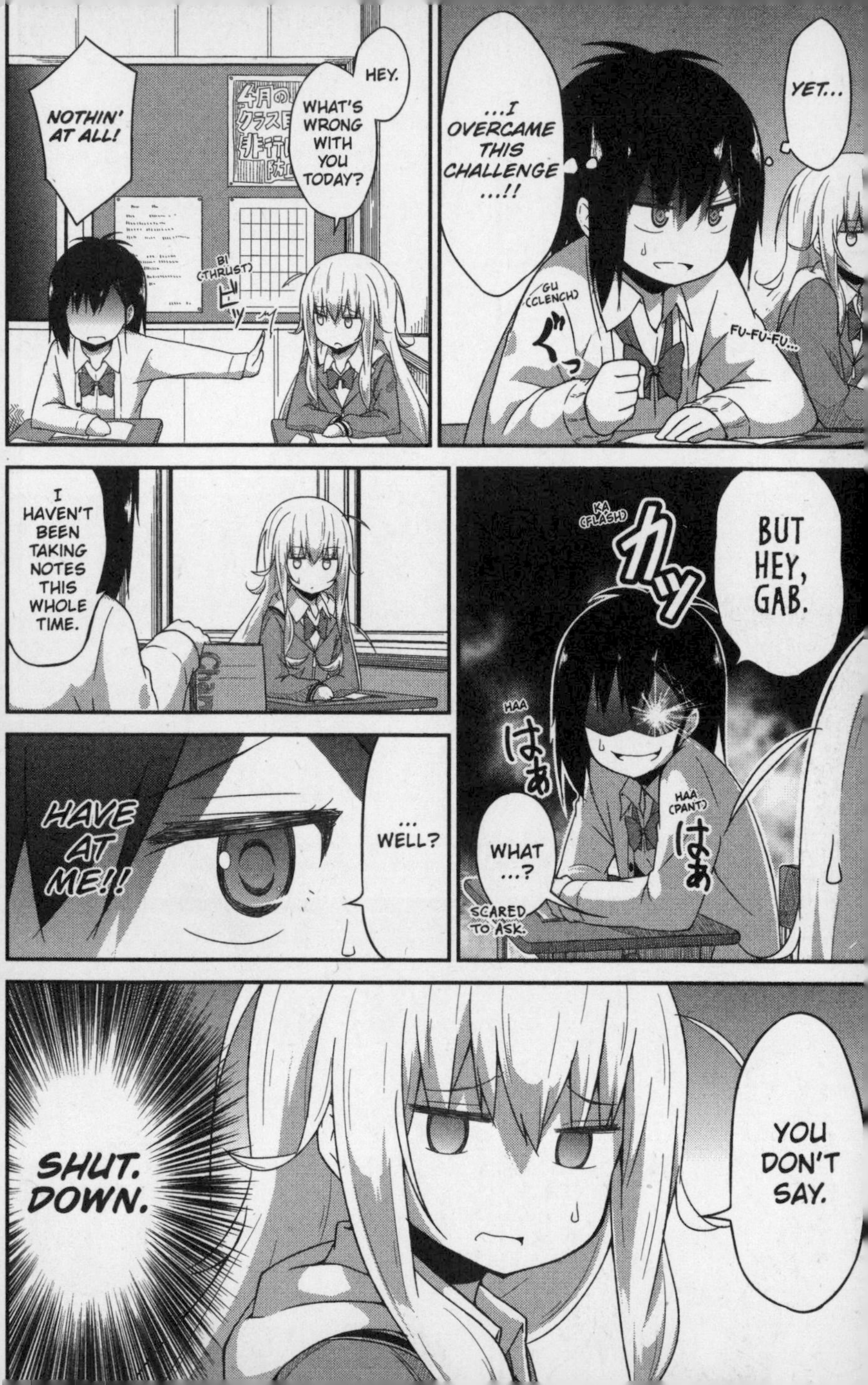
YET...
...I OVERCAME THIS CHALLENGE ...!!
GU (CLENCH)
ぐっ
FU-FU-FU...
HEY.
WHAT'S WRONG WITH YOU TODAY?
NOTHIN' AT ALL!
BI (THRUST)
ビッ
BUT HEY, GAB.
KA (FLASH)
カッ
HAA
はあ
HAA (PANT)
はあ
WHAT ...?
SCARED TO ASK.
I HAVEN'T BEEN TAKING NOTES THIS WHOLE TIME.
... WELL?
HAVE AT ME!!
YOU DON'T SAY.
SHUT. DOWN.

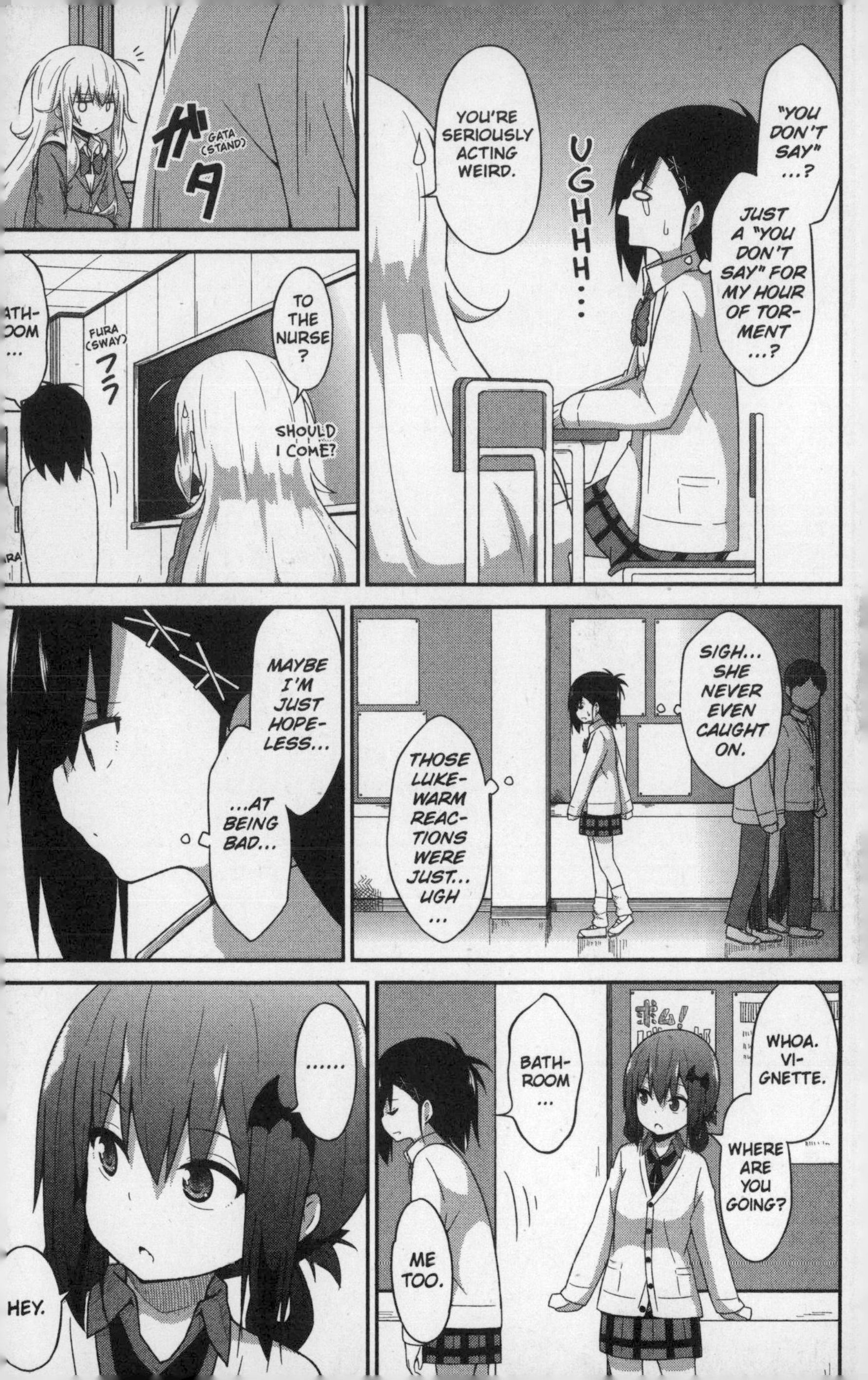
"YOU DON'T SAY" ...?
JUST A "YOU DON'T SAY" FOR MY HOUR OF TOR-MENT ...?
UGHHH...
YOU'RE SERIOUSLY ACTING WEIRD.
GATA (STAND)
ガタ
TO THE NURSE?
SHOULD I COME?
FURA (SWAY)
フラ
SIGH... SHE NEVER EVEN CAUGHT ON.
THOSE LUKE-WARM REAC-TIONS WERE JUST... UGH ...
MAYBE I'M JUST HOPE-LESS...
...AT BEING BAD...
WHOA. VI-GNETTE.
WHERE ARE YOU GOING?
BATH-ROOM ...
ME TOO.
......
HEY.

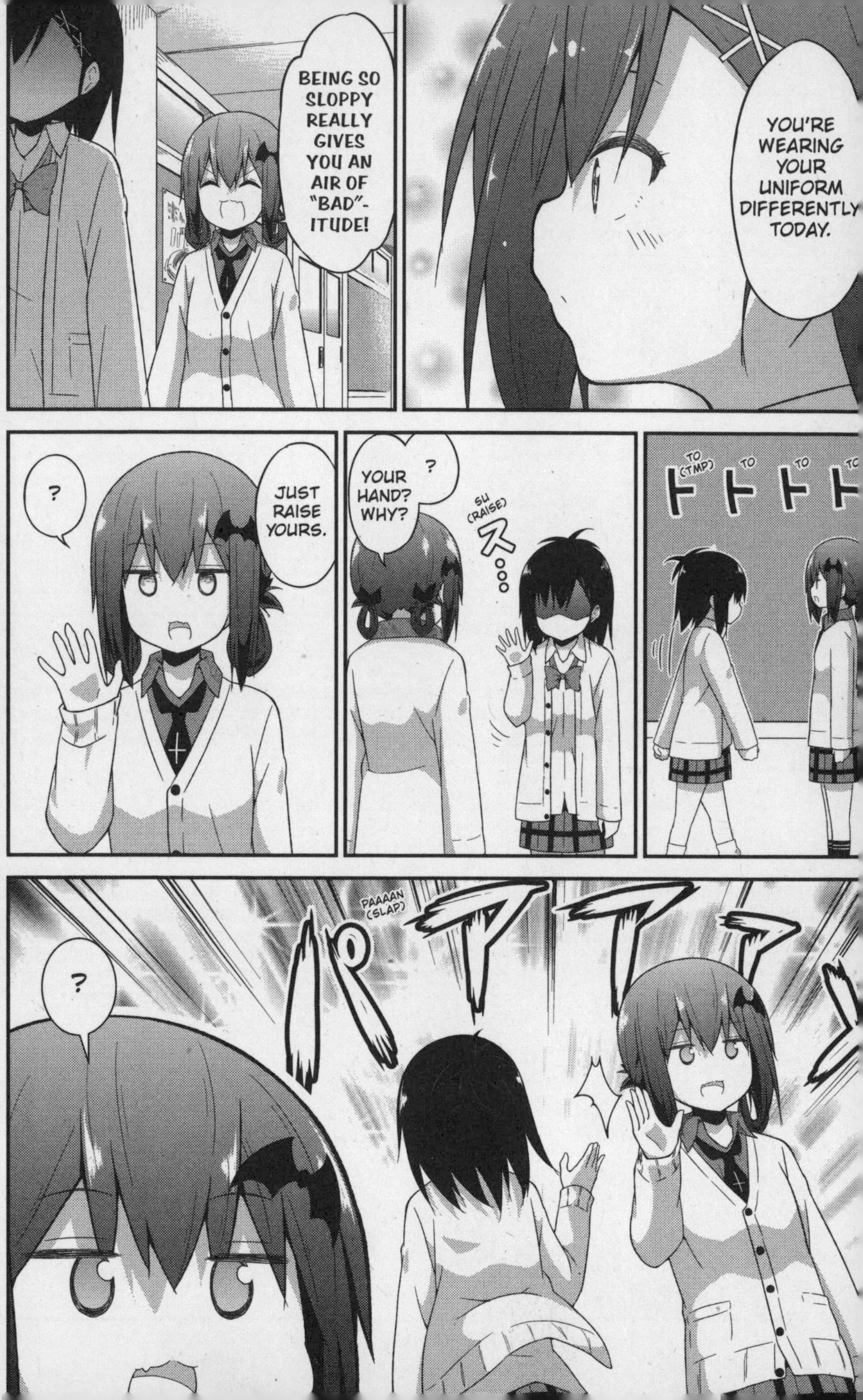
YOU'RE WEARING YOUR UNIFORM DIFFERENTLY TODAY.
BEING SO SLOPPY REALLY GIVES YOU AN AIR OF "BAD"-ITUDE!
TO (TMP) TO TO TO
トトトト
?
YOUR HAND? WHY?
SU (RAISE)
ス…
JUST RAISE YOURS.
?
PAAAAN (SLAP)
パアアン
?

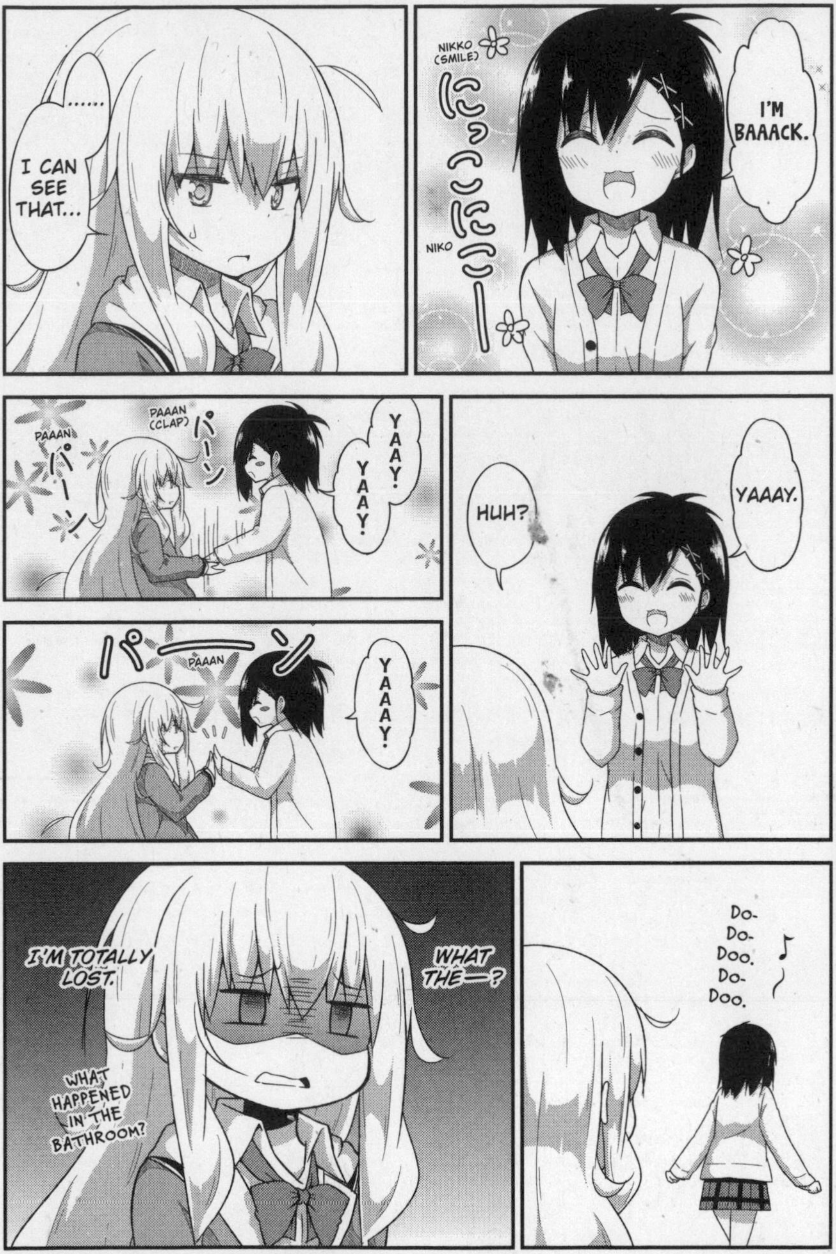
I'M BAAACK.
にっこにこー
NIKKO (SMILE)
NIKO
......
I CAN SEE THAT...
YAAAY.
HUH?
YAAY. YAAY.
パーン
PAAAN (CLAP)
パーン
PAAAN
YAAAY.
パーーン
PAAAN
Do-Do-Doo. Do-Doo. ♪
WHAT THE—?
I'M TOTALLY LOST.
WHAT HAPPENED IN THE BATHROOM?

UKAMI

Translation: Caleb Cook ⁄ Lettering: Rochelle Gancio

This book is a work of fiction. Names, characters, places, and incidents are the product of the author's imagination or are used fictitiously. Any resemblance to actual events, locales, or persons, living or dead, is coincidental.

Gabriel Dropout Vol. 3
©UKAMI 2016
Edited by ASCII MEDIA WORKS
First published in Japan in 2016 by KADOKAWA CORPORATION, Tokyo.
English translation rights arranged with KADOKAWA CORPORATION, Tokyo through TUTTLE-MORI AGENCY, INC., Tokyo.

English translation © 2018 by Yen Press, LLC

Yen Press
1290 Avenue of the Americas
New York, NY 10104

Visit us!
⁄ yenpress.com
⁄ facebook.com/yenpress
⁄ twitter.com/yenpress
⁄ yenpress.tumblr.com
⁄ instagram.com/yenpress

First Yen Press Edition: April 2018

Yen Press is an imprint of Yen Press, LLC.
The Yen Press name and logo are trademarks of Yen Press, LLC.

The publisher is not responsible for websites (or their content) that are not owned by the publisher.

Library of Congress Control Number: 2017945425

ISBNs: 978-0-316-56132-7 (paperback)
       978-0-316-56133-4 (ebook)

10 9 8 7 6 5 4 3 2 1

WOR

Printed in the United States of America